Ann Lovejoy's
Organic Garden Design School

A Rodale Organic Gardening Book

Ann Lovejoy's
Organic Garden Design School

A Guide to Creating Your Own Beautiful, Easy-Care Garden

RODALE

EDITOR: Karen Bolesta
COVER AND INTERIOR BOOK DESIGNERS: Patricia Field
    and Marcella Bove-Huttie
SENIOR BOOK DESIGNER: Nancy Smola Biltcliff
INTERIOR ILLUSTRATOR: Adam McCauley
FRONT AND BACK COVER PHOTOGRAPHER: Susan Seubert
PHOTOGRAPHY EDITOR: Lyn Horst
PHOTO ASSISTANT: Jackie L. Ney
LAYOUT DESIGNER: Keith Biery
RESEARCHERS: Diana Erney and Sarah Wolfgang Heffner
COPY EDITOR: Erana Bumbardatore
MANUFACTURING COORDINATOR: Patrick T. Smith
INDEXER: Kathy Barber
EDITORIAL ASSISTANCE: Kerrie A. Cadden

Rodale Organic Gardening Books
MANAGING EDITOR: Fern Marshall Bradley
EXECUTIVE CREATIVE DIRECTOR: Christin Gangi
ART DIRECTOR: Patricia Field
PRODUCTION MANAGER: Robert V. Anderson Jr.
STUDIO MANAGER: Leslie M. Keefe
ASSOCIATE COPY MANAGER: Jennifer Hornsby
MANUFACTURING MANAGER: Mark Krahforst

On the cover: The ethereal beauty of morning sunshine envelops the front garden at Wardwell Farm on
Bainbridge Island, Washington.

Portions of this book have previously appeared in
significantly different form in several publications,
including *Country Gardens, Fine Gardening,* and the
Seattle Post-Intelligencer.

We're always happy to hear from you. For questions or comments concerning the editorial content
of this book, please write to:
    Rodale Book Readers' Service
    33 East Minor Street
    Emmaus, PA 18098

Look for other Rodale books wherever books are
sold. Or call us at (800) 848-4735.

For more information about Rodale Organic
Gardening magazine and books, visit us at:
    www.organicgardening.com

Library of Congress Cataloging-in-Publication Data

Lovejoy, Ann
    Ann Lovejoy's organic garden design school : a
    guide to creating your own beautiful, easy-care
    garden.
        p.   cm.
    Includes index.
    ISBN 0–87596–836–8 (hc. : alk. paper)
    1. Organic gardening.   2. Low maintenance
gardening.   3. Gardens—Design.   I. Title.
SB453.5.L68   2001
635'.0484—dc21   00–011388

Distributed in the book trade by St. Martin's Press

2 4 6 8 10 9 7 5 3 1   hardcover

For the students who inspired the garden school:

Your ardent, questing spirit keeps life rich.

contents

A Destiny and a Dream

I'VE BEEN A GARDENER ALL MY LIFE AND A GARDEN writer for over 15 years. Back in the '60s, when I was a restless teenager, I discovered a box filled with Rodale's *Organic Gardening and Farming* magazines while tidying an elderly neighbor's garage. My neighbor gladly gave the issues to me, little realizing that he was handing me my life's work and greatest passion. I found a world of wonder in those well-thumbed magazines. Here, at last, were letters and notes from other folks who wanted green, clean gardens, made and maintained without poisons. Those magazines were a treasure trove of tips and techniques for healthy soil building, composting, and edible gardening. I began by growing vegetables and herbs, but soon branched out into making ornamental gardens, as well.

For many years now, my gardens have held plants of all kinds, edible and ornamental, in carefully arranged communities. My plantings echo the layers of nature, from canopy trees to groundcovers. In my herb and vegetable gardens, where I also grow flowers for cutting, the beds have soft, sweeping curves that echo natural shapes such as riverbanks and shoals rather than the harsh, geometric lines found in man-made waterways. I believe that gardens are more serene when they reflect what's found in nature. We've filled our world with plenty of hard edges, so I find it's a welcome change to have gardens overflowing with natural-looking plantings.

I think that plants look most relaxed and at home when they are combined in naturalistic groupings similar to those found in nature. Plants are social; they always put themselves in clusters and groups, never in straight rows. Further, I think we humans grow best when we are in close contact with plants and natural communities. Whether most of us realize it or not, we cannot live without plants, and we live far more richly when we live in cooperative relationships with them. My greatest hope is to promote these ideas, encouraging others to create healthy, self-sufficient gardens that are easy to care for, ecologically sound, and enduringly beautiful.

A School at Your Fingertips

A few years ago, I started a garden school because I felt there was a need to teach garden design and garden care to gardeners who were ready to move beyond the beginner stage. My school is on an island near Seattle. It's a lovely spot, but not exactly centrally located. Since not everybody can visit my school and take classes with me directly, I hope this book will bring the garden school to you. The students who come to my garden school generally fall into one of two camps—about half want to know how to make a garden like mine, and the other half want to focus on matters like seasonal grooming and ongoing maintenance of beds and borders.

My design class is called Practical Garden Design; it addresses the use of space and interior flow in a garden,

> Plants are social; they always put themselves in clusters and groups, never in straight rows.

shows how to create ambiance, and teaches how to develop a regionally appropriate garden that reflects the personal style of the gardener. My other popular class is called Guilt-Free Gardening. Students learn about keeping plants healthy, making divisions and taking cuttings, and caring for plants year-round. The goal is to create healthy plant communities and gardens that can sustain themselves with little intervention, giving the gardener more time to enjoy the garden.

Wherever you live, you will find ideas and resources for personalizing the concepts spelled out for you in this book. Although I now garden in the lush Pacific Northwest, I have lived and gardened in such diverse places as Massachusetts, Ohio, Colorado, Montana, and Italy. I've made shady woodland gardens and sunny, windy, prairie gardens. I've made gardens at 10,000 feet in the Rockies and at the very edge of the ocean. I've gardened in the city on tiny lots and in the country on expansive ones. Each garden was very different, and I learned a lot from every single one.

Cooperation, Not Control

One thing I learned through my travels is that the basics really are the same everywhere. Make great dirt and your plants will grow well. Create healthy, ecologically sound plant communities and the gardens will largely take care of themselves. In fact, my own gardens, which are complex plantings containing thousands of plants, take me only a few hours a week to maintain (once they are established, of course). Most need little supplemental water in summer, and they need little regular care because the plants are chosen for their suitability to my growing conditions.

Each plant must contribute actively to the overall design, but it must do so on its own terms. Asking plants to do what they do best eliminates a lot of the control-oriented chores that are built into the great majority of traditional gardens. I avoid many repetitive chores by thinking about what I want my plants to do, then finding plants to fill the desired role naturally. For instance, when I want a 4-foot-high foundation planting, I use shrubs that mature at 4 feet. (This is a surprisingly radical concept.) When I plant a yard tree, I select one that naturally has all the qualities and seasonal beauties I'm looking for, yet will never outgrow its position. In beds and borders, I choose cooperators, plants that share resources well and grow readily without becoming thugs.

When you work with your plants, rather than trying to bend them to your will, the result is simply beautiful. Designs that are based on what plants do best look natural, rather than contrived. These gardens don't rely on fancy ornaments, expensive furnishings, or the latest imported perennial to make them remarkable. They are remarkable for the harmony they create between plants and place and people. Gardens made like this are cooperative endeavors where both nature and gardeners play a part.

Endless, Enjoyable Rewards

Though I love to garden, I have two kids to raise and a full-time job to hold down. Thus, my goal is to create gardens that don't really need me very much. Even so, my gardens reward the moderate attentions I do offer them with an unstinting flow of beauty all through the year. And they do it quite quickly—even in the first season of growth. Gardens made by the principles in this book will look amazingly full. Within a few years, they'll look close to mature, even though you may have to start with young divisions and small, inexpensive plants. That's because a well-designed, well-prepared, and well-planted garden practically grows itself.

If you would like to get a lot more pleasure and use from your garden without expanding your workload, read on. I think you'll find a lot of practical and functional ideas here that will help you recharge your garden in every way. And before you begin, let me share the most important idea of all with you: A happy garden makes for a happy gardener. I wish you joy in the process and delight in the result. Happy gardening!

Ann Lovejoy

Ann Lovejoy
Bainbridge Island, Washington

1

Creating a Natural Garden

With a new century dawning, we are beginning to discover a new way of gardening, a new way of thinking about our plants, and a new way of interacting with the natural world. This fresh, healthy attitude calls for a new kind of garden design and a new way of making gardens.

These days, few of us have household servants or a small army of gardeners awaiting our orders. We may choose to hire help for the most physically demanding chores. (I happily pay younger people who still have good knees to plant any beds larger than my small car.) Still, most of us will be planting and maintaining our gardens ourselves, in large part because **we enjoy gardening.**

Fortunately, making a garden doesn't have to be a back-breaking experience. **Designing or renovating a garden can be joyful and deeply satisfying.** Though an overall and long-term master plan will be very helpful, no design needs to be implemented all at once. Some ideas may come to life immediately, while others require more time to mature. A good design can be broken into steps and stages that proceed on a timeline and budget that suits your particular needs and abilities.

The point of this book is not just to show you how to make the kinds of gardens that I do, though I am happy to share my experience, design skills, and gardening techniques with you. The real objective is to help you gain the skills you need in order to **make your own garden, just the way you want it.**

Welcome to My Garden School

FOR MANY OF US, JUST BEING IN THE GARDEN IS ONE OF life's simple and lasting pleasures. Working with plants of all kinds, tuning our senses to the needs of those plants, appreciating their beautiful qualities, and relating our activities to seasonal cycles all help to connect us firmly to the natural world. And creating a garden that satisfies the soul is the greatest reward of gardening.

Who hasn't dreamed of having a garden that's a pleasure to explore, tend, and enjoy all year long? A successful garden expresses your personal style as well as the character of your site. Rest assured that you have the skills, knowledge, talent, and creativity it takes to design your garden. You carry within you a native genius for garden making, and it's a skill that develops as you garden. When you begin gardening, you're

Design is about space and the way we move through it.

excited about watching things grow, change, and bloom; every new day brings new discoveries about plants. But as you become more skilled in your interactions with plants, you often begin to want more for and from your gardens.

At my garden school, I teach classes for hundreds of students every year. During every session, my students are certain to ask the same questions about gardening and garden design. I'd like to begin our journey into garden design by addressing the three questions I'm asked most often. The answers will clarify the terms you'll see throughout this book—terms like "garden

design," "naturalistic design," and "organic design." All of these concepts will be developed more fully, but these working definitions should help explain the premise behind my organic gardening school and help you understand why natural and organic principles are the stepping stones to a successful garden.

What Is Garden Design?

Garden design is the process of creating useful and attractive spaces that will be shared by people and plants. Though most of us begin our garden lives by falling in love with flowers or delicious vegetables, design is not really about plants at all. Design is about space and the way we move through it.

The first step in garden design is to look at the way you enter a garden. The entrance or entrances to the garden will influence your choices when you lay out paths and seating areas, and will help you define which part of the yard becomes the garden.

Designing the garden from principal viewpoints—important doorways, windows, patios, and decks—is as important as designing a garden when you're standing in it. And, of course, the expression that "function dictates form" is an essential part of a successful garden. Each garden must serve a variety of needs or functions. And the "form"—the shape of the beds, borders, paths, seating, and work areas—must serve the main function well.

Natural meadow edges offer gardeners both backdrop and layering patterns, from the canopy or treeline layer down through high and low understory to the lowest layers of perennials and groundcovers.

What Is Naturalistic Design?

Naturalistic gardens are based on the concept of natural plant relationships. In any native plant community, there are plant layers that work together to create a landscape. First there is a canopy layer, or treeline—that's what you see against the backdrop of the sky. Next there's an understory, often in layers of high-, mid-, and low-growing plants. The furnishing layer is made up of perennials, dwarf shrubs, and grasses; this is what you usually think of when you use the word "garden." Finally, the carpet layer is made up of groundcovers, creepers, and crawlers, and is often punctuated by bulbs. Vines may knit the whole community together, creeping up from the ground level by clambering through shrubs and trees.

These layers, or tiers, of nature are easy to identify in a woodland, particularly at the edge of a meadow. The pattern may be less evident in a desert or prairie environment, but the relationships between the plants remain similar.

When it's time to design or redesign your garden, you'll need to understand which layer each of your chosen plants fits into. You'll place most of the tallest plants (the canopy layer) around the garden's perimeter to provide enclosure and to create a framework for your secondary plants. In large yards, one or two large trees may serve as a centerpiece for a great expanse of lawn, as a framework for an entry into a meadow, or as the focal point of the view from your home's largest window.

Most of the understory plants you'll plant are shrubs. They serve as visual ladders between the tallest

Under the lightest gardening hand, natural woodlands can become naturalistic gardens, echoing the layering found in native woods.

plants (small trees or large shrubs) and the furnishing layer (mostly flowers). These understory plants provide a backdrop for flowers, but they can also serve multiple functions. Ideally, they will clothe the garden in every season, offer visual privacy, muffle noise, create habitats for birds and beneficial insects, and produce a series of seasonal beauties.

The furnishing and groundcover layers combine typical flowerbed plants (like annuals, perennials, bulbs, and groundcovers) with more structural plants (like compact or dwarf shrubs). Some of the plants in these two layers will be evergreen, clustered to carry year-round presence to the lowest layer of the garden. Others will be deciduous, and these may offer three or four seasons of floral and foliage display.

The idea of layering is what I call "sandwich gardening." (This concept is discussed further on page 112.) Sandwich gardening emulates the natural patterns we see in meadows and prairies, where wave after wave of plants succeed each other. All share the same ground space, so these must be plants that compete well for resources and don't take more than their fair share. The furnishing layer of the garden can be sandwiched with many cooperative plants that take turns blooming with grace, then die off with dignity.

What Is Organic Design?

One of the chief principles of organic design is that you garden where you live. Successful gardens come in all sizes and styles, but they all look comfortably at home in their environments. When you try to copy gardens from distant times and places, you often create a lot of problems for yourself and your plants. When you garden where you really are, you use plants that will enjoy the conditions your garden can naturally offer them.

Gardening where you live also means that you employ garden decorations and design features that make sense in your climate and setting. For example, reflecting pools and lush lawns look utterly out of place in the desert. When you garden where you live, you will employ a garden style that makes sense with the architecture of your home, the natural architecture of the native habitat, and the weather and climatic conditions of your region.

None of this means you can't have the type or style of garden you admire elsewhere. It simply means that your version of those gardens will be healthier, more successful, and easier to care for when you use your common sense and interpret those gardens

I like to say that organic design harnesses the power of the plant.

realistically to your environment. You'll need to adapt those admired plantings by replacing inappropriate plants with others that will have the same effect, but which will thrive in your climate. Thanks to the rapidly increasing presence of regional specialty nurseries, you can almost always find replacement plants that match the originals in size, form, texture, and color.

The essence of any philosophy of garden design is either control or cooperation. Trying to control how plants grow usually doesn't work. This is where organic design comes into play. Organic garden design is about plant cooperation. If you first learn what your plants require in order to flourish and you then combine them into self-reliant communities of plants with like needs, you'll be successful. When you look for plants that, by their nature, mature at the size and shape and habit you want for your design, you'll be satisfied. Above all, when you choose plants that will enjoy the conditions and company you can offer, you'll have a garden design that works.

The idea of plant cooperation also involves eliminating repetitive chores whenever possible. Lawn mowing is a good example. In Denver, I've seen a wonderful lawn of buffalo grass studded with minor bulbs.

ABOVE: This formal garden featuring clipped shrubs is an example of a control-oriented design; a gardener will need to spend many hours keeping these plants inbounds. The plants within the boxlike spaces are often referred to as "infill" by formal designers, since they use the plants sheerly for color and filling in rather than for their natural attributes.

RIGHT: Naturalistic garden designs, on the other hand, are based on green architecture. The shapes and textures of the plants create structure, presence, and impact, without requiring constant care to keep them in check.

It's attractive in any season and never needs mowing because it grows very slowly. In the maritime Northwest, shade and moisture can destroy turf lawns, but moss gardens will thrive with little intervention. In recent years, a number of grass specialists have developed lawn mixtures that require less water and mowing than usual. Many combine tufting, low-growing grasses with meadow flowers such as daisies, chamomile, clovers, and creeping veronicas. These blends are often available through garden centers, nurseries, and mail-order catalogs.

Tasks like shearing and pruning are inherently repetitive as well, because they can only alter plant shape temporarily. Once again, trying to control plants won't work because constant or regular size reduction is never good for plants. If plants require continual whacking to keep them at the size you want, they are in the wrong place. If plants require frequent shearing to give them the shape you want, you have the wrong plants.

In a cooperative organic design, the right plants mature to the desired size and shape naturally. If you want a formal look, it's quite possible to get it without endless clipping and shearing. You simply choose plants like junipers and mugo pines with a naturally formal or symmetrical shape. When planting gardens with more fluid, natural lines, sculptural plants like Harry Lauder's walking stick, also known as corkscrew hazel (*Corylus avellana* 'Contorta'), are equally valuable.

I like to say that organic design harnesses the power of the plant. Our goal is to create a living landscape with potent natural architecture. When we use plants for what they actually are, not for what we wish they would be, they can contribute powerfully to the look and style of the garden with little intervention.

Why I'm an Organic Gardener

To someone who has never tried it, organic gardening sounds great, but it may also sound like a lot of work. Garden making certainly can be hard work, especially when you follow the well-meaning instructions found in most gardening books. For several centuries, the standard guides have explained in detail exactly how to make gardens that by their very design create an enormous workload of continual chores. This kind of gardening was based on the largely unconscious assumption that there would always be a well-trained and inexpensive workforce available. Thus, the gardener would obviously not need to perform any of these tedious, repetitive chores himself. (Gardeners were also assumed to be male for several centuries.)

More recently, the chemical revolution convinced many people that proper gardens had to look perfect. To those who followed this revolution, this meant that their gardens had to be *immaculate,* without a weed or bug in sight. Perfectionism is a loser's game in any case, but in gardening, it has been a force for harm. The concept of a "perfect garden" encourages people to see the natural world as something to be overcome. Domination of nature through poisons like pesticides and herbicides is cruelly easy. Its very simplicity fosters feelings of superiority and makes it seem as if it were right to kill any living thing that might annoy a human. Heaven forbid that a bug or weed should mar the perfection of our acres of lawn or billowing borders!

In my experience, organic gardening is easier than control-oriented power gardening. When you use planting patterns found in nature, you don't need to maintain combative "chainsaw" relationships with your plants. I design beds and borders so a plant's natural attribute (like a gentle weeping form) is an asset, not a detriment, to the surrounding plants. I don't try to alter the essential nature of a plant or my soil; instead, I simply take advantage of their strengths. I'm not an expert on pests and diseases because I rarely deal with either of them. By leaving plenty of native plants along my property edges, I provide habitat, cover, and fodder for wildlife. Those wild edges also support beneficial insects that are natural predators of pesky ones.

What I like best about organic gardening is the result—an easygoing, healthy haven full of birds, blossoms, and beauty. My garden is a place overflowing with ease and comfort, not endless chores and problems. That feels great to me.

Cooperative Plants Are Part of the Plan

WHEN YOU DESIGN A GARDEN, YOU NEED TO THINK NOT only about the shape and structure of the garden, but also about choosing plants that will work on your site. I always begin to develop a garden palette by picking out adaptive plants from a base of what I like to call "natives and allies." When you think in terms of cooperative design, native plants are a logical place to start, especially where conditions may be challenging. Part of organic design is incorporating native plants already present in the garden; it may also mean finding room for native seedlings when they appear.

Naturally, you can always pick and choose. However, our native flora is seldom as honored at home as it is in Europe. Too often, natives are dismissed as "weeds" without being given serious evaluation. When my students complain that nothing will grow under the cedars or maples that are native to this part of the Northwest, I remind them to look in the woods. In my part of the world, even huge old trees are naturally underplanted with a great range of shrubs and perennials, from huckleberries and flowering currants to trilliums and false Solomon's seal.

The Importance of Native Plants

To many gardeners, the term "native plant" can seem quite confusing. Some people feel that only plants that show up persistently in pollen records going back thousands of years can be considered native to a region. Others claim that any plant that was present in North America before Columbus arrived is native here. Some like to include non-native plants that have naturalized comfortably across the country. In my view, naturalized plants are non-natives that make themselves at home in many situations, like common daylilies and Queen Anne's lace. Other gardeners take a broader definition, calling any plant that can and does grow in North America a native plant.

> Too often, natives are dismissed as "weeds" without being given serious evaluation.

For our purposes, let's say that natives are plants that occur in nature in the parts of our region that most closely resemble our garden site. This is an important distinction because it keeps us from making the assumption that every native will like our garden. For instance, I live on an island near Seattle in Washington State. On my side, west of the Cascade Mountains, soils are acid and often clay-based. Gardens tend to be moist and shady, and the native landscape is dominated by forests with a generous understory layer. East of the Cascade mountains, though, soils are alkaline. Gardens tend to be hot and dry, and the native landscape leans toward open grassy savanna, punctuated by bursts of pine. Clearly, plants that thrive on one side of the mountains are not likely to enjoy the other. Only the most adaptable will cross over with ease.

If you're fortunate enough to have a stream tumbling through your site, collect native wetland plants to grace the bank and create a habitat for small animals and birds.

Allies in the Garden

In horticulture, I like to use the term "allies" to refer to plants from the same botanical family or from related genera. An example is the mint family, *Lamiaceae* and the mint-family genera *Mentha*, *Nepeta*, and *Melissa* (plants with square stems and similar flowers, such as peppermint, catnip, and lemon balm). In my garden, I grow six color forms of native red currant, *Ribes sanguineum*, as well as several Californian species and some from Europe and Asia. I call these familial allies.

Allies can also be companion plants or relatives of plants that are found growing in association with our chosen natives in the wild. In the nearby woods, I can find red currant growing with red huckleberry (*Vaccinium parvifolium*) and redtwig dogwood (*Cornus alba*), both of which also grow in my garden. Redtwig dogwood is a terrific hedging plant, and it has several fine garden forms in different sizes and twig colors.

When you are faced with a tough situation, have a challenging site to plant, or simply want to expand a limited plant palette, begin by seeking allies of your native plants. For instance, if I want to make the August garden brighter, I might look for allies of the field goldenrods that seem to glow all summer long. This might lead me to come up with sparkling 'Fireworks' goldenrod (*Solidago rugosa* 'Fireworks') as the perfect choice.

By drawing on your native flora and by imitating the natural plant relationships around you, you can develop core plantings that will not need much summer water, will take winters in stride, and can thrive on a steady diet of nutritive mulches such as compost, instead of artificial fertilizers.

Developing a Garden Style

YOUR GARDEN MAY BE CHARACTERIZED BY COLORFUL combinations of perennials and foliage shrubs, by whimsical or beautiful garden sculpture, or by a vast collection of birdhouses. Quite simply, garden style is what puts your personal stamp on the garden. Such personal expressions of taste give each garden its own character and personality.

The phrase "garden style" often refers to the school or type of garden design that determines the shape and plantings of the garden. A cottage garden will have simple paths and billowing beds filled with a mixture of edible and flowering plants. An Asian-inspired garden will be spare, uncrowded, and thoughtfully planted. Each component, whether living or artificial, will be placed with attention to its sculptural qualities. Formal gardens are generally laid out symmetrically, using straight lines and geometrical axes. Plants are nearly always clipped and are rarely allowed to keep their natural forms. Informal gardens are based on curves and sweeps instead of straight lines. The plantings generally look more casual than contrived, and are sometimes based on natural relationships.

This artist's garden is full of style and personality. The low garden wall and eclectic path heighten the drama of the garden just beyond the arbor arch.

Combining traditional elements from Asian and Western garden design, this Japanese garden uniquely celebrates powerful sculpted forms and natural layering. A gardener extraordinaire is clearly at work here, using touches of color and texture to create a memorable living canvas.

The Liveliest Art

All artists are creative, but I consider the art of garden making the liveliest of the arts. By mingling plants of many kinds in rich profusion, we can create thriving communities that echo the natural relationships of plants in native habitats. You can shape these communities as you please, creating a potent but informal structure with curving beds and sweeping paths that echo the purposeful but sinuous meandering of streams through meadows or woodlands.

Some gardeners may initially feel more comfortable with a more formal design, using artificial planting patterns based on symmetry and geometry. Because these traditional patterns are based on control rather than on cooperation between people and plants, it is a great deal more challenging to create

naturalistic, plant-centered gardenscapes using those rigid parameters. However, you can freely adapt any school or style you admire and strive to create spaces that invite visitors in and make your plants appear comfortably at home.

Once you have given your garden shape, your personal taste will direct the way you group and cluster your plants. Your own sense of beauty will direct the way you arrange those partnerships so that color, form, texture, and mass are emphasized and repeated in the garden. You can go on, developing season after season of color and interest, until at last you have created a palette of plants that provide structure, beauty, privacy, and powerful visual pleasure throughout the entire year.

The Garden as Art

To make a garden that suits both your needs and your sense of beauty, you must define your personal taste and style. This can be trickier than it sounds. You may be quite aware of what you admire in general terms: You know how you like to dress, what sorts of colors and objects you prefer to have around you in your home, and even the kind of artwork you enjoy. However, it's not always easy to understand why you made the choices you did. Very often, you are simply buying or selecting one object from many, and you may be refining your choice by comparing it to the others close at hand: This shirt or that one? This lamp or that one? This paint color or that one?

one

Many people with naturally fine taste are baffled when garden design proves so much more challenging than furnishing a home or pursuing artistic endeavors such as painting, sculpting, or quiltmaking. The first reason for this is that it's often difficult to know what will happen in your garden as plants grow and become more mature. You can choose and arrange them with care, but you can't really control how they will react in their new home. Some will settle in willingly, appreciating the conditions you can offer them. There are others that will perform all too well, requiring you to replace them with less-ambitious substitutes or making you alter a pathway to accommodate the now-mature size and shape of the plantings.

Second, making a garden is often a more complex process than creating artwork because it forces you to think and create from many angles. Many kinds of art (especially flat paintings) can only be seen properly from certain vantage points. This gives the artist implicit control over the way the images are viewed. The garden is much different. It's certainly three-dimensional, like sculpture, and it involves many architectural elements, some more dramatic than others. What's more, the viewer is often able to approach beds and borders from numerous angles: the front, the back, both sides, or head-on. This means you need to figure out how to create layers, combinations, and vignettes that are as visually appealing across the distance of a lawn as they are when close at hand.

Third, when you design a garden, you have to take into account the fourth dimension—time. Plants change their shape, size, and color seasonally, and your carefully chosen plant relationships change with the seasons and years. What was once the tallest anchor plant in the grouping may become one of the smaller ones as the shrubs and trees reach maturity.

It takes time to appreciate the fullness of a garden. It also takes time for the garden to come into being. And it takes time to learn how to make a garden that rewards your attentions many times over. Fortunately, the process of learning to make a garden is as rewarding as having a garden—perhaps even more so.

ABOVE: Historically accurate formal gardens complement this Colonial Williamsburg home. The same home would look equally comfortable if enveloped in a simple, naturalistic garden based on trees, shrubs, and old-fashioned flowers.

RIGHT: Loosely knit masses of bold native penstemons and verbenas give this hillside garden a distinctively West Coast flavor. The garden becomes more naturalistic as it transitions into the woodlands behind the sloping beds.

Making Garden Dreams a Reality

IT'S TIME TO TURN YOUR ATTENTION TO YOUR SITE, YOUR wants, and your needs. The "Organic Garden Design School Workbook" on page 232 will take you through the processes of assessing your garden and site as they are today and dreaming about how you want your garden and site to be a few years down the road. To garden realistically, you need to know what you have to work with, both on and above ground level. If you have an established garden, it's easy to identify paths and large plants that are already in place. If you are starting with bare earth, the possibilities can feel crippling. It's helpful to review the various aspects of your site, empty or full, before making any big decisions. And the easiest way to see what's really there, or not there, is to draw a site map.

Your site map doesn't need to be complex, but it does need to be fairly complete. The drawing should indicate the shape and size of the site, as well as all its key elements. These can be physical characteristics, such as aspect (which way is north?) and changes of grade (are there moderate or steep slopes or rises?). They can also be situational: The front yard is always sunny, the prevailing winds come from the west, rainwater puddles persistently along the north side of the garage.

The site map also records the locations of structures, starting with the house and garage and including the driveway and any paths. The drawing should also include "hardscape"—man-made structures such as walls and fences, arbors and arches, and patios and pergolas.

An inventory of important plants will reveal the location and relative size of large trees and shrubs, all of which should be noted. Underground features such as power and sewer lines, septic fields, drains, and water infiltration lines should also be included. Overhead features like telephone wires, power lines, and the canopy line of large trees are equally relevant.

You may already be well acquainted with your property and therefore think this kind of review is not really needed. If so, you can probably make your basic map from memory. If you feel you know your site inside and out, making the map will still prove helpful when you begin to think about how you might design, or redesign, the available space. Even when you are completely aware of the dog's favorite nap spot, it's surprisingly easy to overlook such facts when designing a hypothetical garden on paper.

If you are not very familiar with the site, if it has many complicated features, or if you aren't sure just what you should be looking for, the workbook exercises will help you make a functional map simply and quickly. And as you work your way through the workbook, you'll also find that you'll need to look beyond what you see on the surface and start assessing what's really working and what's not working in your garden. It may be difficult to identify areas that need improving and even more difficult to figure out how to make changes, but the exercises will get you on the right path.

The 5 Senses of the Garden

When I design a garden, I always rely on a series of concepts that I describe as the five senses of the garden. Rather than physical attributes, these are more subtle aspects that give each garden its own flavor and character. These key senses are those of welcome, enclosure, entry, flow, and place.

A Sense of Welcome

Every designer has a favorite place to begin the design process, and each has a favorite starting principle. Mine is that of welcome. A well-designed garden welcomes us in. In welcoming gardens, the garden maker and visitors alike may feel at home, satisfied, at ease, and at times deeply joyful.

If being in our own garden creates feelings of stress or guilt (usually triggered by the sight of un-completed chores), its design may need a thor-ough overhaul. If gardening sessions involve a series of small exasperations, the design may simply need some practical fine-tuning.

Evaluating the sense of welcome begins with an examination of the main entrances to both home and garden. To do this well, you need to try to see past your assumptions about your home and garden. What you think you know can influence what you see. Thinking in terms of strengths and weaknesses helps you view almost anything a bit dispassionately, and this allows you to see it more as others do.

In the workbook section beginning on page 232, you'll find an entry assessment guide with questions that will help you identify the strengths and weak-nesses of this crucial part of your garden's design.

A Sense of Enclosure

Welcoming spaces are nearly always well defined. To give an open space definition and make it a place to be in its own right, you must clarify its perimeter, which means that you automatically create a sense of enclosure. You can do this symbolically, using low plantings or see-through fencing. Or you can approach it more tangibly, using informal and irregularly tiered plantings, solid fences, walls, or some combination of the three.

In either case, such an enclosure immediately declares the garden space as set apart, a place to be. Enclosure also makes it instantly attractive. We humans tend to use and enjoy enclosed space far more than we do open, undefined areas, which we generally avoid. This is why our front yards are so often rather sterile, empty places, while all the life and fun take place in our relatively private backyards.

A Sense of Entry

Next, you need an entrance, a gate, or a portal: a place to come in. Like enclosure, entry further defines the garden as a place apart, separate from the ordinary world. By breaking the enclosure with an arch, an arbor, or a gate, and by providing glimpses of open space beyond the constriction of the entry-way, you create a powerful invitation to enter.

A well-designed entry will be welcoming without giving up all the garden's secrets at a glance. Entries that allow enticing glimpses of the garden are more tantalizing than those that majestically frame the entire yard. The entry must be wide enough to permit comfortable access, yet it should also provide a stimulating bit of mystery. What lies behind that gate, that arch, that subtly winding path?

Entries that are enclosed overhead reinforce this mysterious aspect nicely, often creating a strong wish to see more. Arches, arbors, pergolas, and plant "tunnels" that seem to cut through a hedge all create a feeling of passage and entry. By making someone pass from a lighted area, through shadow, and back into light, you make both a physical and an emotional transition to the beckoning space.

A Sense of Flow

"Flow" is a term designers use to describe the way people move through space. In a house, you might say that a certain cluster of rooms has good flow, because it's easy to get from place to place in a natural manner. Good interior flow is also visual, leading the eye from object to object or room to room. When rooms and hallways feel awkward and are difficult to use well, you say they lack flow. An interior designer may use low walls, tall counters, mirrors, and arrangements of furniture to improve flow indoors.

In the garden, the same concepts apply. In gardens with good flow, the paths lead both the eye and foot in ways that maintain our interest and offer pleasing surprises. Each seating area is alluring. Each vista, however small, calls you onward. Paths curve, creating a sense of expansive space and adding a touch of mystery.

A good garden designer will analyze the transition zones between the house and the garden space and create a free flow between the inside and out, either visually or in terms of foot traffic.

A Sense of Place

A well-designed garden has a definite sense of place. This can mean several things, beginning with character. A garden that looks as if it belongs where it is always shares something of the character of the house it belongs to, and it also reflects the character of its owner. No matter what their style or kind, gardens should suitably reflect their surroundings, both in terms of the immediate area and in terms of the greater community.

This does not mean that you should mimic the planting patterns of suburbia! Most suburban design denies its place, trading character and presence for anonymous neatness. Often it is impossible to tell from a photograph whether a typical suburban home is in Ohio or Oregon. By contrast, gardens that belong to their settings will reflect local habitat, incorporate regional plants, and echo native plant relationships.

Organic Design Principles

When you begin to think about designing a garden, analyzing the site and making a site map should be your first steps, and they're relatively simple ones. It's also important to identify which elements of the garden are wonderful keepers and which might be disposable, and that's not particularly difficult either. But finding the best replacements for existing plants and successful solutions for problem areas can seem a lot harder. **The good news is that you don't have to get everything right to make a wonderful garden.** Indeed, one of the great mysteries of garden design is why some gardens that do everything "right" in terms of design are stiff, unwelcoming spaces, while others that are "wrong" in terms of design can be enchanting.

The secret ingredient in many successful gardens is heart, pure and simple. Made-to-order gardens seldom have the warmth that deeply beloved gardens do. A garden that's been a labor of love will welcome visitors with open arms.

In addition to heart, clarity of vision is important to achieving a satisfying garden design. It is certainly far easier to create an attractive, serviceable garden when you are clear about what you want the garden to be and do. Your vision may also involve identifying missing elements or figuring out how to **make do with what you have available.**

Very often, however, it's easy to become impatient with planning. Before you're really ready with a comprehensive plan, you jump in and start planting things more or less at random. If you find this to be true in your garden, your first project when designing or redesigning might be to make a nursery bed or holding area for new acquisitions. In such a spot, randomness does no harm, as long as you don't crowd the plants. Indeed, **chance juxtapositions** from the nursery bed often suggest rewarding border combinations.

On the other hand, if you think your entire garden looks like a holding area, the result is rarely restful, alluring, or satisfying. The wisest policy is to put a temporary moratorium on buying new plants and to concentrate instead on deciding what to do with what you already have.

Starting a Design the Right Way

WHEN I DESIGN A GARDEN, THE FIRST THINGS I THINK about are spaces and access; I try to create interesting places within the garden, and then figure out how to get there efficiently and attractively. Then I turn my thoughts to privacy and screening. If I want a garden that will be used, it has to have space that's out of view of neighbors and passersby. Next comes problem solving, where I deal with practical considerations such as poor drainage or difficult changes of grade. Only after I've dealt with spaces, access, privacy, screening, and problem solving do I find places for key specimen

Cut with a stone chisel, old concrete makes natural-looking walls that border various sections of the garden and provide continuity in this large setting.

plants and planting beds. These fall into place quite easily after thinking about the other issues.

I believe that it's always helpful to have real-life examples that utilize the principles you're learning. To make this sequence of thinking about spaces, access, privacy, screening, problem solving, and planting more clear for you, I'd like to share a few examples of how I designed gardens for my home on Bainbridge Island. I used the same process that I teach at my garden school (called The Sequoia Center) to actually create the gardens around my home and school. Many of the site details and settings may not mirror your situation exactly, but most of the ideas will be applicable in some way to your home garden.

My situation is somewhat unique because I have a building that houses a healing arts center in my backyard. You, on the other hand, may have an equally challenging garage to deal with, or close-set neighbors whose homes are a willy-nilly part of your skyline. You may not have poor soil, steep slopes, persistent standing water, a noisy road, deer, slugs, or wandering sheep like I do, but I'm sure you have problems in your landscape that you'd like to resolve. Some of the design ideas I'm presenting are for large-scale sites, while others apply to spaces that are actually quite small. In nearly all cases, these plans can be scaled up or down to fit into larger or smaller spaces. This is easily done by paying attention to plant size (using small plants in small settings) and by adapting portions of designs you like to fit into your space.

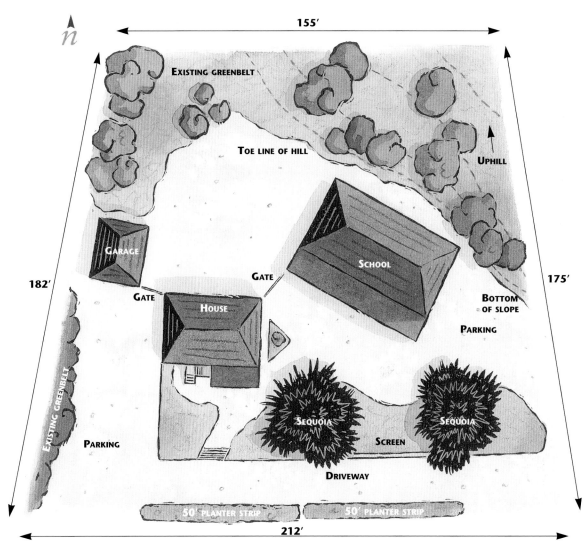

This ¾-acre site sits at the foot of a sloping hillside with a dense greenbelt on two sides. Two large sequoia trees screen the garden school from the busy road that runs in front of the house.

Spaces and Access

MY PROPERTY FEATURES A HOUSE, AN OUTDOOR GARDEN school, and a healing arts center, and is home base for the various activities of my two teenage sons. We bought this home a few years ago. It's located on a ¾-acre lot on a fairly busy road. When we bought it, the sloping site included a modest but well-built older home with a great deal of concrete paving on the flat portions of ground. (The former owners had a catering business and needed loading docks.) The uphill area behind the house was lightly wooded and full of old stumps and scrubby second growth (younger, smaller plants that move in after mature forest has been clear-cut). Nearly all of the existing outbuildings were dilapidated and needed to be removed. Scruffy grass covered the spaces between the concrete pads. The only plants of note were two magnificent sequoia trees by the roadside and some pretty stands of mixed native trees such as fir, hemlock, yew, alder, and cascara, and many species of maples.

Apart from its accessibility and size (which allowed us to add the large healing arts center building), the site's main assets were a view of a wonderful tree line and deep woods bordering the lot on two sides. Its main drawbacks were very poor soil and the noise from the busy road. Back in the 1940s, when the site was cleared, all the topsoil had been pushed across the road to build up a neighbor's soggy building site. That left an unpromising subsoil layer exposed, most of

which was hardpan. It's no wonder that the grass looked scruffy when we moved in.

Of course, we began by measuring and mapping the site, so we would have a tool to work with as we analyzed spaces and access. In our case, there was a lot of clutter—unwanted hardscape and unwanted plants—that we had to get rid of first.

Clear Clutter First

The aging outbuildings were demolished and the concrete pads were broken up into usable pieces. These were cut with a stone chisel to give them a clean edge, then stacked into unmortared retaining walls to hold up several eroding slopes. We were fortunate that we could recycle our concrete pieces into walls. You may want to do something similar, or you can use the pieces for pathways, stepping stones, or garden structures like a water garden or a wishing well.

The sinuous retaining walls that hold the hillside in place in front of my house are made from recycled concrete that was already on the site. An excavator broke the old concrete pads into chunks, and these larger pieces were trimmed and stacked into loose, unmortared walls that allow hillside runoff to drain freely. We are often asked where we got the "granite" for our walls, and some people flatly refuse to believe that it's recycled concrete until we show them the stripes on a piece that had been part of an old tennis court.

New buildings often fit uneasily into existing plantings, but the school building seems to have been in place for years. We left the lower branches on the backdrop trees so they would envelop the building in a natural-looking manner. Even though it made the construction process slightly more difficult, the result was worth the extra trouble. Even the building crew agreed—in the end!

We had an excavator peel off all the struggling turf, and we cleared the few small trees and understory shrubs from the area we planned to build in. And yes, we composted the turf in one pile, then heaped the brush into another large pile that now supports a variety of wildlife.

Once the land behind our house was cleared, we selected the site for our new healing arts building. We knew that we had to do this before we could tackle any specifics of our garden design. (This is true for anyone who plans to add a garage or an addition to their home—it will have a significant impact on the spaces you'll end up designing.) Building code restrictions gave us little choice about where the healing arts center would go on the property, but we wanted to position the building so that the area between the house and the center would have interesting angles and spaces for the gardens we wanted to add.

We spent a long time playing with sticks and colored surveyor's tape, marking out the parameters of the building in various places. Because the existing house sits low on the land, it would be easy for the large, barn-like structure to overwhelm it. We used different colors of tape to show each possibility, angling the shape back and forth over the narrow lot. This type of playing and imagining is always helpful, even for siting a small storage shed or your children's swing set.

When large buildings like a home and a garage are aligned in rows or set at right angles, the space between them often feels static—architects of space call this "dead space." Even a slight change in the angles at which they sit can make for far more intriguing spaces that are easier to turn into attractive, alluring gardens.

When we found just the right angle for the school, the result was amazing. It's hard to believe that a

Named for its beautiful trees, The Sequoia Center for the Healing Arts is a dedicated place of service. The center offers classes in tai chi, yoga, meditation, kung fu, Nia, and dance; sponsors community council circles; and is home to the garden school.

40 × 60-foot building that stands 20 feet tall could fail to loom over a modest home, yet the school is hardly visible from the main windows of the house, despite the fact that it stands mere feet away. To further soften the look of the big building, we stepped down the front side to create a lower face in scale with the entry to our home. If you have a similar situation, such as where your two-story garage or another outbuilding overshadows a single-story house, try lowering part of the facade to help integrate the taller building into the surrounding landscaping.

The Power of the Path

Once we decided on the placement and architecture of the healing arts center, we were ready to start the garden design process. The first task we turned our attention to was creating access to the building by developing paths. Paths have a great deal to do with a garden's flow. Well-made paths visually lead us ever onward, suggesting infinite space with a gentle curve and a veiling screen of foliage. Curves, even slight ones, are the gardener's best friend where spaces are small or confined. Nothing more powerfully suggests the continuation of space than a curving line. In contrast, when paths are dead straight they expose the full extent of the space, often with no more reward than an empty birdbath.

The shape of our lot and the desired flow of foot traffic offered us only a few options for paths. I wanted to make the paths from the parking area to the school building very obvious because I wanted to direct students away from the entryway to our home and toward the school. The main entry paths are 8 feet wide, swelling into a small courtyard in front of the school and house and swelling again into parking lots where they meet the driveway and roadway. The effect is like a little river pouring smoothly through the property. The broad paths make it clear where students should enter the school and gardens.

We chose soft curves instead of angles for the paths because we wanted to emphasize the natural fall and flow of the property. Though the path end is never fully obscured, the gentle curves are alluring, coaxing eye and foot onward to see what comes next. Smaller paths that are 4 to 6 feet wide lead to more intimate areas, such as our home, the tai chi practice garden, and a shady garden tucked into the wooded hillside.

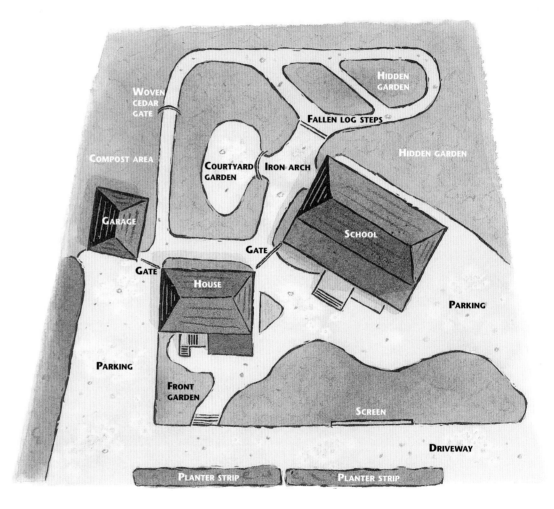

The flow of paths becomes extremely important when there is considerable foot traffic on a site. With over 100 visitors each day, the garden school pathways must be generous enough to serve several people at once. Near the school building and parking lots, where folks often linger and chat, the paths broaden even more to accommodate the to-and-fro of students and the casual seating areas that are enjoyed almost year-round.

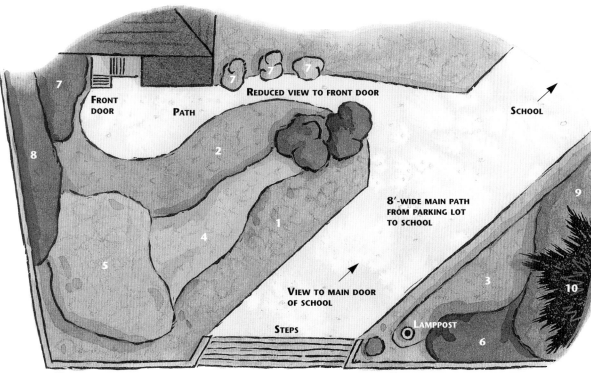

FRONT DOOR

REDUCED VIEW TO FRONT DOOR

PATH

SCHOOL

7

8

2

1

4

5

8'-WIDE MAIN PATH FROM PARKING LOT TO SCHOOL

9

3

10

VIEW TO MAIN DOOR OF SCHOOL

STEPS

LAMPPOST

6

5'-HIGH RETAINING WALL

5'-HIGH RETAINING WALL

To provide privacy throughout the year, the front beds hold a mixture of screening shrubs such as redtwig dogwoods and brooms. About half the bed's plants are small evergreen shrubs and grasses that give the bed a sturdy structure, with bulbs and perennials tucked into the pockets between the evergreens for ongoing flow of seasonal color.

PLANT KEY

1. HARDY SHRUBS AND EVERGREEN PERENNIALS (1'–2' HIGH)
2. HARDY SHRUBS AND PERENNIALS (1'–3' HIGH)
3. HARDY SHRUBS AND PERENNIALS (2'–6' HIGH)
4. HARDY SHRUBS AND GRASSES (2'–4' HIGH)
5. HARDY SHRUBS AND GRASSES (3'–6' HIGH)
6. HARDY SHRUBS AND PERENNIALS (4'–8' HIGH)
7. HARDY SHRUBS (6'–8' HIGH)
8. LARGE SHRUBS (8'–12' HIGH)
9. TALL SHRUBS (8'–15' HIGH)
10. SEQUOIA
11. FALSE CYPRESS
12. JAPANESE TANBARK OAK
13. ROSEMARY

If you've been working through the exercises in the workbook, you know that easy access between the house and garden is vital to an effective design. In our case, I used the back door when I wanted to go into the garden because the front door was inconvenient. I realized I had to downplay access to the front door of the house and steer visitors away from it, encouraging them to use a different door to the house. In actual design terms, this meant minimizing the path to one door and making an inviting and very obvious pathway to the preferred one.

We decided to build a wide set of steps on the slope in front of the house to direct visitors to an equally broad, 8-foot-wide gravel pathway. The flowing curve of the path powerfully pulls both eye and foot toward the new main entrance. To subtly minimize the importance of the front door, we created a narrowing, 5-foot-wide access path that hugs the house. An upright evergreen shrub hides the former front entrance. We also painted the white metal porch trim the same gray-black as the house, fading it out behind a curtain of clematis vines. This combination of factors turned the main entry into a quiet backwater, just as we had hoped.

Emphasizing Entrance

Throughout the school site, we have created gates, entryways, and portals that announce a change of style, atmosphere, or intention. If we can create a powerful sense of entry and access as we come into our gardens, they will be perceived as places with distinct character. Even when they're not fully enclosed, garden spaces evoke the presence of a room when the entrance to them is strongly delineated. When you plan to use various areas in very different ways, marking the entrance to each in a manner that accentuates the intended use will make your intentions more obvious to others.

We wanted the two entrances to the woodland garden (affectionately known as the Hidden Garden) behind the school to be distinctive and clearly unlike the lower gardens near the school. Where the first Hidden Garden entry path winds past the school building, we reduced it to just over 2 feet wide. Though the constricted section of path is only a few feet long, it makes the Hidden Garden seem hidden indeed, and gives an immediate sense of intimacy to the short journey uphill. There are shrubs on both sides of this narrow stretch, so even though the actual distance is quite short, you can't really see where you are going until you are almost there. This small access path winds between several large trees before leading into the Hidden Garden clearing.

A sense of mystery and adventure helps set gardens apart and gives them a particular character. When we can see everything at a glance, we are less intrigued than when we are made curious about what comes next. The sensation of passing from an open space through a constricted one, then reemerging into relative emptiness is intriguing (as long as the actual passageway is easily traveled and not lined with scratchy

Deeply layered gravel pathways have a lot of benefits: They offer safe footing for our many visitors, and they're firm enough for wheelchair access. Also, the dark-color native basalt gravel we used at the school is never glaringly reflective of light, and it drains perfectly in all types of weather.

plants). Because of this, we placed several large shrubs so that they obscure the actual dimensions of the garden space and conceal the windings of the path. These screening plants also help to create a sense of mystery and make the small area seem much larger than it actually is.

The second entrance to the Hidden Garden is off a secondary path that leads to our composting units and a large brush pile. Here, the climbing path passes between two sets of triple-trunked trees—a vine maple and a birch. Because this spot is over-looked from several key positions, it gains a visual importance that its actual function doesn't quite merit. To take advantage of the drama of the clus-tered, pale trunks against the dimness of the deep woods behind them, we commissioned a talented local artist, Sue Skelly, to create an arching gate with winged side pieces that taper into the sur-rounding woods. Made from naturally curved pieces of local cedar, this gateway powerfully proclaims the entrance into the woods.

In one sense, the change from woodland to a utility path is not a very important one; few people ac-tually enter the upper garden that way. However, be-cause the archway can be seen across the lower Courtyard Garden, its flowing lines dominate the scene so that the gateway becomes the focal point of the entire space. The Courtyard Garden is located just off the back door of our school. When this door is open, the garden is reflected onto the long, mirrored back wall of the practice hall. This mirror assists stu-dents with body alignment and movement practice, but it also serves to bring the garden into the school building. From within, we already see the young Courtyard Garden as an enclosed space, with the

arching gateway leading enticingly upward from be-yond the low plantings.

Even if the archway didn't really lead anywhere, it would still convince the eye and the imagination. In-deed, this device—setting up a gate to nowhere—is just as effective psychologically as visually. In sug-gesting physical extension, it lets us mentally expand our sense of space. Glimpsed through an enticing archway, the garden might be never ending (though as its main caretaker, I'm glad it's not).

Enclosed by foliage plants, the meditative Courtyard Garden is reflected in a wall of mirrors inside the school building. The garden beds feature plants for every season and contain a blend of structural evergreens, perennials, bulbs, and grasses.

The entry gate to the woodland Hidden Garden is woven from native red cedar branches and wild cherry bark. The artist, Sue Skelly, employs techniques that have been used by Native American woodworkers for millennia. The feet of the arch supports are burned to prevent rotting, and every piece is hand-tied with long-lasting native bark and vines.

Privacy and Screening

CREATING A RESTFUL GARDEN RETREAT IS AS MUCH ABOUT creating intimacy as it is about plants. Who wants to garden in a wide open space that offers little connection to tangible elements like shade and enclosure, and that allows the whole world to see your every move? Planning for privacy and screening can be easy once you've tackled the issues of spaces and access. When you've defined the parameters of your garden space, you can use trees, shrubs, and plants, plus hardscape features like fences and gates, to limit unwanted views and to create other, more scenic views and viewpoints. As the gardens on the property developed, issues of privacy and screening were foremost in our minds.

Peace, Tranquility, and Privacy

The Hidden Garden on the hillside overlooks a lower courtyard area created between the house and the school building. The native vegetation along the lower slope of the Hidden Garden makes an effective screen between the upper and lower gardens, even in the wintertime. The clusters of vegetation offer only a couple of functional view corridors and create a feeling of privacy. We've taken advantage of these scenic overlooks by providing benches where people can sit in a cool, shady spot and look down into the open, sunny Courtyard Garden below. One bench overlooks our cat shrine, the resting place for family

pets that have been gathered home. As time passes, this area is filling up with sculpture and mementos that family and friends bring to it. There are also several commemorative plants that mark the passing of dear friends. We even planted a 'Rex' rhododendron to remind us of a favorite cat whom we now speak of as "The King on the Hill."

This little sculpture corner creates an enticing inner view that holds its own in any season. We use sculptural pieces as simple as a rock, a piece of driftwood, or a lovely fallen branch for accents. If you create a sculpture corner on a site where electricity is available, you could add water features of all sizes, from the simplest bubbler to the tumble of a recirculating cascade, to function as sculptural elements. Even without electricity, broad, shallow bowls can serve as water mirrors. During the summer, we often keep a full water jar in the shade garden, where the smooth surface reflects passing clouds and glimpses of sunny or moonlit skies into the shaded retreat. When ruffled by wind, these water mirrors send shimmering sparkles of light into every corner of the shade garden.

In the Hidden Garden, the wandering path of shredded bark meanders down to the cedar entry gate. In just a few seasons, the young understory layers will knit seamlessly into the established woodland plants, which have been edited with a light hand.

We use sculptural pieces as simple as a rock, a piece of driftwood, or a lovely fallen branch for accents.

Screens for All Seasons

When we were designing the gardens for the courtyard behind the house, we knew that there were several considerations. We needed to enclose the courtyard to block out street views and traffic noise, create a pathway from the parking lot to the school, and screen the view into the house from the pathway. The original space was a rough rectangle, largely enclosed on all sides. The house and school provide walls on two sides, while the other two are backed by mature woods of varying depth. Several gaps in this enclosure allowed views out to the busy road.

Both the school and my house have a view of this area, and I wanted it to look attractive in all seasons from both viewpoints. Because many people walk through it to get from the parking area to the school, we needed to provide a major path and night lighting. We also needed privacy screening for the house windows.

We began by building large cedar gates for both corners that opened out to street views. Both pieces are oversize and almost sculptural in quality. Linking house and school on one side and house and garage on the other, the gate panels needed to have architectural strength and serious bulk just to relate properly to the scale of the buildings and the setting as a whole.

Cedar gates mark the passage from the main school entry to the courtyard area. The gates also serve to flatten a tight corner, reducing the angularity of the overall space.

In winter, the salmon-and-gold stems glisten in the somber rain, drawing gasps of admiration from everyone who walks the path through the garden.

Set at oblique angles, these gates alter the feeling and form of the garden by making the courtyard space seem more enclosed; their angles also make the interior space feel less geometrically defined. When shut, these gates effectively reduce street noise (though nothing can eliminate it entirely, unfortunately) and reinforce the sense of place for the garden as a whole. The cedar panels are starting to age to a beautiful silvery gray that sets off plants almost as well as our dusky building walls.

When we created the main pathway to the school from the parking lot, we also defined a shallow crescent-shaped planting bed alongside the house specifically for shrubs that would create a privacy screen for the house windows. A simple, rhythmic planting now screens the view entirely, to the satisfaction of viewers from all angles. Five stunning 'Midwinter Fire' twiggy dogwoods (*Cornus sanguinea* 'Midwinter Fire') are spaced on 8-foot centers along the 40-odd-foot expanse of the house wall. In winter, the salmon-and-gold stems

glisten in the somber rain, drawing gasps of admiration from everyone who walks the path through the garden. When lit at night, these red-and-gold stems are among the most impressive pieces in the whole garden, with a beauty that never palls.

Between the dogwoods are clumps of a gold-leaved whitewashed bramble (*Rubus idaeus* 'Aureus') with powdery white stems that gleam out in winter against the dusky house and school walls. Spills of golden-variegated hakone grass (*Hakonechloa macra* 'Aureola') line the front of the bed, accompanied in season by softball-size purple ornamental onions (*Allium christophii*). The effect, I must admit, is breathtaking and memorable.

Naturalistic gardens rely on plants to serve many purposes, from adding screens and enclosures to filtering noise and views. When privacy and screening are the topics at hand, you can count on finding dozens of ways to use plantings to create enclosure and intimacy for your garden spaces.

Though many dogwoods are grown for their flowers, 'Midwinter Fire' twiggy dogwood (*Cornus sanguinea* 'Midwinter Fire') could easily be grown just for the spectacular showing of colorful stems. Reaching 10 feet high, this dogwood is useful as a scrim plant where only a partial view is desired.

Problem Solving

Our site presented a number of large challenges and more than a few small problems we had to correct. When faced with decision making about a small or large problem, be sure to keep an open mind. Review your site map and all the notes you've taken, and discuss a variety of options before you proceed. Sometimes the answer has been apparent from the start, but more often than not, the best solution is one that takes a while to percolate.

Building Better Beds

We decided to tackle the front garden area early in our site transformation. The excavations for the school building showed us that the hardpan layer under the front gardens was at least 15 feet deep. Despite this drawback, we wanted to grow a mixture of evergreen and deciduous plants that could take advantage of the full blast of western sun in the afternoon. Although the front garden banks steeply, it does not drain particularly well. Winter root rots carry off more plants than winter cold, so we would clearly need to improve drainage in this area.

We did this in two ways. First, we replaced several cracked, old sidewalks with deep gravel paths that would drain water quickly. Next, we created raised beds above the hardpan. Over the past decade or so, all the gardens I've made have been raised above soil level. In these beds and borders, plants of all kinds flourish for years with no commercial fertilizers and very little summer watering. I know that whether I want ornamental or edible gardens, layered raised beds will give me good results without my having to resort to tilling or double-digging (which is good because both tasks are basically impossible with our hardpan soil). I use annual feeding mulches (4-inch layers of compost) to keep the soil in good health indefinitely.

After much debate over siding colors, we chose a soft, receding shade of charcoal black steel for both the house and the school building. It may sound gloomy, but the effect is powerful. It is the perfect backdrop for plants of every color.

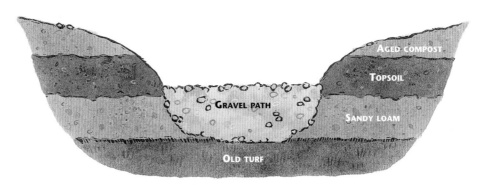

Raised beds mean less toil for gardeners dealing with poor native soil. Layers of sandy loam, topsoil, and aged compost create a hospitable environment for plants of all kinds. Raised beds are the perfect partners for garden paths because the high soil level keeps the gravel in place effortlessly.

Since the site drains poorly, we gave our raised beds a deep base of sandy loam, which drains freely but has enough loamy content to hold its shape. Sandy loam is available in some regions; if you have difficulty finding a source, you may have to use a topsoil and sand mixture. On sites with clay, hardpan, or subsoil, this bottom layer of sandy loam should be at least 6 to 8 inches deep. In large gardens, or where the land is very irregular, the base layer may be a foot deep or more.

You can use this relatively inexpensive material to fill holes, even out irregularities, and make privacy berms. You can also shape beds to create visually interesting topography. Subtle ridges and dips make good places to set attractive rocks, and sculptural plants can be showcased by setting them a bit higher

than their less-shapely neighbors. If your site already drains well, you don't need the sandy loam layer, but it is a less expensive way to get bulk and height for large projects than using all topsoil is.

We covered our sandy loam base with a layer of clean topsoil. The topsoil layer of the beds can be as little as 6 or 8 inches or as much as a foot deep. The goal is to have a deep enough bed so that you won't need to dig into often-poor native soil when planting. Since raised beds will settle with time (and rain), make them several inches higher than you really want them. If most of the plants you use are in quarts or gallon containers, a foot of depth (after settling) is sufficient. If you're using larger nursery stock, deeper beds (or deeper areas in designated beds) will be needed.

Naturally, where the underlying soil is better than hardpan or heavy clay, these precautions are not necessary. Even so, making layered raised beds is far less intensive and time-consuming work than standard double-digging or tilling, especially since the preparatory part only needs to be done once. Once the garden beds are installed, feeding mulches of compost keep plants growing well. Raised beds made this way don't need edging strips, bender board, or wooden sides. We simply sloped the sides attractively, smoothing the edges as they reached the gravel paths. Gravity keeps both soil and gravel in place, and even heavy rains won't wash good topsoil into the paths. These layered raised beds do not need to be mixed or tilled—we just work a little compost into each planting hole and adjust the topdressing after planting.

Restoring Integrity

Whether you're gardening on an established lot or creating a garden around a newly constructed home, you'll probably discover site problems or construction aftermath that will need correcting. When we bought our property, I had no intention of altering the native greenbelt of trees and shrubs that clothed the hillside that backs the site. Unfortunately, because of the hardpan elsewhere, the hillside was the only possible place to put a drainfield for the school.

Curving walls create a clean-lined but natural-looking retaining wall for the front entry garden. This steeply pitched slope formerly held ragged grass and weeds. Now the front wall garden is one of the most handsome features of the property. The plantings have grown enough to help mask the front entry, effectively directing the eye away from the house and toward the school building behind it.

Happily, we found a company that was willing to create a hand-dug drainfield that required the removal of just a few young trees, leaving our majestic old ones intact.

The septic field excavator left a road-size scar running down the hillside, though, so we backfilled the high side of the tracks to restore the original line of the slope and to cover any exposed roots that were left high and dry during the construction process. We also reshaped the slope to match its former line and covered the exposed roots of the remaining native plants.

What remained of the raw excavator track was converted into a sinuous path that fools the eye by

The former understory was covered with ancient moss, and we wanted to re-create the look as much as possible.

wandering between the existing mature trees and by curving gently across the former truck-wide track. We added a few steps in sections of the path where the steepness of the slope might encourage erosion.

We deliberately made the pathways in this Hidden Garden narrower than those in more public parts of the garden. Here they vary between 3 and 4 feet wide, which is enough to accommodate a loaded wheelbarrow, but too narrow for two to walk abreast. This idea was inspired by the celebrated garden at Wave Hill in the Bronx, New York, where garden director Marco Stufano created narrow paths in a wooded section. His goal was to make it difficult for people to walk through the garden while conversing with others, because he felt that this particular part of the garden is best experienced alone. To encourage visitors to have a solitary experience, he cut down the usual path size until it was still functional as a working path for wheelbarrows but just wide enough for one strolling person.

Here at the garden school, we gradually reduced the 5-foot width of the secondary paths that lead to the Hidden Garden to a 3-foot width where they enter the woodland. To emphasize the change in atmosphere, we also changed path materials from gravel to coarse wood chips. These chips are a free resource in many communities where tall trees are common; they're available from the power line crews that clear

roadside vegetation. (Although I rarely admire the crew's pruning skill or their feeling for plants, I am willing to receive the results of their work. I figure the best way to honor the dead is by recycling fallen trees and shrubs back into a woodland garden, where they can molder peacefully.)

The former understory was covered with ancient moss, and we wanted to re-create the look as much as possible. By simply editing the woods, clearing out dead twigs and branches, and cleaning up elderly native shrubs, we succeeded in making a garden out of the tangled understory that existed when we purchased the land. The remaining plants responded very well to the renewed resources that weed removal and fresh soil offered them. Already, native understory plants like mosses, ferns, huckleberries, and creeping mahonias are returning to carpet these new pathside "beds."

Site problems can range from a seriously eroding hillside to a path that's uninviting. When finding a solution seems overwhelming, consider a consultation with a garden designer or landscape architect. Technically challenging problems are best handled by a professional. Smaller site challenges may keep you busy for years, but one of the rewards of gardening is the satisfaction of transforming a poorly used space into one that's alive with spirit, usefulness, and a sense of welcome.

Plants and Planting Beds

Where bulldozers left a wide scar, mounded beds now shrink the path back to human scale. We are planting native understory shrubs that will knit the garden back into the surrounding woodlands.

DESIGNING A GARDEN IS AN EVOLVING PROCESS. ONCE space and access have been addressed, issues of privacy and screening are worked through, and problem areas are corrected, you can have fun with the plants that inspired you to garden in the first place. Creating planting beds and plant communities is a challenging and richly rewarding activity, and if you're like me, you'll never run out of ideas for changing and improving your gardens.

Gardening High and Low

In our current backyard, we've created a set of upper and lower gardens between the school building and the house. Our beds are designed to merge naturally into the native plant community and greenbelt that borders our property. Behind the school, the hillside is filled with regal old trees and handsome natives. The winding path will lead visitors through a collection of species rhododendrons, native and not, and many of their natural allies. As the evergreen shrubs we planted in this area mature, they will mask the actual entry into this section of the garden, which will eventually become fully enclosed.

For quite a while, I was calling this area the "Septic Garden." Though apt, that name definitely lacked charm. Perhaps for that reason, this potentially intriguing area received very little attention for the first year or so that we lived there. When I started calling it the "Hidden Garden" everybody's attitude changed, including mine. Now, the newly named Hidden Garden is filled with rhodies and fragrant woodland witch hazels, including my particular favorite, the sumptuously scented *Hamamelis mollis* 'Pallida'.

At the feet of these shrubs are clusters of evergreen ferns and perennials, as well as lots of deciduous woodlanders that flower early in the year. The carpet is made of several kinds of native evergreen creepers, including wood sorrel (*Oxalis oregana* 'Wintergreen') and the same piggyback plant (*Tolmiea menziesii*) that I used to grow as a houseplant back in the East. All of the groundcovers are easygoing spreaders that are very easily removed when they wander past their designated areas.

After fighting thuggish groundcovers like yellow archangel (*Lamium galeobdolon*) and bishop's weed (*Aegopodium podagraria*), both of which make beautiful but formidable enemies in this climate, I've learned to choose my carpeters with caution. Beware of neighbors bearing groundcovers! As a rule of thumb, any groundcover that is offered to you for free by the truckload is probably not a choice plant. Many plants that behave fairly well in established, mature gardens, where there is plenty of root competition to keep them in check, can run wild in new ones, where empty beds are just waiting to be annexed.

My mannerly woodland carpet is punctuated by hundreds of Spanish bluebells (*Hyacinthoides hispanica*). These are not the choice English bluebells

of poetry and song, but humble, ragtag bulbs that are scrupulously dug out by local gardeners who dislike their untidy ways. I beg everybody's castoffs for my woodland garden, where they can ramble around without disturbing anything. In spring, these eager, hardworking bulbs provide a sheet of tender blue that mirrors the distant sky—all for free.

If this sounds like a direct contradiction to the above advice on groundcovers, I can only say that thuggishness is relative; some plants take no prisoners, while others are modestly content to wind underneath everybody else without interfering with their needs. If you're in doubt as to a plant's proclivities, ask a long-term local gardener. It's also a good idea to start looking around and making notes about how various plants behave in your region. Plants that seem modest in young gardens may have taken over completely in older ones, while some that do just fine in relatively empty young gardens dwindle in health and number as other plants take over in turn.

Overcoming Geometry

When you design naturalistic gardens, you should always push yourself to look beyond the obvious and expected outcome. The Courtyard Garden between the house and the school is a perfect example of finding a soft solution for a hard shape. Once the pathways for the courtyard were in place, this space

Designing by problem solving sounds negative to some ears, but to me it makes perfect sense.

loosely resembled a small pond. To completely erase the last traces of the original rectangular shape, we surrounded the courtyard with softly curving raised beds that look like the banks of a small, natural pool. These narrow beds run the whole way around the courtyard, leaving only one entryway into the space. In time, the courtyard will become completely enclosed with living green walls that will lap the space in foliage at any time of year.

To further set off the area and reinforce the sense of entrance to the Courtyard Garden, we commissioned a large iron arch for the entry. As luck would have it, while we were debating about how to deal with the entry, a fellow named Elvis drove up with a truck full of unusual and well-crafted ironwork. When he saw the space we wanted to fill, he created a beautiful, oversize double arch that was just the right solution. Decorated with naturalistic forms and the Chinese symbols for good health and happiness, this arch is set at a slight angle across the courtyard entrance so the intricate ironwork patterns can be seen against a plain background.

The long, narrow beds in the courtyard are an average of 8 to 10 feet wide, though they alter considerably as they wind about the site. Like the other beds in this garden, these have a 6-inch base of sandy loam covered with 8 inches of topsoil. Made in chilly winter, the beds were topped off with dairy manure, which kept them free of weeds until we were ready to plant them later in the spring.

By that time, the courtyard had taken on a decidedly Asian character, so we decided to fill the beds with a mixture of native plants and their Asian allies. Native vine maples are joined by several low-growing Japanese maples that perch like living sculptures on their sloping beds. The woodsy backdrop includes several large native rhododendrons, so we added dwarf and compact species rhodies with an intriguing variety of foliage forms and colors, as well as evergreen azaleas. Native Oregon grape and creeping leatherleaf were given glamorous Asian companions such as Leatherleaf mahonia (*Mahonia japonica* 'Bealei') and several mahonia hybrids (*M. × media hybrids*).

Our native ferns now have plenty of cousins with them, as do a goodly number of native wildflowers such as trillium, violets, false Solomon's seal, and umbrella plant (*Darmera peltata*). We have no native hostas, but I used them anyway, since they contrast so pleasingly with ferns and cutleaf astilbes, which are kin to our native false goatsbeard (*Astilbe biternata*). It's fun to plant a garden with an overall theme of this kind, but if a certain non-native and non-Asian plant looks at home in such company and would grow beautifully in those conditions, I would rather use it than to stick rigidly to the terms of my original proposition.

Now nearing completion (though I can always think of improvements), the Courtyard Garden is a good example of a simple but successful design that turned an undistinguished side yard into an unusual and attractive place with a distinctive character. The quality I am most pleased with here is its seeming inevitability; to most eyes, the courtyard garden looks like a natural opening in the woods around it. It provides pleasing views from the house and also effortlessly becomes an extension of the school practice hall by simply opening a door.

An oversize iron arch combines the Chinese symbols for good health and happiness at the top of the arch with vinelike, naturalistic forms on the sides of the arch. Elvis Whittingham, a local ironworker who emigrated from Jamaica, crafted this stunning arch that displays the kind of cultural design fusion often found on the West Coast.

Nearly everybody who offered "helpful" suggestions during the planning stage started by assuming that this area would best be treated geometrically. My feeling was that, precisely because it *did* have such geometrical surroundings, it was all the more important to link the design to the natural sides of the setting, relegating the buildings to being mere backdrops. By doing this, the garden gained the refreshing quality of a natural setting, making those who enter it feel that they are truly surrounded by nature.

Designing by problem solving sounds negative to some ears, but to me it makes perfect sense. The deep gravel paths that resolved our drainage difficulties help to protect the huge old sequoias, they set off plants nicely, and they look elegant in every season. The raised beds are filling in quickly, and after only a season or two they are providing color and interest continually through the year.

The needs of our property were certainly unique (we have 100 or so visitors each day), but the overall design is flexible and adaptable enough to suit more intimate use, as well. When I work in the young beds, listening to birds and seeing new growth, I feel that this is exactly the kind of garden I would want even if I didn't have to accommodate foot traffic through the property. It feels great to have created a place of peace that brings pleasure to many visitors (including wild things), but it feels even better to have made a haven that nourishes and replenishes me.

Gardening Where You Are

Gardening where you are is a simple way of saying that you have to face up to regional realities. We are a very mobile society, and many of us move frequently. One very common mistake we gardeners make is trying to have the same kind of garden wherever we go. This rarely works well, even when we stick to vegetables and herbs, simply because this **big, beautiful country** of ours is so amazingly diverse. Even if you stay within a USDA Hardiness Zone (say, moving from one part of Zone 8 to another, perhaps from North Carolina to western Oregon), you will very likely need to **alter at least some of your gardening habits and assumptions.** With the recent popularity of regional gardening styles and a new emphasis on using regionally appropriate plants, it's becoming easier to find accurate regional information, rather than relying on generic gardening instructions that are supposed to be equally useful in both Arizona and Maine.

To be good stewards of the land, we need to educate ourselves about weather, soil, elevation, and native flora. **By learning all we can** about the natural ecology of an unusual site, we can figure out how to go about developing it in a nondestructive way, and sometimes even healing it. This is a highly rewarding process, and **those who own or take care of a piece of the wild will never be bored.**

Working with Weather

Climate and weather patterns can (and should) powerfully influence the way we garden. I garden in what's known as Cascadia, the maritime part of the Pacific Northwest. Back in Massachusetts, I learned to garden in ways that would be wildly inappropriate for where I live now. If I fail to take Cascadia's climate into account, my garden is going to look sad and I am going to be frustrated.

Making climatically appropriate choices doesn't mean that you have to throw away everything you know already or make gardens you don't like. It's almost always possible to capture the overall look or feeling of a garden in a far-away place by substituting regionally appropriate plants for those that would otherwise languish miserably in your yard.

The key to successful regional gardening is understanding the climate in which you live. In Cascadia, the main point that we local gardeners need to grasp is that we have a modified Mediterranean climate. Now, anyone who has actually lived in Seattle knows that "modified" is the key word here. (A local joke says that summer begins on July 5 and is over by July 7.) The good news is that northwestern garden styles have taken the climate into account, and well-designed Cascadian gardens often reflect the fact that a day in January may be as nice as a day in June.

Though the climate in Cascadia isn't much like that of Italy (drat!), it does share the crucial Mediterranean weather pattern of dry summers and wet winters. Because our winters also tend to be mild, gardeners here spend a lot of time outdoors all year-round, despite the ceaseless rain. Most Cascadian gardeners have learned to appreciate the climate's nuances and have created gardens that celebrate the weather patterns found here.

To stay true to organic design practices, you need to accept and work with the idea that your climate should greatly influence the design of your garden. Your climate may also dictate which elements are important to include and which may not be suitable. When considering pathways, garden "rooms," seating areas, and planting beds, think about how often and how long you'll use and appreciate garden features like these through the four seasons. As a general rule, spend your time planning and planting areas that you'll enjoy the most—and the most frequently.

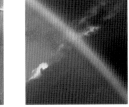

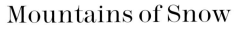

Mountains of Snow

In places where winters are long and fierce, it's not important to create an outdoor space for year-round use because you'll be inside for many months of the year. All your ideas about creating windbreaks and weather-worthy shelters, plus planting perennials and shrubs with winter interest, won't change the fact that your winter climate is brutal. I grew up in New England, where the snow falls long and hard. I learned that it was more important to focus on placing plants where they wouldn't be crushed by wet snow sliding off a roof than it was to focus on creating wonderful little pockets of evergreen ferns and hellebores for picture-window enjoyment. You can make a case for using plants that create interesting patterns under snow, but it's hard to get worked up about the beauty of berries and bark that you can't even see because of massive amounts of snowfall.

When I lived in Montana, I thought more about how we were going to get out of the house in winter, when snow lay some 10 feet deep, than about which plants might still look great. Winter changed the look of the whole mountain range dramatically, burying most vegetation. I finally found out how the tops of young birch trees got so ratty— when snowdrifts make sagging treetops easily accessible from the ground, rabbits can eat right off of them in winter. In this severe climate, garden design was more about choosing tough-as-nails plants than about selecting plants for color or beauty.

From Rain to Snow

In moderate winter areas, gardeners need to think about deliberately creating winter shelter, retreats, and winter interest. To begin, locate the places in your yard that are mostly sunny and sheltered in winter and the places that are the least exposed to high winds during the rainy season. If a large garden structure such as a gazebo seems out of proportion on your site, consider adding a small covered arbor where you can spend time during seasonably good weather.

Once you find just the right place for a shelter, think about what you will see during those off months. If the site lacks winter interest, this will be a great place to begin developing more interesting gardens. Winter-blooming hellebores, evergreen ferns, twiggy dogwoods, and rhododendrons are good possibilities for a cold-season garden. You should also look for plants that have decorative fruit that holds throughout winter, such as cotoneasters, crabapples, and beautyberries.

Mild and Mannerly

In areas of the country where winter is only a mild inconvenience, garden shelters and seating areas can be used year-round. Mild-climate gardeners like me can design gardens and choose plants that will satisfy the soul even on rainy days, since we're never housebound by extreme weather. Here in Cascadia, snow is rare. So rare, in fact, that nobody I know owns a snow shovel. This also means that we can't rely on snow insulation to bring plants unscathed through the occasional storms that send Alaska's weather suddenly south. In much of America's Northern Tier states, very cold winters are balanced by a heavy blanket of snow that keeps plants snug when temperatures plummet. That's why you can grow a surprising range of plants in Anchorage that don't always do well in Seattle—our lack of snow cover makes plants more vulnerable to cold damage.

In mild winter areas, storms can be sudden and predictions unreliable, so wise gardeners stockpile defenses against unexpected icy blasts. My garage always holds a few bales of straw, big bags of dried leaves, old sheets and blankets, and plenty of Reemay to cover young or tender plants. I also use foam pipe insulation to protect rose canes and the trunks of newly transplanted young trees. But all this planning ahead can actually work against me. If I wrap plants in leaves or straw and winter never really materializes, my plants may fall prey to molds, mildews, and root rots. My pampering can also encourage mice to nest among the plants, which can prove more fatal than any icy wind.

Regardless of the climate in which you garden, it's important to make design and plant decisions with your weather in mind. If you can be outdoors 12 months of the year, by all means create a garden you can enjoy year-round. If winter weather sends you indoors, concentrate on designing gardens that you can see from inside the house or design gardens and outdoor rooms that let you pack 12 months of enjoyment into a 6-month gardening season.

The Soil Effect

The best all-around tilth builder is compost. Even though its beginnings are humble (from kitchen scraps and grass clippings to weeds and fallen leaves), the resulting compost is rich, dark, and nutrient-filled. A layer of compost on your garden fertilizes and conditions the soil and slows soil erosion in harsh climates.

NATIVE SOILS COME IN VARIOUS TYPES, AND EACH WILL generally support certain kinds of plants better than others. It makes sense to work with what you have, seeking out plant families that have already adapted to whatever kind of soil you have. However, working with what you have doesn't mean that you can't amend your native soil to make it more comfortable and nutritious for your plants. Where native soils are challenging, adding humus builders to improve tilth is never a mistake.

Clay soils can be generously amended with tilth-builders like compost and aged manure two or three times a year, indefinitely. Indeed, where clay soils are heavy and intractable, you may find yourself amending regularly. How much to use depends entirely on where you are. In much of the Midwest and along the Eastern seaboard, adding an inch or two of compost as mulch each spring and fall will suffice. Where topsoils are deep, you may not need to amend at all; your top mulch can then be useful as a weed suppressor. In parts of the South and the Northwest, where intractable clay soils dominate, you'll need to add far more tilth-building amendments just to improve the soil slightly. Take heart, though—clay soils tend to be quite nutritious, and can be amended to support a terrific range of plants. Sandy soils may need generous amendments simply to create good tilth and adequate nutrition.

Proponents of wild gardening often suggest that it is a bad idea to bring in lots of amendments or to alter native soils. That's because if you're growing native plants in undisturbed native soils, the balance should be just right for the plants, and they won't need the extra fertility that added organic matter provides. But this theory doesn't hold true if you're gardening on a degraded site. It's quite true that it takes an incredible amount of time, effort, and raw materials to significantly alter the basic nature of any soil. (I know, because I've tried.) But adding amendments can make poor or inhospitable soils more welcoming to the plants you've decided to grow in your garden.

Water-Wise Gardening

NO MATTER THE CLIMATE, YOU HAVE TO CONSIDER rainfall, whether heavy or light, and drought, whether moderate or severe, when planning a garden. The extremes of both weather patterns can be difficult to cope with, but happily, most of us have climates that fall somewhat in between these polar opposites. Rainfall and gardening usually go hand in hand, but a gardener can feel challenged by a perpetually wet site, especially if most of the moisture comes from runoff. Gardeners in dry climates (or areas that have a history of summertime drought) may have to think beyond the most popular plants and carefully evaluate their selections when designing or redesigning a garden.

Dealing with Drainage

As house lots in suburban neighborhoods get smaller and closer together (a significant trend over the past decade), drainage becomes a very important issue. Many gardeners are forced to deal with runoff from neighboring properties where excess water has simply been channeled to the property line. This pattern can set off a series of ecological misfortunes, creating serious erosion as well as artificial bogs, perpetually soggy lawns, failing drain fields, and destabilized slopes. Whole neighborhoods suffer when the natural ecological patterns are destroyed by heedless building that does not adequately consider drainage control.

In contrast, organic design principles suggest trying first to work with what you have. One approach would be to fill that boggy ground with incredible bog plants. If the wet place remains wet year-round, that's a fine solution. A small pond might be created to take advantage of the constant moisture and a water feature of some kind could be worked in. However, where the wet ground dries out partially in summer, true bog plants would suffer without significant supplemental watering.

In situations where summer watering would prove difficult or expensive, it's more practical to fill such a spot with hardy marginals—plants that appear naturally along streams and rivers. (The term "marginals" refers to plants that live in the margins or edges of wetlands, not those that are marginally hardy.) Streamside marginals such as lobelia, swamp milkweed (*Asclepias incarnata*), and monkey flower (*Mimulus* spp.) are well adapted to seasonal cycles of wetter and drier soil.

There are plants for almost every place, but not all are equally adaptable. Some marginals thrive in

Soggy soil can spell garden disaster, but here the inventive gardener takes a hint from nature. This naturalized bog contains natives and allies—companion plants with similar cultural and climatic requirements that prefer moist conditions.

acid soils and others prefer alkaline situations. Many like rich clay soils that would drown lesser plants, but a few demand sandy soils. By looking at native flora near your home and consulting with local nurseries that specialize in water gardens, it becomes a lot easier to figure out which kinds of hardy marginals will enjoy the conditions in the damp areas of your garden.

Where a site abuts genuine wetlands, there may be laws that restrict gardening. Many folks buy a piece of land with a natural stream, bog, or pond, and they happily begin development, only to learn that they are not free to change or impact these sites. The impulse to tidy things up is laudable in most situations, but not in natural woods or wetlands, where a complex but fragile ecology preserves a delicate balance between plants and critters of many kinds. It is not a good idea to "park out" a wetland meadow, turning it into a mowed lawn accented with bog plants.

It is, however, a great idea to bone up on native wetland plants. That way, you can edit the site knowledgeably, perhaps weeding out overly ardent native reed grasses in favor of skunk cabbage (*Lysichiton* spp.)

or cleaning out Euro-trash weeds like purple loosestrife (*Lythrum salicaria* and *L. virgatum*). You can also choose the wetland lovers that you like the looks of and add more of them or introduce them with care. For guidance, find the nearest native plant society and attend a few meetings. There may well be a study group on wetlands where you can meet folks with similar yards who can give you advice, guidance, and even starts of some great, site-appropriate plants.

In many regions, the Department of Natural Resources holds native plant sales (at very reasonable prices) each spring. You can buy woodland and wetland plants that will adapt well to your conditions, and you can often pick up handy brochures that tell you just what to do with the plants, as well. These sales are usually announced through the local Cooperative Extension Service. Your local extension agent can help you find lots of great resources, including native plant groups and Master Gardeners. Local libraries are great places to start looking; many have wonderful resource centers and can help you track down all sorts of information and contacts.

Lobelias relish plenty of moisture and even thrive in soggy soil, but they'll also be content in average garden soil if they're watered between rainfalls. Lobelias self-sow in moist conditions. This is a welcome occurrence in most gardens because the plants tend to be short-lived, lasting only about 3 years.

Gardening without Water

In dryland communities, completely different issues arise around water use. Water is precious and it needs to be treated like the commodity it is. When shared wells run dry or water rights are disputed, gardeners can find themselves boning up on xeriscape in a hurry. The goal of xeriscape gardening is to have beautiful yards and gardens with little or no supplemental water. In Denver, where the movement started, this can mean replacing thirsty turfgrass with handsome lawns of drought-tolerant buffalo grass (*Buchloe dactyloides*). When buffalo grass is studded with bulbs like crocus, species tulips, and ornamental onions, the effect is stunning. By filling beds with hardy alpine plants and borders with native shrubs and perennials, we can create a matrix (a community of permanent plants) of tough, hardy plants that like where they are and look great without us fussing over them.

Savvy westerners have long understood xeriscaping. Instead of clearing away the high desert flora when they build a new home, they treat the gorgeous native scrub oaks, low-growing sumacs, and wild roses as the basis for gardens that expand off this basic palette with Mexican hat plant (*Ratibida columnifera*), colorful sages, and penstemons galore.

Dryland gardens in the Southwest rely on native plants that are already adapted to local conditions and that thrive on native soils. In this New Mexican garden, the existing native flora has been respectfully edited and amplified with artfully placed stones.

When buffalo grass is studded with bulbs like crocus, species tulips, and ornamental onions, the effect is stunning.

If you garden in sandy soil that won't hold a drop of moisture, seek out blue sea holly (*Eryngium alpinum*). These plants thrive in the harsh seaside conditions (hot sun, drying winds, and salty soils) that are detrimental to so many other plants.

Similarly, Great Plains gardeners can grow splendid grasses and dramatic wildflowers such as cup-plant (*Silphium perfoliatum*), goldenrods, coneflowers, and sunflowers without watering their beds.

Most people laugh when I begin talking about xeriscaping in the Pacific Northwest, but the idea is actually of far more importance here than in New England or the Midwest, where summer rain is frequent and, in some cases, generous. The envious often refer to the Pacific Northwest as "Little England," but the title is misleading. In England, summers are typically rainy, but here in the Northwest, they are dry. It's quite true that a terrific palette of plants grows here, but if the goal is to create a self-sustaining ecosystem that doesn't need supplemental water in summer, the picture changes dramatically.

My goal, no matter where I've lived, has always been to make gardens that can get by just fine with very little help from me. New gardens are obviously more vulnerable to drought and will need frequent summer water to keep growing well. But I try to create gardens that, once established, can survive and look good with a once-a-month deep watering in July and August (and sometimes September). In Cascadia, it may be necessary to water twice a month during hot years (a rare occurrence, but still a possibility).

Xeriscape plantings make good sense anywhere that summers are not reliably rainy. Unfortunately, many gardeners buy standard border beauties like phlox and daylilies and expect them to perform beautifully in any climate—but in areas where there may be no measurable rainfall from May into October, these old favorites look dreadful without regular watering. Lawns, too, require at least an inch of water once or twice a week to stay green. Advice on planting and transplanting is peppered with remarks like "divide early bloomers after the rains return," or "don't move young trees until the rains come." Many newcomers to Cascadia assume that because the skies have been gray all summer and they are still wearing their winter sweaters, they don't need to water to keep plants happy. Sadly, this is not the case. Even where summers tend to be cool, drought counts.

In any region where gardeners have to balance factors like dry summers with wet winters, it's not enough to choose plants that don't need a lot of summer water, such as globe thistles, phlomis, and sea hollies. You'll also need to identify those that can tolerate being wet up to their crowns all winter, such as daylilies, hostas, and ligularias. Similarly, where summers are reliably wet, it's important to avoid plants that can't tolerate summer water. This is a very common reason for the disappearance of otherwise long-lasting bulbs such as species tulips. Summer wetness can cause many kinds of bulbs that require a dry dormant period to rot. Dryland plants such as junipers, rosemary, and sages that are adapted to long periods without water may also develop root rots when they receive the regular moisture that keeps most border beauties fat and happy. The solution to all of these problems is the same one I've offered as a reliable strategy earlier in the book: Plant a matrix of native plants and plants from similar climate regions, and you'll eliminate many of the problems your plants have.

Playing the Angles

IN ORGANIC GARDEN DESIGN TERMS, GARDENING WHERE you live also means playing the hand you are dealt, at least in part. Years ago, it was standard practice for designers to come into a new site with a bulldozer and simply eradicate all traces of its original plants, let alone the lay of the land. These days, many if not most designers prefer to work with what's already in place. Indeed, some of the most exciting and unusual designs are those that play up existing features such as majestic old trees, dramatic changes of grade, natural rock outcroppings, or permanently soggy areas.

This attitude has come about just in time, for a great deal has changed in recent years. Most people still think of a typical yard as a flat rectangle covered with grass, with perhaps a shade tree or two and some simple foundation plantings. Though initially uninteresting, potential garden sites like this offer plenty of scope, allowing the designer's imagination free rein. There are still plenty of lots like these being created in areas where farmland is available to develop. But in populated areas and top vacation regions where all the prime flat land has already been built on, development is stretching onto wetland verges, sloping hillsides, and steep ravines. Developers are creating new building lots on sites that were previously considered unbuildable or simply too difficult to bother with. Increasing population pressure has boosted the value of this formerly marginal land so that it's now worth a fortune.

This means that many new home sites present difficulties that standard design books don't even mention. These nonstandard sites often have many limitations and problems to solve, leaving the property owner with few options. To get the most from a challenging situation, it's helpful to try to turn what may initially look like drawbacks into assets.

Nonlevel sites make a lot of folks lose their nerve. They rush to call in a designer, which is not a bad move in itself. Even small slopes can be tricky (and dangerous) to work with, and it's especially easy to make expensive and inconvenient mistakes when working with steeper slopes. It's important, though, to find a designer who has experience with irregular sites and who actually likes the challenge. And be sure you agree about what you're trying to create right from the beginning. Otherwise, you may find yourself paying for advice that runs counter to what you are trying to accomplish, then paying again to have the wrong approach corrected.

When homes are built on difficult sites, steep slopes and berms may be created during the construction process. Instead of making an ordinary retaining wall, a slope may be planted with a tightly knit variety of plants. Good bank-holders have thirsty, clinging roots that help hold the soil in place and reduce runoff.

Working with Gentle Slopes

A new and increasingly common design challenge is occurring all across the country—the significantly nonlevel site. Slight and moderate slopes can often be groomed and planted with care and made even more stable than nature left them. (Nature is not in the real estate trade and owns no homes, so our goal for a given area may or may not be consistent with what might happen there if nature had its way.) It's still well worth exploring local and regional resources for advice on proper planting techniques, best plant choices, and best timing for such work.

Where a lesser slope tempts you to simply smooth it away, it is worth considering that many designers deliberately introduce changes of grade to provide interest within a flat garden. Artificial berms are big these days, so why not take advantage of any natural ones? Gentle or steep, gardening on a slope provides wonderful opportunities to showcase plants in dramatic positions.

You can make shallow flights of steps with chunks of recycled concrete or timbers. Generosity counts here: Risers should be about 7 inches high, and the run of the step should be at least 11 or 12 inches wide. When you create steps that are 2 to 3 feet wide, you can use the steps as a seating area and as a means of getting up the hillside. Fill the step area with gravel to provide drainage in sunny areas, then plant creeping herbs such as Corsican mint (*Mentha requienii*) or thyme (both grow happily without minding light foot traffic). In a shady setting, coarse bark will be a better filler for the step areas.

Keep in mind that steps do not have to be linear; they can curve a bit or fan out as the slope requires. You can interrupt longer paths at irregular intervals to create an interesting effect, or you can evenly divide your slope for a more formal look. For artistic plantings, alternate a few flights with three steps each with a five-step flight. This gives you the opportunity to make simple, repetitive plantings that vary enough not to be boring or predictable.

Working with a moderate slope can be great fun, too, providing you with the chance to make a dramatic and unusual garden. Any large-scale projects for such a site will probably be best carried out by a professional. Earthmoving equipment can be rented, but unless you know exactly what you are doing, it's best to leave earth work on sloping sites to those with lots of experience and terrific insurance policies. That said, a bold stairway with steps broad enough for seating, a series of angled decks, or interestingly terraced gardens can transform an unremarkable slope into a place of beauty and distinction. For ideas, consult several local designers as well as a landscape architect or two. Professional consultations are usually worth every penny, for the trained eye sees all kinds of possibilities in the most ordinary setting.

Nature seldom leaves slopes unclothed. On this California hillside, masses of wildflowers knit with native grasses to stabilize the terrain. Such healthy natural communities should be disturbed as little as possible because erosion almost inevitably follows any attempt to improve on native plantings.

A Hillside of Beauty

Sloping hillsides can be feasts for the eyes. One of the most incredible sloped sites I've seen is the public teaching garden created by the Northwest Perennial Alliance (NPA) at the Bellevue Botanic Garden near Seattle. The sight is unforgettable—5,000 perennials in a mixed border with deciduous shrubs, bulbs, groundcovers, and a few ancient apple trees. The border is made on a sloping hillside of heavy clay soil punctuated by several small seeps or underground springs. Rather than trying to alter the nature of the soil or the general shape of the slope, the design committee decided to use these natural attributes to their advantage. Now, the wet spots hold water-loving plants such as ligularias and water iris (*Iris pseudacorus*). Looking up from below the well-planted slope, you see the plant shapes and colors against a dramatic backdrop of sky; from above, you see the deep-toned woods as a backdrop for this incredible mixed border.

Though the site lacks territorial views, several borrowed views of distant woods are employed to give greater perspective to the site. Where long views are not available, the designers have created viewpoints that refer back to other parts of the garden, rather than outward. This is done by creating view corridors or long "windows" into other parts of the garden. As you wander the paths, you get tantalizing glimpses of what lies just beyond your view. These view corridors are created with tall plants or by careful pruning of distant shrubs and trees. Garden glimpses can also be created by making curving paths with dense plantings that periodically open up to allow sudden views into other areas.

This idea can also be applied to very small gardens, where views and vistas are less than glorious. A glimpse of a distant but lovely tree can be as rewarding to the eye as a mountain or water view, and it can be equally satisfying to look back at a handsome planting, a piece of sculpture, or a sculptural old stump that is located within the garden itself.

American gardeners have embraced naturalistic design ideas, yet English visitors are amazed when they see beds that follow the natural slope of the land. A similarly sized English border would be made flat and framed by a perfectly flat lawn and a clipped, rectangular hedge instead of the rolling turf and natural woodlands found at the NPA teaching border. Roy Lancaster, a distinguished horticulturist, told me, "It's extraordinarily beautiful to see the plants silhouetted against the sky at the top of the beds as you walk along the lower path. It's truly remarkable; I've never seen a border like this in England."

Less Is Best with Steep Slopes

I'm going to speak out against a very common practice—leveling slopes. Even when faced with a steep slope, many landscapers choose to level out large sections, reshaping the earth to make it conform to suburban standards of comfort. There certainly are times when bringing in fresh soil and creating some level areas will make a garden far more comfortable and practical to use. However, extensive resculpting is not only expensive, but it will also utterly destroy any native soil (and plants) that may have escaped the home construction vehicles and process. Earthmoving also alters the character of the site, making it look less like itself and more like everything else.

Significant reshaping of slopes often creates serious drainage problems that can be avoided by less-intrusive garden practices such as shallow terracing or using switchback paths. Often the best solution of all is to simply give a natural site a light editing or tidying session and then leave it alone.

Alternatively, organic design principles teach us that it's wise to create a garden that takes advantage of the fall of land. Add wandering switchback paths with short flights of steps to prevent erosion. If the slope is in a woodland setting, leave native trees and shrubs in place to help hold the soil, then do a bit of judicious thinning of the understory to make room for pocket garden beds where you can grow some favorite plants.

When designing a pathway on a steep slope, allow for broad curves in the path that will accommodate a bench or seat so you can take advantage of surprising and attractive views. Think about including sections of wooden staircases, small bridges, and wooden walkways to allow visitors to travel through fragile areas that would be damaged by foot traffic. Wherever possible, use simple trails of bark chips to guide people through the shifting levels of the terrain.

If your home is on a nonlevel site that isn't already planted, you'll find that it can be quite difficult to plant it. Mismanagement of steep plantings can cause serious problems with erosion and slippage. Some towns have a planning department, and officials may be able to advise you on how to handle lots of situations, from drainage to bluff or cliff planting. You could also contact your local extension office to see if they have any regionally appropriate information for difficult sites. If you are getting ready to work on a nonlevel site or are considering buying one, do some research first, either through local officials or your local extension office, or by consulting with an experienced excavation or earthmoving company. This simple step can save you time, money, and heartache.

On significantly nonlevel sites, preserve as much native flora as possible. Keep formal garden areas well away from the edges of any slopes or bluffs. You can further protect steep slopes by leaving a green belt of native plants intact. Even if the property is sparsely planted by nature, don't try to improve upon what works—even seemingly innocuous changes such as removing dead trees can trigger a cascade of results that are not at all what you had in mind. When working with any challenging slope, the best way to proceed is slowly and with great respect for what is already in place.

In dryland areas, gentle slopes can be stabilized with plantings of native wildflowers and shrubs that have extremely moderate water requirements. This almost eliminates the need for summer water.

Right Plant, Right Place

A windbreak of small trees and shrubs can prolong the growing season by sheltering plants that are likely to fall prey to chilly nights, damaging early frosts, and drying autumn winds.

ANYWHERE IN THE WORLD, GARDENING WHERE YOU LIVE also means finding plants that will like where you live without too much coaxing. I have been in gardens (east and west) where enormous labor was directed toward keeping unsuitable plants alive as a point of pride and to earn some measure of horticultural acclaim. A stroll through your city's arboretum or many a private garden will prove that this kind of forceful, artificial approach is not really necessary. It's quite possible to grow a large and varied assortment of plants almost anywhere.

The secret is in paying attention to where a given plant comes from; if its climate, soil, and overall ecology is very similar to yours, chances are you can grow it well and without a lot of fuss. In recent years, a number of books on plant origins have been published, making it easier to find out such information. It's also possible to use the natives-and-allies approach (see page 10), whereby we seek out relatives of native plants from other parts of the world. This is not an infallible way to find new successes, but at the very least it's quite interesting to see how the same plant family adapts itself to differing conditions.

It's also good practice to make a point of visiting public gardens where many kinds of plants are grown. At Denver's Botanic Garden, there are over 6,000 species in the rock garden alone. You'll see a huge range of plants there, growing in several kinds of environments. How the plants look in each place tells regional gardeners a lot about how the plants will adapt to similar microclimates in their own gardens.

For my garden in Cascadia, I had to find plants that were adapted to our pattern of wet winters and dry summers. First, I looked to the Northwest's own splendid flora and identified plants that naturally occur in this region of the country. I also looked for plants from other parts of the world with similar climate patterns. Obviously, the real Mediterranean was a starting place, followed by New Zealand and Australia, South Africa, and certain parts of Central and South America.

The next task was finding out which plants from the identified areas could also tolerate other climate features that are specific to my region. Most importantly, I need to match temperature averages and fluctuations and patterns of wet winters and dry summers. For instance, my min-max recording thermometer showed me that Cascadia often had cold nights (with temperatures in the 30s and 40s) well into July. That means the soil doesn't really heat up until late, which slows the growth of corn, tomatoes, petunias, and other tropical heat lovers. I learned that gardeners here tend to grow a range of reliable performers with cultivar names that reflect this particular region, such as 'Seattle's Best' and 'Oregon Spring' tomatoes.

It is not unusual to have a month of solid rain, and some years we may get close to 100 days of rain without a break. After a while, there's simply nowhere for the excess water to go. The water table is often barely below soil level, so that any hole you dig fills immediately with water, and seasonal flooding (which can last for months) is very common. Thus, it's not too surprising that root rots are common here. For example, most woody ornamental plants can tolerate cool soil, but they can suffer significant root damage

A Little Indulgence Won't Hurt

I'm sure there are many plants that have simply captivated you despite their unsuitability to your climate. Well, just go ahead and buy them, if you have a plan in place! Collectors of rarities often create sections of the garden where they try to coax plants from very different ecosystems to grow well. They might create a peat bog for acid-loving water plants, a clay bed for plants that prefer heavy soils, or a sandy-soil bed for those plants that demand quick drainage. There is nothing wrong with doing this, but it's best to keep such plans small. Although it's hard to alter the basic nature of native soils in any substantial way, you can probably pamper a few exotic treasures in a bed created just for them. Just keep the plant collection and the garden simple enough so you won't have to spend all your time caring for high-maintenance specimens.

during relentlessly wet winters. Indeed, wherever this wet-winter pattern reigns, finding plants that tolerate phytopthora, verticillium, and similar blights, fungi, and pests is another key to happy gardening. The lesson to remember in every region is that native plants tend to be well adapted to soil pathogens that would quickly kill off less-stalwart stock from other ecosystems.

Wherever you live, learning as much as you can about local and regional conditions will help you plan well, select plants wisely, and place your garden so it takes full advantage of natural phenomena such as fog, shade, sun, moisture, or wind. Master Gardeners, local and regional nurseries, native plant societies, local extension offices, and libraries are all great places to start the search for specific information. Your own observations and your garden journal will help you to fine-tune the information you gather. As you locate and chart the microclimates on your property, you can directly apply what you learn about regional weather and soil to your garden.

Hope Springs Eternal

FOCUSING ONLY ON PROBLEMS CAN OBSCURE WHAT'S right about where we live. Sometimes when I explain to visitors just how much it rains and how very bad our native soils are in the Northwest, they say in amazement, "Why don't you just move?" Having gardened in a lot of places, I know that every region and every climate zone has its own little peculiarities. True, we do have tsunami warning signs on every coastal highway and we do get woken up frequently by little earthquakes, but we don't get tornadoes or hurricanes and I don't need to wear snake boots in the garden (okay, I do wear slug boots, but that's another story). I love where I live and I don't view these various aspects of Cascadia as drawbacks, but as regional realities that I must take into account when I design and plant my garden. When I garden with all these factors in mind, I'm apt to make very good plant and planting choices that will remain satisfying and beautiful for a long time. When flukes of climate or weather prove those choices wrong, they also provide a chance to try something new.

Over the years, I've made gardens in New England, Ohio, Colorado, Montana, France, and Italy, as well as here in the Northwest. Each one of those places had wonderful strengths and significant drawbacks. What made gardening in each environment a joy rather than a struggle was focusing on regional "bests"—the things that grew well with very little coaxing. At 10,000 feet in Montana, it was much more fun to enjoy a meadow of gentians and gather lots of excellent potatoes and rhubarb than to try to convince tomatoes and eggplants to ripen when the cold nights constantly offset the warm days. The rose and lavender fields of France were surrounded by wild crops of thyme, rosemary, and sage that grew in aromatic abundance with no husbandry at all. Achieving a garden of fragrant herbal delights was all but effortless in the South of France, but growing a lush, English-looking garden there involved a huge amount of work, endless watering, and lots of frustration. So why bother?

Native plants will almost always outperform non-natives, so don't fight nature. I was very fortunate to grow up with a large Victorian garden in Massachusetts that boasted a host of elderly plants that I rarely saw elsewhere. All sorts of flowering shrubs thrived, from enormous native rhododendrons that reached the second story of the house to sunny Exbury azaleas, billowing hydrangeas, and groves of tree-size lilacs. As a child, I especially admired Carolina allspice, bush honeysuckles, and sturdy mountain laurels. There were native birch, maple, and nut trees, and the understory was rich with trilliums, species tulips, and masses of minor bulbs. And there were pockets of Job's tears, a grass with hard, beadlike seeds that could be strung into necklaces. The garden was an endless treasure trove for a child, and I'm still trying to make gardens as magical as that one for others to enjoy.

As I grew older and visited more gardens, I noticed that very few of them had anything like the variety or profusion of native plants in the aging garden we inherited when we bought that house in Massachusetts. It was a wonderful experience to grow up amid the gift of that long-ago adventurous gardener who planted such an unusual range of plants that grew well even when neglected, as those had been for many years.

I'd like to pass on gardens of that kind for the next homeowners—gardens so well planted and placed that they achieve independence like a native habitat does. Naturally, the finesse and details that personalize our gardens will vanish with us, but plants with compatible needs, set in companionable arrangements that create miniature ecosystems, can persist well after our time.

In Wisconsin, this naturalistic garden is modeled after the native tall grass prairie, where a profusion of wildflowers provides waves of color for this rural gardener. Native grasses have a rugged adaptability and tolerate a variety of weather conditions, making them superior choices for large-scale use.

Green Architecture

Garden designers often talk about "garden bones," or "the backbone of the border." This analogy to the skeleton of a body relates so well because a garden is a living entity made up of living parts. The bones of a garden are the elements that change little over the course of the year; they define a garden's perimeter and give it shape and presence in every season. If you aren't really sure what this means, **take a stroll through the garden** (or any park or landscape) in winter. Without the distraction of foliage and flowers, it's quite easy to assess the garden's bones, making winter the logical time to take a visual inventory of your site.

Garden bones can be living or man-made. Naturalistic gardens and landscapes rely on what I call "green architecture," **employing the natural shapes of the plants** themselves to create the garden's structure. More traditional garden styles define plant architecture in terms of clipped hedges or topiaries, and they rely on hardscape for garden bones, using hardscape structures like **paths, patios, pergolas, porches, decks, and arbors** to hold the garden together.

Green architecture proposes that flowers placed among supportive, shapely companions will be **showcased rather than overwhelmed.** In most traditional English and European gardens, however, the structure comes from hardscape like walls and fences and arbors and trellises, or from plants that gardeners force to have geometric qualities. (I've yet to see a rectangular yew in nature!) Where they exist, walls and arbors can be a boon and can serve as solid bones to the **garden maker.** But English gardens in particular, with their stately walled garden rooms, set up unrealistic and inappropriate expectations for North American gardeners whose garden centers rarely stock Elizabethan stone walls and who have to rely on less-traditional hardscape.

With green architecture, you can **frame your gardens in living walls,** using tall, fast-growing grasses as temporary fillers while your shrub and tree "hedges" mature. You can place multi-trunked trees and **intriguingly shaped shrubs** in your gardens to act as living sculptures that direct both foot and eye through the garden just as well as any wall does. You can arrange powerful, sculptural combinations in your borders that command attention from early spring well into winter.

When we allow plants to define and dominate our gardens, they provide an invaluable counterpoint to the ceaseless geometry of hard-edged modern life. **Our gardens become green havens** where plants flourish and the balance between humans and nature is harmonious.

Sculptural Planting

GREEN ARCHITECTURE IS ALL ABOUT PLANTS. IT INVOLVES choosing plants of all kinds with powerful forms, then placing them like sculpture among similarly strong companions. I can find similarities between green architecture and Asian gardening traditions, where plants are placed with the same respectful attention to their sculptural properties as a stone or a lantern would be. The idea is to consider plants as three-dimensional objects, bringing depth, width, and height to a site. A fourth-dimension quality—time—is of equal importance. Unlike objects, plants change over time, growing and spreading from season to season and year to year. When you select garden ingredients that lend structure over a long period, your borders won't be as dependent on flower color to create drama.

In the typical summer border, flowers play too great a role. Perennials may make terrific minglers when they're in bloom, bringing blobs of color to a larger mass planting, but many of them lack distinction when they're out of bloom. Without its flowers, the average perennial is relatively shapeless and its foliage is indistinguishable. If you put a moratorium on blobby perennials and deliberately bolster your palette with shapely plants of many kinds, your gardens will soon display a delightfully stimulating play of form and texture that holds your attention before and after the floral highlights.

You can arrange shapely plants in powerful compositions that read vividly across the garden, in or out of bloom. For example, the spiky foliage and bloom spires of hardy yuccas will balance a fussy flurry of

LEFT: Asian gardens may look spare and lean to Western eyes accustomed to fuller, lusher plantings. Zen garden spacing gives equal weight to plants and objects and also values the negative space surrounding them.

BELOW: Naturalistic designs rely on the natural, innate architecture of plants, emphasizing their true shapes. This more cooperative approach makes for low maintenance and healthy plants.

finer-textured perennials like coreopsis. A spreading fan of variegated iris or a spill of luxuriant ornamental grass will punctuate an undifferentiated mass of flowers, offering pleasing contrasts of form and texture.

Here's an example of how to build a composition starting with a shrub that has three-season interest. 'Goldflame' spirea is compact, and its leaves are copper in spring, gold in summer, and tawny pumpkin in fall. Its shape is irregularly mounded, so set a fan-shape plant—perhaps creamy variegated iris (*Iris pallida* 'Argentea Variegata') or dainty variegated maiden grass (*Miscanthus sinensis* 'Arabesque' or 'Adagio')—beside it.

Then tuck a foamy, chocolate-colored mound of 'Chameleon' spurge (*Euphorbia dulcis* 'Chameleon') in front of the upright fan and add a coppery sedge (*Carex* spp.), a tumble of golden oregano (*Origanum vulgare*), or a silvery sprawl of carpeting artemisia (*Artemisia stellerina* 'Broughton Silver').

There are many contrasts here—of plant form and leaf shape, of foliage color and tonal value, and of texture and surface. There will also be plenty of flowers, from the raspberry blossoms of the spirea, bright blue or yellow standards of the iris, lemon-lime bracts of the spurge, and golden daisies of the artemisia.

In traditional design, garden bones are often created by formal planting patterns that impose an artificial shape on plants of many kinds. This style of garden requires a great deal of continual maintenance and is stressful for plants, but it is still the design of choice for many gardeners and noted botanical gardens.

Bone Plants

When winter winds blow, the architectural structure of this garden comes to life. Absent the vibrant colors that entertain in the growing season, these shapely plants feature a mix of textures, heights, and interesting seedheads.

ONCE YOU DECIDE TO EXPLORE THE POSSIBILITY OF USING green architecture, you need to begin looking for bone plants. Evergreen trees and shrubs are often referred to as bone plants. However, deciduous plants that have a strong silhouette and retain significant mass even when bare of leaves may also be considered garden bones. As with hardscape, the three-dimensional quality of deciduous plants is emphasized in winter, when skeletal shapes may dominate the garden as they do the greater landscape or countryside.

Evergreen plants provide both backdrop and contrast to the open architecture of naked deciduous trees and shrubs. Though many broad-leaved evergreens are restricted in range by a lack of hardiness, you can employ a wide array of conifers to create living walls, privacy screening, and focal points for the garden in colder climates. In milder parts of the country, the palette of evergreen plants increases dramatically, since you can also use the great conifer clan. In either case, seeking out bone plants in a stimulating variety of sizes, shapes, and foliage tints will help reduce the static quality of gardens that are overly dominated by structural evergreen plants.

In design terms, static spaces have little or no visual movement or flow. Such spaces tend to feel inert and lifeless. They do not command attention or draw visitors in to explore their mysteries. When garden spaces are dominated by structure (in the sense of man-made hardscape), they become less inviting to human interactions. In my travels, I've seen many classic French parterre gardens (which are almost entirely structural) that are not intended for strollers; they are made to be seen from windows or walkways. Gardens with tall hedges and narrow, hedge-lined paths often suffer from this overly structured effect.

When a garden that is largely dependent on seasonal color is hedged or walled, it can look sadly empty and dull in winter. To soften the garden and add visual interest, a gardener could add compact conifers with strong natural architecture to the confined space to create powerful contrasts of form and texture. False cypress such as hinoki cypress (*Chamaecyparis obtusa* 'Filicoides') and the golden hinoki cypress (*Chamaecyparis obtusa* 'Nana Lutea') are terrific choices for such a role. Deciduous plants with interesting shapes, such as dragon's claw willow (*Salix sachalinensis* 'Sekka') or Harry Lauder's walking stick, also known as corkscrew hazel (*Corylus avellana* 'Contorta'), also bring enlivening movement and visual flow to a static setting. So will grasses that retain winter interest, from feather grass (*Stipa tenuissima*) to taller Indian grass (*Sorghastrum nutans*).

> Evergreen plants provide both backdrop and contrast to the open architecture of naked deciduous trees and shrubs.

The Rule of Thirds

A_N_ INFORMAL RULE OF THIRDS MAKES FOR PLEASING combinations. This means that when about a third of the garden's plants are evergreen, with another third structural deciduous plants, the final third can consist of seasonal color plants (bulbs, perennials, and annuals) without sacrificing coherence. North American gardens can suffer from one of two extremes: they are short on structure and long on seasonal color (all flowers and no trees) or they are long on structure and short on seasonal flow (all trees and hedges and no color). Striking a balance between structure and seasonal interest should be one of the goals of a naturalistic garden.

Evergreens

I use the rule of thirds for framing the entire garden and defining its perimeters, and for framing and defining each part of the garden. I use the evergreen third to integrate the garden with its setting and to create patterns that hold the garden together during winter. These evergreens are part of the garden's bones; they establish the lines and flow of the garden from within the house, from within the garden itself, and from outside of the property.

I place the largest evergreens first, setting them where they can frame, create, or minimize views. I cluster smaller evergreens (including compact shrubs and evergreen perennials) to make island groups, each of which will read as an integrated unit in winter, but which will merge easily into the richer tapestry of seasonal color plants in summer.

Choice Structural Evergreens

When you begin seeking out attractive, easy-growing structural evergreens, investigate these reliable performers. Regional reference guides will help you select species that grow best in your area.

COMMON NAME (BOTANICAL NAME)	HEIGHT (IN FEET)	HABIT	GARDEN NOTES
Arborvitae (*Thuja* spp.)	8–50	Upright or broad	Flat, wide foliage
False cypress (*Chamaecyparis* spp.)	8–20	Upright or broad	Varied foliage colors; many tall, columnar species
Hemlock (*Tsuga* spp.)	18–30	Upright or broad	Small, soft needles
Japanese fatsia (*Fatsia japonica*)	To 15	Rounded	Bold, large leaves; white fall blooms
Juniper (*Juniperus* spp.)	1–30	Species vary from groundcovers to tall trees	Blue-green, needlelike foliage
Leatherleaf viburnum (*Viburnum rhytidophyllum*)	To 15	Upright	Textured foliage; billowing white flowers in spring
Pine (*Pinus* spp.)	15–30	Upright or broad	Long needles
Rhododendron (*Rhododendron* spp.)	1–20 or more	Shape varies by species	Spectacular spring bloomers
Spruce (*Picea* spp.)	15–30	Upright or broad	Fine-textured, needlelike foliage
Yew (*Taxus* spp.)	3–30	Upright hedge	Fine-textured foliage; good as a focal plant

> Striking a balance between structure and seasonal interest should be one of the goals of a naturalistic garden.

Choice Structural Deciduous Plants

The more we ask from our deciduous shrubs, the more they deliver. Get picky and choose shrubs with spring flowers, handsome summer foliage, showy fall color, and striking winter skeletons.

COMMON NAME (BOTANICAL NAME)	HEIGHT (IN FEET)	HABIT	GARDEN NOTES
Almond, cherry, peach, and plum (*Prunus* spp.)	12–40	Habits vary by species	Spring bloom; summer fruit; some fall foliage color
Apple, crabapple (*Malus* spp.)	12–40	Round-headed	Spring bloom; fall color and fruit
Dogwood (*Cornus* spp.)	12–20	Spreading	Spring bloom; fall color and fruit
Filbert (*Corylus* spp.)	4–20	Broad and twiggy	Edible nuts
Hawthorn (*Crataegus* spp.)	15–30	Spreading or round-headed	Spring bloom; fall fruit
Hornbeam (*Carpinus* spp.)	20–60	Varies by species	Fine-textured foliage; can be sheared for hedge
Locust (*Robinia* spp.)	15–50	Columnar	Fragrant pealike bloom; fall color
Maple (*Acer* spp.)	2–50	Mounding	Both deciduous and evergreen species available; deciduous species present brilliant fall color
Mountain ash (*Sorbus* spp.)	10–50	Varies by species	White spring flowers; fall color and fruit
Willow (*Salix* spp.)	3–50	Varies by species	Fall color

Structural Deciduous Plants

After evergreens, the next third of a naturalistic garden should consist of deciduous structural plants. These secondary furnishing plants are less visually dominating than the evergreens, but they are still powerful in form and line. Small deciduous trees or large shrubs are the largest plants in the category; they should nearly always be sited for maximum winter effect. The simple, solid backdrop of evergreens gives a sense of order to the complex shapes of deciduous trees and shrubs, which could otherwise lose their impact if placed against chaotic or jumbled plantings. And in turn, a graceful, fluid shrub or a small tree, such as a flowering dogwood or a cascading weeping cherry, can soften the naturally stiff and unchanging evergreens when flower petals drift onto the evergreen branches.

Smaller deciduous shrubs (such as the colorful border barberries, compact spireas, and shrubby potentillas) may lack leaves in winter, but their densely twiggy structure holds power even when bare. Mushy, indistinct plants like forsythia and butterfly bushes don't count in this category. One exception is hydrangeas, which hardly qualify as structural shrubs but which can look marvelous in winter if left unpruned—their skeletal flowerheads seem to rebloom when heaped with snow. Like the smaller evergreens, deciduous shrubs with natural strength of form can be clustered in patterns that read well in any season, with or without lots of snow cover.

Seasonal Color Plants

The final third of the garden's contents consists of what I affectionately call fluff-and-flow plants. These plants bring a vital sense of change and liveliness to an otherwise static garden scene. Though their beauty is ephemeral, perennials in particular may be considered the lifeblood of bed and border.

When considering perennials for inclusion in a garden, always evaluate them for their overall contribution, not simply in terms of what color they bloom and when. Many perennials have little intrinsic architecture, while others offer a handsome shape and attractive foliage, as well as beautiful blooms. A choice few may be considered structural plants, contributing as much in their own way as the garden-framing evergreens and privacy-screening shrubs. In my own gardens, I prefer to use a high proportion of plants that boast strong natural architecture. Fans of iris, fountains of Frikart asters (*Aster* × *frikartii*), spikes of yucca, sheaves of maiden grass, and spills of sedum all contribute sturdy shapes as well as colorful flowers.

I use many plants with colorful foliage that contributes as much as or more than their flowers. In shady settings, a tapestry of broad hostas and lacy ferns, spiky bear's breeches (*Acanthus* spp.) and arching

Evergreens give an entryway year-round structure, but seasonal color changes keep the view fresh. Dogwood, Japanese maple, geranium, and alyssum offer bloom and foliage in a pleasing mix of colors that persists from spring to fall.

I use many plants whose colorful foliage contributes as much as or more than their flowers.

toad lilies (*Tricyrtis* spp.), delicate epimediums and bold rodgersias will hold up in good years and tough ones, weather-wise. In sunnier settings, jagged cardoons (*Cynara cardunculus*), swordlike yuccas, bronze fennel (*Foeniculum vulgare*), and red orache (*Atriplex hortensis*) mingle with silvery artemisias and blue rue (*Ruta graveolens*). These hardworking foliage plants have significant visual interest of their own, and they ably support their flowery companions over the course of many weeks and months.

I keep tabs on many of the plants I've grown over the years and have identified what I call "A-List" perennials—plants that make several kinds of contributions over a prolonged season. These well-favored perennials are the ones I tend to use often and in quantity. Plants that are compelling for a shorter time or that lack intrinsic architecture are "B-List" perennials, and I use them in smaller quantities. The B-List also includes those plants that have little more than pretty flowers to recommend them; I plant these sparingly, if at all. Lists such as these are a bit tricky to develop in a general way, since plants that are top-notch performers in one region may be slackers (or outright thugs) in another.

To develop your own A-List, track the performance and overall good looks of your favorite candidates over the course of a few years. As you evaluate their efforts, keep in mind that A-List status is as much a question of character as of appearances. Plants that quickly outgrow their positions or lose their youthful good looks go on the B-List, while those that mature with dignity and grace are definite A-List material. Plants that need division every year to look great, such as 'Moonbeam' threadleaf coreopsis (*Coreopsis verticillata* 'Moonbeam') get a B-List rating, while slow clumpers that bloom well even when congested, such as 'Happy Returns' daylily, may move up to A-List status.

Extended seasonal appeal also counts for a lot. Certain perennials, such as many astilbes, Russian sages (*Perovskia* spp.), and globe thistles (*Echinops* spp.) have attractive seedheads that remain lovely well into winter, especially when their stark, stripped-down forms are dramatically framed by sheets of snow. As you find new and better plants, you can make room for them by removing plants with fewer attractions. Unless the plants you're removing have truly bad habits, they can be passed along for public plantings at nearby

From the stunning red tinge of its young leaves to the crimson and cream of its late-spring flowers, *Epimedium* × *rubrum* is a nonstop visual treat. Although they're slow to establish, epimediums need virtually no care once they're up and growing.

Often, our old favorites are beloved because of a whole host of wonderful attributes, and they are likely to remain so for a lifetime.

schools, traffic circles, libraries, and so on. One woman I know has planted the sidewalk strip along a nearby fish packing plant with her garden outcasts. The workers often tell her that this impromptu garden is the only bright spot in their day—such is the power of these public plantings! Programs such as Habitat for Humanity are always glad to receive free plants, especially easygoing ones that grow well with little care or extra water.

Naturally, new does not automatically supersede old. The idea is to try out unfamiliar plants that sound promising; however, new plants must prove themselves before earning permanent placement. Often, our old favorites are beloved because of a whole host of wonderful attributes, and they are likely to remain so for a lifetime. Even plants without a lot of horticultural merit are worth keeping if they remind you pleasurably of people and places from your past.

In order to bolster attributes the garden is lacking, stretch past your current strengths. If you love spring flowers, your garden is probably terrific in May, but duller in late summer. Seek out late bloomers with good summer form, such as goldenrods and sea hollies. Visit nurseries during your garden's quieter periods to find great candidates to spark up those dim corners.

Remember that seeking out perennials that will reward you with a whole year's worth of attractions is a long-term project. It may take years to assemble a garden full of flowers and foliage that you deeply enjoy.

A-List Perennials

Stroll through woods and meadows in every season to find native perennials with great year-round form. Nurseries and gardens (public and private) are also great places to glean ideas.

COMMON NAME (BOTANICAL NAME)	HEIGHT	HABIT	GARDEN NOTES
Astilbe (*Astilbe* spp.)	10–48 inches	Flower plumes in summer	Full sun to light shade; moist soil; Zones 4–8
Globe thistle (*Echinops* spp.)	1½–6 feet	Round flower heads	Full sun; well-drained soil; Zones 3–9
Goatsbeard (*Aruncus dioicus*)	5 feet	Flower plumes	Full sun to light shade; moist soil; Zones 6–9
Hellebore (*Helleborus* spp.)	8–24 inches	Nodding, cup-shaped flowers on a soft mound	Shade; moist, well-drained soil; Zones 4–9
Russian sage (*Perovskia* spp.)	3–5 feet	Shrublike clump of flowering stems	Full sun; well-drained soil; Zones 3–9
Sea holly (*Eryngium* spp.)	1–5 feet	Stiffly upright with spiny leaves and flowers	Full sun; dry soil; Zones 3–9
Sedum (*Sedum* spp.)	4–24 inches	Varies by species	Exposure varies by species; well-drained soil; Zones 3–9
Spurge (*Euphorbia* spp.)	Most 1–3 feet	Varies by species	Most need sun and well-drained soil; Zones 6–9
Yarrow (*Achillea* spp.)	1½–4 feet	Dense mounds	Full sun; well-drained soil; Zones 3–8
Yucca (*Yucca* spp.)	1–25 feet	Dramatic spike foliage	Full sun; well-drained soil; zones vary by species

Placing Specimen Trees and Shrubs

SPECIMEN TREES AND SHRUBS ARE ALSO PART OF A landscape's bones. A specimen plant is one that has significant visual importance in the garden. Which woody plants you choose as specimen trees and shrubs are at least as important as where you put them, because if you choose the wrong plant, it may mature to a size that's not proportional to the landscape around it. A great many reference and design books continue to suggest large ornamental and shade trees that are no longer appropriate choices for most American yards, and many nurseries continue to sell large trees because that's what most homeowners request and buy. But as the average lot size gets smaller, so do the gardens. This usually means that big trees will outgrow their positions in as few as 5 years. Unless your garden is acres wide, you are wise to stick with trees that will remain in proportion to your site.

It's sad to realize that cities and suburbs no longer afford room for some of the majestic native trees—they are coming down quickly as rampant growth crowds them out. The average tree line of the future will certainly be less dramatic than the few pockets of magnificence we still enjoy in many urban and suburban settings. Indeed, on the rare sites where it is possible to place a large tree well, that tree becomes a civic gift to the entire neighborhood for generations to come.

Unfortunately, trees in the city are more often a source of contention than a focal point for admiration and gratitude; trees have been vandalized or even illicitly removed by neighbors who want to improve their own view. Few people realize that a fabulous tree *is* a view. What's more, trees help us see better: Over time, you most appreciate views that are partial. In a fairly short time, you tend to stop admiring panoramic views, even when they are the ostensible reason for buying or building a home in a certain spot. In contrast, views that stay fresh remain rewarding over time. Trees can play an important role in framing and revealing important views, and they always keep views fresh, lively, and interesting. So when you place key trees, you should be considering not only how the tree itself will look, but how it will reshape and reframe everything around it.

Despite what you see growing in many developments, a static tree line of maples isn't the only choice you have for your garden. This fall landscape proves that a variety of flowering and fruiting species of evergreen and deciduous trees, shrubs, and perennials creates a woven tapestry that's immeasurably more interesting.

Borrowing Trees

In small gardens, you can often "borrow" trees from the neighboring tree line for the canopy layer. In any garden, large or small, you can link upward to the borrowed tree line by using secondary layer plants (mainly shrubs) to make visual ladders. Nearly all settings afford views of trees, near or distant. Trees that are across the street or in a neighbor's yard are quite easy to incorporate into the gardenscape. More distant trees can be framed by tall shrubs to produce the impression of a generous vista even when the actual area is fairly small. Even a modest implication that the garden is set within a well-treed community helps to establish a more natural-feeling ambiance.

Trees That Fit

Within the garden, there may not be room for many—or any—trees, except quite small ones. In little gardens, it's almost always best to fill these classic tree positions with large shrubs, such as the Sargent crabapple (*Malus sargentii*), which rarely exceeds 15 feet, and golden privet, which can be shaped as a multi-trunked, round-headed "tree." Multi-trunked specimens of any large shrub, from laurel to privet, can be pruned to create a tree shape. Professional pruners call this process "arborizing." This involves lifting the skirts of the shrub by pruning to reveal the bare trunk. The canopy can then be kept to a practical and attractive height (preferably one that clears the head of the designated lawn mower).

Single Specimen Trees

Specimen trees are commonly planted in the midst of a large lawn, either alone or surrounded by secondary plants such as low-growing evergreen shrubs or a groundcover. Giving young trees company is a good idea, both practically and visually. For starters, a carpeting understory of lower shrubs and perennials will help to protect the trunk of a vulnerable young tree from inadvertent damage during lawn care. String-trimmer scars are a common cause of tree death and disfigurement, so it's always better for the tree to have as large a circle of plants around it as is practical and attractive. Underplantings also help to visually integrate the relatively small trunk of a young tree into a large expanse of lawn. The accompanying bed may at first dwarf the young tree, but within a few seasons its increasing height and spreading branches will balance out the picture nicely.

By the time specimen trees mature, they often gain enough girth that they no longer need the assistance or protection of an underplanting. If you do decide to underplant the tree, you should select plants that are adaptable to both sun and shade to go under the tree, or accept the fact that the plantings will need to be altered altogether at a later date. As trees grow, they can cast so much shade that lawns and other sun-loving plants will no longer thrive beneath their branches. In such situations, a bed of shade-tolerant plants and a luxuriant mossy carpet will look far more attractive than a struggling lawn and sad perennials.

Trees in Mixed Borders

Specimen trees and shrubs can also be placed within planting beds, where they become the focal point of a mixed border. Mixed borders hold combinations of plants of all kinds, usually integrated into layered communities. The garden's interior canopy layer might be created with small trees or large shrubs, with intermediate understory shrubs making the transition to border shrubs, perennials, and groundcovers effortlessly.

A choice small tree can also become the focal point for the entire border. Placed as the centerpiece, all its subsidiary companions will help lead the eye back to the main attraction. In a sunny spot, a weeping 'Red Jade' crabapple (*Malus* 'Red Jade') might be flanked by masses of peachy 'Daybreak' potentillas, pink floribunda roses like 'The Fairy', and white coneflowers (*Echinacea purpurea*).

In a shadier place, a goat willow (*Salix caprea*) could be surrounded by wintergreen (*Gaultheria procumbens*), fluffy astilbes, evergreen ferns, and hellebores. In both cases, the small, shrublike tree has enough of a sculptural quality that it will carry quite a large planting with panache.

If you'd like to use an evergreen tree as a focal point, you could try a multi-trunked strawberry tree (*Arbutus unedo*). This madroña relative has white bell flowers followed by fat little fruits that have a sour tang (they're great in salads!). In colder climates, a viburnum, rhododendron, or small holly could be arborized to fill this role.

An expanded understory planting becomes a garden bed in its own right. The flowering dogwood acts as its centerpiece in spring and is an anchoring focal point in any season.

Siting Trees Successfully

EMPHASIZING THE SCULPTURAL QUALITY OF A SPECIMEN tree is the key to successful placement. If the tree is too crowded in its setting, it won't be able to develop its characteristic shape—presumably one of the qualities we found desirable—properly. If the understory plantings are too dense, too complex, or too tall, we won't be able to see the lead player very well. Allowing enough room for trees to grow is common sense, yet is surprisingly difficult to do.

In order to place a tree well, it's vital to have a clear sense of how it is supposed to look. Naturally, you will consider its ultimate height first. To find this accurately, it's best to seek out local resources such as parks, arboretums, or botanic gardens. What some tree labels give as mature heights are actually the probable height at 10 years. Some nursery staffs will be able to tell you just how big a certain tree will get in your region, but you should do a little research on your own as well, because your site conditions can affect a tree's growth and its ultimate height.

Standard reference books are not always very helpful either, since many are intended for use over such a broad range that they become generic. Trees may behave quite differently in various parts of their natural range, and when they are taken further afield, the result is not generically predictable. For instance, here in the Pacific Northwest, we can usually count on plants getting 20 to 25 percent larger than they do elsewhere. However, a sourwood (*Oxydendrum arboreum*) that may grow 60 to 75 feet high in Kentucky (where it occurs by nature) rarely reaches 20 feet here. Finding local specimens will help, as will checking with Master Gardeners or your local Cooperative Extension Service.

Because the natural shape of each species varies, part of good placement lies in selecting a tree whose own proper shape and size will look terrific in the available space for many years to come. Where space is limited, you can use upright, narrow, and columnar trees—they will look less crowded than those with spreading limbs and broad crowns. In a wide-open space, tall trees with high, billowing crowns will look majestic in every season. In moderately sized settings, a tree that begins branching close to ground level anchors itself firmly to the garden plantings around it.

It's also useful to think about what a key tree will offer you in every season. Even if you are choosing a tree mainly for its sumptuous spring flowers, you still need to think about how its shade may affect the garden's light in high summer. Winter silhouettes are

> Perhaps the most useful preparation for planting a tree is to stroll through a well-planted neighborhood.

also a consideration, as is autumn color. If the tree is deciduous, it's even worth thinking about the size and texture of its foliage. If you prefer not to do a lot of raking, choose trees with small, fine-textured foliage that breaks down without smothering lawns or plants when it hits ground level. If you have your heart set on a tree with oversize foliage, you need to think creatively about what to plant beneath and around it in order to avoid creating an ongoing chore (for you and for your neighbors). Frequent raking can be rough on many border plants, and big leaves often clump together to form slimy, impenetrable mats that are slippery underfoot (especially on walkways and patios) and very tough on lawns.

All of these factors taken together will help you make good, informed decisions about where a key tree will have a great chance of growing up beautifully. Perhaps the most useful preparation for planting a tree is to stroll through a well-planted neighborhood. Make mental notes about which trees look terrific and which look less than healthy or attractive. Look at the spacing of the best examples, and jot down the approximate distances involved. How far is the tree from the house? From other trees?

If you can identify the trees you like best, it will help you at selection time. If you aren't sure what you are looking at, sketch a leaf and any flowers, or note any distinctive branching patterns. You can then identify the plant by using a tree key (many tree reference books have keys to help you locate an unknown plant).

Planting for the Golden Bowl Effect

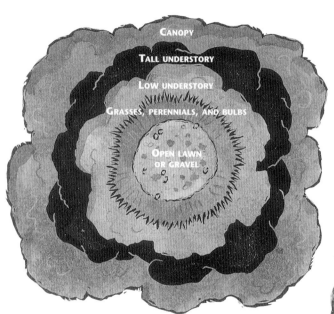

EVERY GARDENER YOU TALK TO MAY HAVE A DIFFERENT idea when you ask about their dream garden, but most folks want two basic things: sunshine and privacy. One way you can get both is to design a sunny central area, then surround the area with plants and key trees for privacy. I call this the golden bowl effect. Think of the garden space as a bowl full of sunshine. The center of the bowl will be broad and shallow, with gently sloping green sides. Key trees and shrubs will be placed at the corners of a square or rectangular plot to round out the angles of the bowl and minimize the geometrical effect. In a golden bowl garden, you keep the central part of the space open. You can cover it with grass, ground-covers, or gravel if you want to encourage great

If you want a sunny area in your yard, create a design based on the plant layers found in nature; I call this the golden bowl effect. The base is an open seating area surrounded by gently tiered plantings that frame the open space like the sides of a bowl.

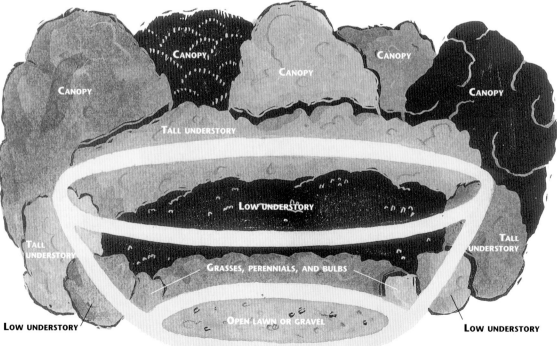

drainage year-round. If drainage isn't a problem, you can use pavers for the central area, but permeable surfaces are always more desirable. Turf sheds water, so consider it an impermeable surface as well, and use it with discretion. In places where you want lawn, seek out regionally appropriate seed mixtures that won't require excessive summer watering.

Many gardeners make the mistake of plopping a specimen tree right in the middle of the lawn. If you consider the flow of movement (both visual and physical) through the garden, you'll realize that plunking a large tree in the middle of the largest open space on the property isn't always a good idea. If you enjoy sitting, playing, and gardening in the sun, think long and hard before you eliminate a great deal of it with a specimen tree. If you want a sunny yard, you'll be better off planting for the golden bowl effect.

To begin building the green walls of your golden bowl, use low-growing plants to line the edges of the center area. Next, add shrubs and trees, layering back to the canopy line, which may be actual or borrowed. When placing trees, keep in mind that even though a tree no longer functions as the centerpiece of the yard in golden bowl planting, you still need to think about how a tree will grow over the seasons and throughout its lifetime. The structure of a key tree will not dominate as it would if it were centrally located in a garden, but it may take center stage while it blooms or puts on a fabulous fall display.

Planting for the Future

IT'S WORTH REPEATING THAT PLACING TREES IS SOMETHING that should only be done after much thought. If you've ever seen U-shaped trees along Main Street, you'll understand what I'm talking about. When you plant a tree, you need to not only think about the next 10 years, but also about the next 25 and 50. It's sad when a lovely, healthy, mature tree has to be removed because it's outgrown its allotted space.

Room to Grow

Planting a specimen tree smack against the wall of your house (or any wall) is not a good idea. In such a position, a plant can only achieve half its true shape. What's worse, the back side of plants placed too close to walls are nearly always plagued by mildews, molds, and other problems. The main culprits are poor air circulation and dry soil (because rain can't reach under roof soffits).

The one exception is weeping trees that are naturally rather one-sided. This is not true of all weeping trees (weeping willows, for example, get equally big in all directions), but it's possible to find wonderfully shaped trees that will live a full and happy life in what would be crowded quarters for others. Weeping purple beech (*Fagus sylvatica* cultivars), weeping Camperdown elm (*Ulmus glabra* 'Camperdownii'), weeping 'Red Jade' crabapple, and 'Weeping Sally' goat willow are all great candidates for a position near a house or other wall. So are vine maples

(*Acer circinatum*) and many Japanese maples, particularly smaller forms with multiple trunks, such as *Acer palmatum* 'Butterfly'.

Even so, it's best to allow such a tree breathing room. As a rule of thumb, never plant a tree closer than 6 or 8 feet out from the roofline (which means at least 6 feet beyond the soffits and gutters). That way, when it comes time to wash the windows, your tree won't be damaged or in the way of your work. It will receive any rainwater that falls, reducing its need for supplemental water. What's more, if you live in an area with snowy winters, your tree won't be in line for a direct hit when wet winter snow crashes off the roof.

A perfect specimen tree can indeed be a treasure for the whole neighborhood, but it can also prove to be troublesome to your neighbors. Always plant anything that will mature to over 10 feet with thoughtful care. Never put a tree where it will grow into overhead wires of any kind. Likewise, keep those deep roots well away from underground water mains and sewage lines. It certainly makes sense to place specimen trees where they will frame a desirable view or screen a regrettable one, but it is absolutely vital that you also consider the views—present and future—of others around you. If your favorite tree will get 40, 60, or 100 feet tall, what will happen to the view from nearby homes? Also, might roots and leaves and litter from your tree eventually fill other folks' yards?

If not, you are lucky. Those with large properties can indulge in almost any kind of tree and revel in the results for years. Evergreen magnolias, bigleaf maples, copper beech, and pink-flowered chestnuts are all spectacular large trees that increase in magnificence decade after decade. However, unless you can be sure that your actions will not unfavorably impinge on the lives of others, you must resist the urge to reforest the country by starting in your own yard. To avoid a host of expensive problems, plant smaller and more compact trees if you have a modest lot.

My Favorite Small Trees

Fortunately, there are dozens of exceptional small trees that offer beauty in every season. Among my favorites in the 20- to 30-foot category are the stewartias. These graceful small trees have subtly dappled bark that grows increasingly complex in its patterning as the trees age. Stewartias also have a handsome branching habit, with wide but upswept arms and twigs that offer a lovely lacelike effect in winter. All have white flowers in summer, some quite fragrant (notably *Stewartia sinensis*), though most are only mildly so. The small, tapering oval leaves take on brilliant tints in fall, when they look like a living sunset. The most commonly grown species, tall stewartia (*S. monadelpha*), can reach over 30 feet, but may take more than 40 years to do so. Smaller Japanese stewartia (*S. pseudocamellia*) has larger flowers, incredible fall color, and looks splendid rising behind large rhododendrons.

In small gardens, you can let the tree grow naturally for 4 or 5 years, then begin selectively removing lower branches to keep them from encroaching on paths or crowding borders. This will also create a more treelike, less shrubby silhouette. In larger

Choice Small Trees

Each region has its own native trees, some of which may be appropriate as yard and garden specimens. To learn which make good choices in your area, contact local arboretums and native plant societies.

COMMON NAME (BOTANICAL NAME)	HEIGHT (IN FEET)	HARDINESS ZONES	GARDEN NOTES
Amur cherry (*Prunus mackii*)	20–40	3–6	White spring flowers; exfoliating bark
Carolina silverbell (*Halesia tetraptera*)	25–40	5–8	Clusters of white flowers; spreading, rounded habit
Fragrant snowbell tree (*Styrax obassia*)	20–40	5–8	Fragrant, bell-shaped white flowers in spring; oval habit
Fringe tree (*Chionanthus virginicus*)	12–20	4–9	Plumes of white flowers in spring; blue-black fruit
Japanese flowering crabapple (*Malus floribunda*)	15–25	4–7	Deep pink flowers; yellow and red fruit; rounded habit
Japanese stewartia (*Stewartia pseudocamellia*)	20–40	5–7	Roselike white flowers in spring; pyramidal habit
'Sango-kaku' Japanese maple (*Acer palmatum* 'Sango-kaku')	To 20	5–8	Striking coral bark and yellow foliage in fall
Sargent crabapple (*Malus sargentii*)	6–8	4–8	White flowers; red fruit; mounding habit
'Taihaku' Japanese flowering cherry (*Prunus serrulata* 'Taihaku')	20–25	5–8	White flowers in spring; reddish-tinged foliage
'Weeping Sally' goat willow (*Salix caprea* 'Weeping Sally')	12–30	4–8	Grafted on standard for upright habit

As brilliant as a golden sunset, the fall color of Japanese stewartia (*Stewartia pseudocamellia*) takes a back seat only to the peeling bark that's characteristic of even young trees. Stewartias prefer moist, well-drained soil and transplant most successfully when they're container-size. Best of all, they're rarely bothered by pests and diseases.

gardens, a stewartia can be allowed to remain clothed down to the ground. Grown this way, it will mingle attractively with large shrubs and oversize perennials such as maiden grass and Indian pokeweed (*Phytolacca acinosa*). In the West, American pokeweed (*P. americana*) can also be used.

Fragrant snowbell (*Styrax obassia*) is a sculptural Asian tree with boldly rounded leaves and small, honey-scented white flowers that drip like fringe from the slim twigs in June. It's often multi-trunked, which tends to keep the plant more compact (closer to 20 feet than 30). In winter, the wet bark takes on a tawny orange glow. Hardy only to Zone 6, it needs evenly moist (but not waterlogged) soil to grow well,

and in colder gardens it should be given the warmest possible spot out of the wind.

Smaller Japanese snowbell tree (*S. japonicus*) is hardy to Zone 5 and has handsomely stippled gray-brown bark. Its arching arms bear slimmer foliage that turns a clear, pale gold in autumn. In summer, it carries astonishing masses of pendant, drooping little bell flowers in white or pink, followed by round little seedpods. This is a great little tree to put where it will be viewed from beneath, perhaps at the top of a staircase, atop a gentle bank, or on a retaining wall.

Persian ironwood (*Parrotia persica*) is an Arabian witch hazel relative with big, bold leaves and fabulous fall color. Multi-trunked specimens are often wider than their height, and they look really gorgeous when their long branches reach out over a reflecting pool. The bark is marbled in gray and cream, and the branches grow increasingly gnarled with age. It gets big (30 to 50 feet, in time), but is a garden gem where space permits its planting.

Smaller still are the crabapples. This large and mixed group can be confusing to the novice—who can sort the best of the bunch from so many dazzling beauties? Here again, it's a good idea to consult a reliable regional resource (such as Master Gardeners or the Cooperative Extension Service). The idea is to look for crabs that resist scab and other apple diseases. My own favorites include the narrowly upright 'Centurion', with rosy flowers, round red fruit, and ruddy-tinted foliage. I'm also fond of the new 'Centennial' crab, with large, snowy blossoms and fat little apples big enough to use as garnishes. It's very disease-resistant, but deer love it. My particular pet, a plant I grow in every garden I make, is the Sargent crab (*Malus sargentii*), a low grower (generally to 15 feet) with extraordinary fall color.

Layering to Scale

Once the structural plants that define your landscape are in place, you'll want to fill in the details of the picture by adding plant layers. Layering allows you to re-create the haphazardly beautiful lines, textures, and shapes found in nature, but lets you be selective about what and where to plant. I've created gardens full of layers—layers of trees, shrubs, evergreens, deciduous plants, grasses, perennials, vines, and groundcovers—to tie the tree line to the ground. The boldly shaped beds that flank the main pathway from the parking lot to the school on my property are similar in character, so there is visual unity, yet they are planted quite differently in terms of layering, since they must perform different tasks.

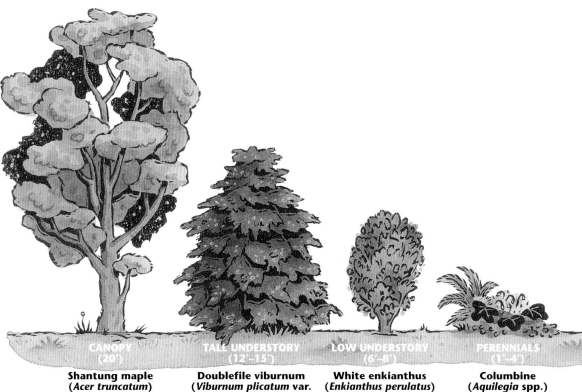

CANOPY (20')

Shantung maple (*Acer truncatum*)

TALL UNDERSTORY (12'–15')

Doublefile viburnum (*Viburnum plicatum* var. *tomentosum* 'Mariesii')

LOW UNDERSTORY (6'–8')

White enkianthus (*Enkianthus perulatus*)

PERENNIALS (1'–4')

Columbine (*Aquilegia* spp.)

Cinnamon fern (*Osmunda cinnamomea*)

Mayapple (*Podophyllum peltatum*)

Transitional Layering

The bed on the right of the main pathway to my garden school, a slightly inflated triangle, is backed by an adolescent sequoia that is now a mere 60 feet high and still growing. I needed to create plantings that would relate to this tall tree. They needed to include visual ladders—transitional plantings that would carry the eye to the treetops and back. The bed is about 25 feet deep at the widest point, which allowed us to use small trees and large shrubs to create the necessary layers.

We chose a mixture of large- and medium-size shrubs and small, narrow trees for the transitional layers between our big sequoia tree and the garden. About a third of the key elements are evergreen and the rest are deciduous. This blend of sizes and types creates the kind of ruffled, irregular tiering that is commonly seen where meadows merge with woodlands. By re-creating the look of these woodland edges, we can make visually effective and attractive transitions between lawn and garden or garden and stands of large trees.

My specific mixture was developed for the mild northwestern climate and includes many plants that

When creating naturalistic layers in the garden, you may have a tree line as part of your garden already, or you may need to visually borrow trees from neighboring properties. Tall understory shrubs will link the trees to the lower layers of the garden. Low understory plants form the border, offering a supportive framework for the seasonal flowers that carpet the garden's "floor."

One of the goals of a naturalistically layered garden is to link taller trees with understory shrubs and plantings. Here, the gracefully arched branches of a 60-foot-tall sequoia are used to provide a visual ladder between the tree and the ground level.

are not hardy in most parts of the country. No matter where you live, though, you can achieve a similar effect by using a base of native or site-adaptive plants that grow well in your region. To create a visually intriguing mixture, select plants that provide a range of leaf forms and textures. For instance, sumacs, elders, and tall hydrangeas provide large, bold leaves, while spireas and mock oranges offer smaller, fine-textured ones.

In cold places where broad-leaved evergreens are difficult to please, a judicious mixture of conifers will give your transitional plantings depth, weight, and solidity. Rather than creating a formal, straight hedge, the idea is to mingle the conifers with deciduous shrubs in an appealing array. For greater contrast, consider using some blue or gold-tipped conifers, some with weeping branches, or some with eccentric forms such as 'Hollywood' junipers or Hinoki false cypress. Except where a wall-like effect is wanted, it's best to limit evergreen elements to no more than a third of the total. Otherwise, the effect can be stiff and stodgy, rather than lively.

Shrubs with contrasting habits (forms and shapes) will add even greater interest to your visual ladders. Open, airy Japanese maples contrast well with narrow, upright lilacs and arching, bushy barberries. Weeping or cascading plants emphasize those with uplifted arms, while shrubs with intricately cut or variegated foliage look best next to solid, unfussy plants with simple leaves.

In a smaller garden, you could achieve the same link between a tree and ground level by growing vines on sturdy, free-standing trellis frames and transitional shrubs that are naturally columnar or narrow in form. These would provide the desired height without much bulk.

In my garden, the transitional mixture that fills the back of this important bed along the main path includes a small Japanese maple, some buttery yellow euonymus, both golden and blue conifers, large butterfly bushes, and several climbing vines. These tall plants are stepped down with compact border shrubs, including dwarf spireas with colorful foliage, dwarf butterfly bushes, evergreen herbs, and low-growing roses. We filled the spaces between the shrubs with a variety of hardy bulbs and long-blooming perennials for ongoing seasonal color.

When you plan a layered planting like this, it's a very good idea to place evergreens and key structural plants first, and to be sure that each is allowed enough room to achieve its proper size and shape. Where thoughtful placement leaves unsightly gaps, try using annuals, easily moved plants, or short-lived fillers such as castor beans, tall grasses, and Spanish broom to fill in between the growing shrubs. Where climate permits fall or winter planting, it's useful to place these key structural plants without the distractions of seasonal color. In the quiet off months, you can easily see whether your backbone plantings make a satisfyingly harmonious whole.

Even in the first season after planting, the matrix of plants in my triangular bed knit together well. By the second year, the taller shrubs had already begun to forge the visual links that make the garden look like part of the greater landscape. Because of the high percentage of appropriately sized woody plants, maintenance is very low in this bed.

However, as the plants mature, ongoing editing will be required. This is always true, even of professionally designed gardens filled with well-chosen plants. Real gardens never quite match the perfect ones we so carefully draw up on paper for our garden plans.

Top Broad-Leaved Evergreens for Transitional Layers

Where winters are fierce, broad-leaved evergreens are rare. But gardeners in climates just a bit more mild can choose from evergreen shrubs that will thrive in those conditions.

COMMON NAME (BOTANICAL NAME)	HEIGHT (IN FEET)	FOLIAGE	HARDINESS ZONES	GARDEN NOTES
Abelia (*Abelia* spp.)	3–6	Fine textured; bronze-red in fall	7–9	Upright, wide habit; profusion of flowers in summer
Blueberry, cranberry (*Vaccinium* spp.)	5–20	Fine textured, fall color	3–8, varies by species	Upright or broad habit; colorful fruit
Holly (*Ilex* spp.)	4–60	Glossy, often spiny leaves	5–9, varies by species	Upright or broad habit; noted for red, yellow, or blue-black berries
Mahonia (*Mahonia* spp.)	5–10	Stiff, glossy leaves	6–9	Upright habit; yellow spring flowers; drab blue fall fruit; protect from wind
Mountain laurel (*Kalmia latifolia*)	7–15	Glossy, dark green	4–9	Upright or broad habit; white to deep rose blooms
Pieris (*Pieris* spp.)	8–20	Tapering leaves often reddish when young	6–8	Upright or broad habit; fragrant white flowers in spring
Rhododendron (*Rhododendron* spp.)	5–20	Broad, dark green leaves	4–9, varies by species	Upright or broad habit; many colors of spring blooms
Viburnum (*Viburnum* × *burkwoodi*, *V. davidii*, or *V. rhytidophyllum*)	5–20	Various types	4–8, varies by species	Upright or broad habit; spring blooms; fall fruit

What's more, plants don't follow the directions. Some that don't succeed will be replaced with better choices, while those that succeed all too well will need to be curbed or removed.

Transitional Trees and Shrubs

Mixtures of deciduous and evergreen shrubs make natural-looking layers that create context, please the eye, and provide excellent cover for birds. Finding interesting deciduous shrubs is not hard; even if you stick to a few prolific families such as barberries, buddleias, spireas, hydrangeas, and elders, you'll find hundreds of excellent and showy choices.

It can be trickier to track down broad-leaved evergreens that will perform well in the colder parts of the country. Again, a few reliable genera such as rhododendron, pieris, mountain laurel, and viburnum offer many splendid and solidly hardy choices. Protection from desiccating winter winds will also help get broad-leaved evergreens through harsh winters. Use regional references or a good local nursery to find the best specific options for your garden.

Small-Scale Layering

Along the main pathway that passes by the house, I wanted to develop a combination of evergreen plants that would screen both the parking area and the busy road without taking up too much space or robbing the small garden of light and air. This bed has an eccentrically curving shape that serves both to screen the former front door and to steer people toward the main entry. It's also bordered on two sides by a 5-foot-high retaining wall that divides it from the parking lot.

Though the rest of the lot is fairly shady, this bed gets full sun all day long, offering me a rare opportunity to grow prairie and meadow plants.

Overscreening is a common problem in small gardens, where blocking out more view than is desirable can result in little usable space. By measuring from inside the house and from the pathways, we determined that a scrim (visual curtain) of plants 6 to 8 feet tall would effectively block out the roadway, which is somewhat lower than my property. The houses on the far side of the road are set lower still, and a screen of modest height would easily hide them.

We wanted to link the garden in front of the house to the trees across the parking area. There we had a mature stand of native vine maples, small trees that reach 15 or 20 feet tall. We determined that bed plantings of moderate height would eliminate the unwanted view of the parking lot and make the desired visual connection to these nearby trees, which would then become the borrowed canopy layer. By integrating a palette of smaller-scale plants into this bed, we could accomplish two things: create effective layering and provide necessary screening.

Our palette included a combination of dwarf and compact border shrubs, some of which were deciduous

The textured plantings in front of my home include shrubs that screen the road and parking areas from window view. To avoid constant pruning, I used compact and dwarf forms to create the beds and borders.

and others evergreen. To preserve the open feeling of this section, we decided to use scrim plants (chiefly deciduous shrubs with colorful stems in winter) rather than trying to create a solid visual barrier. A dense, hedgelike planting might easily feel confining in such a small space. Deciduous scrim plants would provide plenty of privacy and help baffle street noise without limiting our vistas.

For this role, I used several kinds of twiggy dogwoods whose stems are beautifully colored in winter. Among my favorites is bloodtwig dogwood 'Midwinter Fire' (*Cornus sanguinea* 'Midwinter Fire'), an airy, 6- to 8-footer with green summer foliage, creamy flowers, blue-black berries, and stunning coral-and-peach stems in winter. Although deer feed freely on three or four other twiggy dogwoods in the garden, including our native red osier (*Cornus stolonifera*), they content themselves with just a few leaves from 'Midwinter Fire', which must not be as tasty as the others.

There are a great many twiggy dogwoods to consider, some with brilliant green stems, others with stems of old gold, sunny yellow, hot red, or even plumblack. Their foliage may be green or gold, plain or variegated with gold, silver, or even cream and pink. Some, such as redtwig dogwood (*Cornus alba*), are fully hardy to Zone 2, while others need some protection to come through winters in Zone 4, especially where snow cover is erratic.

Another wonderful scrim plant is a blueberry relative from the American southeast called dusty zenobia (*Zenobia pulverulenta*). Once rare in gardens, this handsome shrub is becoming better known as growers and gardeners alike discover its pleasing ways. Hardy to Zone 4, zenobia is an upright shrub that reaches 5 to 6 feet in a few seasons. The slim stems are set with rounded, pewtery grey-blue leaves that look as if they were lightly powdered with flour. In early summer, the branch tips carry clusters of large and showy white bell flowers that are followed by green and blue fruits.

Like their cousins the blueberries, these shrubs produce reliable fall color, usually in glowing reds and oranges. In winter, the slim apricot-color stems gleam enticingly, yet are rarely sampled by our local deer. Isn't a shrub with so many charms well worth seeking out? Zenobia is easy to root, either from hardwood cuttings taken in fall or by layering the lax outer branches. Simply pin them down with a rock and you'll soon find healthy new roots coming from each leaf node that touches the soil.

Go on a Fact-Finding Mission for Plants

With a bit of research, it's possible to develop a long list of rock-hardy plants that can fill any garden with a full range of forms, textures, and foliage colors. This may sound like a daunting task, but what it really means is spending some free time visiting public gardens and making notes about likely plants. Garden touring is more popular than ever, and many communities boast a steady stream of fund-raising garden tours all summer long. Another excellent way to broaden your practical plant palette is by cruising nurseries in every season, not just spring. Large garden centers will provide plenty of reliable and well-known war horses that will never let you down. This is always a good place to start, but for those who want to branch out, small specialty nurseries will expand the possibilities with less familiar plants to try. Plant sales sponsored by local garden groups and plant societies will offer still more possibilities.

If you are most interested in using a base of native plants that are well adapted to your region, contact your local extension office or the Department of Natural Resources. Both are splendid resources for helping you to connect with local or regional groups interested in native plants. Even if you can't often attend meetings, many groups publish newsletters and bulletins with regionally reliable information. They will also provide you with notice of upcoming sales and events, such as lectures and workshops.

Midborder Layering

Naturalistic layering that continues down to the ground level can add an exciting flow of change and color to beds and borders in every season. Obviously, this is most important where snow cover does not hide the garden for months at a stretch. Because snow cover is rare and fleeting where I live, the garden can be seen at all times. I wanted to fill both the right and left front beds along the main pathway with plants that remain attractive for as long as possible. Here, as almost anywhere, having lively beds and borders in spring and summer is not very difficult, but having a great deal of fall and winter interest was an important goal. To meet this requirement, I developed what I call a texture garden matrix—a collection of low-growing evergreens that includes small shrubs, hardy perennials, small grasses, sedums, and succulents.

Here in the maritime Northwest, we can grow a large array of small evergreen shrubs, such as evergreen Mediterranean herbs (rosemary, sage, and lavender), swordlike flaxes (*Phormium* spp.), and fine-textured hebes from New Zealand. Other New Zealanders that do well here are grasses like carex that come in lustrous shades of copper, tawny orange, gold, or green.

It's easy to assume that this exotic West Coast palette is what gives our gardens their distinctive look and color scheme. But for gardeners who choose to do so, this or any look can be emulated almost anywhere simply by seeking out plants that are hardy equivalents of tender ones. Designers who want to re-create the overflowing look of ebullient English borders in, say, Chicago, are well advised to replace those classic but prima donna border beauties with easygoing prairie plants. Those who fall for the potent shapes and deep colors of New Zealand plants or the salsa-based

Small-Scale Evergreen Layering Plants

Medium and compact shrubs are the building blocks of layered gardens. Before placing an evergreen in the garden, though, it's vital that you consider the plant's ultimate height.

COMMON NAME (BOTANICAL NAME)	HEIGHT (IN FEET)	FOLIAGE	HARDINESS ZONES	GARDEN NOTES
Arborvitae (*Thuja* spp.)	1–50	Fine textured	2–7	Upright habit; check height at maturity when selecting
Blueberry, cranberry (*Vaccinium* spp.)	5–20	Fall color (some species are deciduous)	3–8, varies by species	Upright or broad habit; attractive fruit
Bog rosemary (*Andromeda polifolia*)	1–2	Blue-green	2–6	Low, mounded habit; spring flowers; requires moist peaty or sandy soil
False cypress (*Chamaecyparis* spp.)	2–100	Many foliage colors	5–8, varies by species	Upright or broad habit; many small cultivars, check height at maturity when selecting
Gaultheria (*Gaultheria* spp.)	½–5	Glossy, smooth leaves	4–8, varies by species	Upright or broad habit; spring flowers; white, pink, or red fruit
Japanese cedar (*Cryptomeria japonica*)	6–60	Bronze in winter	5–6	Upright habit; handsome, red-brown bark
Japanese holly (*Ilex crenata*)	3–10	Dark green in winter	5–7	Upright or broad habit; blue-black fruit
Kalmia (*Kalmia* spp.)	2–10	Leathery, dark green leaves	4–9, varies by species	Upright or broad habit; white, pink, or deep red spring blooms
Leucothoe (*Leucothoe* spp.)	3–6	Bronze in fall	5–8, varies by species	Arching branches; white, fragrant flowers in spring
Mahonia (*Mahonia* spp.)	5–10	Bronze in winter	6–9	Upright or broad habit; yellow spring flowers

My goal is to build plant communities that are as close to self-sustaining as I can make them.

tropicalismo so popular in the West can match the look by combining bold foliage plants with oversize hardy perennials and flamboyant annuals (many of which are really tender perennials or shrubs). For example, hardy yuccas can replace the beautiful but tender New Zealand flaxes. Several native and exotic yucca species adapt well to most parts of the country, providing dramatically spiky or sword-shaped foliage.

However, the real secret of these luxuriant plantings is less the specific plants than how they are employed. The key is in two principles—the first is the ability of naturalistic layering to link the garden to its tree line, then continue right down to the ground, and the second is the emphasis on natural architecture. This involves the selection of plants with naturally sculptural forms, the placement of such plants to emphasize their architectural qualities, and the development of shapely combinations and vignettes. Interior layering and the emphasis on sculptural plants are what really gives the West Coast gardens their strikingly dramatic appearance.

Gardeners in colder climates may choose from thousands of excellent hardy plants, starting with small trees and shrubs. Many perennials will grow almost anywhere. Annuals, too, are adaptable, as are many bulbs and grasses. Any or all can be arranged with flair and distinction simply by placing them in ways that make their natural attributes assets to the overall design. However for me, the point of creating these exciting-looking naturalistically layered gardens is not just their powerful appearance, but also their ease of care. I am less interested in growing the hottest (or coolest) new horticultural introductions than I am in finding good-looking plants that enjoy the conditions I have to offer and that get along well with others. My goal is to build plant communities that are as close to self-sustaining as I can make them. If, in addition, they are also lastingly lovely (as they nearly always are), so much the better.

When I've gardened in other parts of the world, I've based my midborder layers on beautiful, low-growing, native evergreen shrubs. Among my favorite dwarf shrubs is bog rosemary (*Andromeda polifolia*), especially choice forms like 'Green Ice', with gray-blue foliage and fragrant, rosy flowers. I also love box huckleberry (*Gaylussacia brachycera*), with lovely, fine-textured foliage and red-striped white flowers followed by matte black berries.

Indeed, dwarf and low-growing shrubs of all kinds can mingle in our beds and borders. We can draw on the great *Vaccinium* clan, which includes blueberries, huckleberries, cranberries, and lingonberries. Several native gaultherias (*Gaultheria* spp.) and winterberries (*Ilex verticillata*) are also excellent little plants for mixed gardens.

The rhododendron family is increased yearly with new hardy shrubs of all sizes. Dwarf mountain laurel (*Kalmia latifolia*) has contributed its cold-hardiness to a race of charming little shrubs with beautiful flowers like small, octagonal chalices.

The entry bed in front of the house is an experiment in texture gardening. Every plant was chosen for year-round good looks and natural architecture, and textural contrasts got preference over floral combinations.

Seeing the Possibilities

Designing a naturalistic garden takes time and energy (in a good way!), and the results are so rewarding and so low maintenance that you'll want to spread the word to other gardeners. Throughout this book, I've given you many ideas about creating a garden space and shown you how to create an effective garden design. I applied the principles to my own garden and I thought it would be worthwhile to show you how I used the same problem-solving approach to design a garden on another property. This site was large, but you can **use these same ideas** on a smaller scale for your garden.

This property, affectionately known as Wardwell Farm, is the perfect example of how good garden design can transform a diverse, unassuming property into an **inviting, usable,** multipurpose garden. We centered a series of large gardens around the small, elderly farmhouse that had been charmingly restored. The site is over 7 acres, and is a sunny upland with generally poor soil (it's very low in tilth and nutrients), but few drainage problems and **plenty of space.** When we began working on the gardens, nearly all the property was in meadow.

The owner wanted to create small-scale gardens around the house that would suit the style and size of the **simple farmhouse.** He also hoped these gardens would screen the road and driveway and allow for seating areas and small trees. He wanted to expand the existing small orchard of **heirloom fruit trees,** and he wanted several large beds for **herbs, vegetables, and cut flowers.**

Large and small properties require designs made to decidedly different scales. In order to make sense of this large site, **we divided the whole place** into several sections so that each section could be tackled individually.

We were fortunate to have several **extraordinary specimen trees** already on the property. Though the place had been logged years ago, big second-growth firs, hemlocks, and cedars still stood. There were also a number of madrona trees, and the lower meadow was dominated by **one of the region's largest bigleaf maples.** These anchor trees helped to define garden areas, and they turned out to be great assets in creating focal points on this large site.

First Things First

THE POTENTIAL OF THE FARMHOUSE AND ENVIRONS WAS inspiring, and the owner and I had many great ideas for gardens. However, before we made any major decisions, we completed a more formal site assessment (see the "Organic Garden Design School Workbook" on page 232) to make sure we were clear about our wants and needs. After an initial site examination, we were able to clarify and define a number of goals for our garden design. We had to think about the site as a whole, then evaluate what we wanted to accomplish in each area of the garden. Here are the highlights of our assessment, the details of what our evaluation found, and what we tackled as part of the garden plan.

The Site Specifics

The site plan for the property was simple to draw, but it showed everything we needed to know about the site. The house faces east, and the prevailing winds come from the south and west. These aspects were important to know when we started choosing and siting plants. We located all the overhead power lines and underground pipes and wires (not included on this basic site map) so we could avoid planting anything that might get in the way. We also added existing features to the map, including buildings, trees, sidewalks, stairs, and porches, plus large areas on the site, such as meadows and greenbelts. We marked the site of two large well tanks near the front door because they would need special handling during the garden

redesign; we were pretty sure we wouldn't "lose" them, though, because both tank covers were painted a vivid artificial green!

We identified the trees and shrubs on the property on a separate list so we could make decisions about whether or not to remove them. We knew we wanted to leave some for protection from wind or to provide screening from the road, but we were sure we wanted to remove others.

The owner was unsure about the location of the septic field on the property. It's always a good idea to locate the field before bringing heavy equipment onto a site, but in this case we had to take our chances. Our laid-back attitude worked in our favor. We sowed winter rye in one area behind the house, and it came up thick and fast, growing twice as well as anywhere else. Voilà! The septic field revealed itself without effort.

> The majestic bigleaf maple in the background may be over 300 years old. Its presence is awesome in any season. One of many incredible trees on the property, this maple tree helped us create a focal point in the meadow.

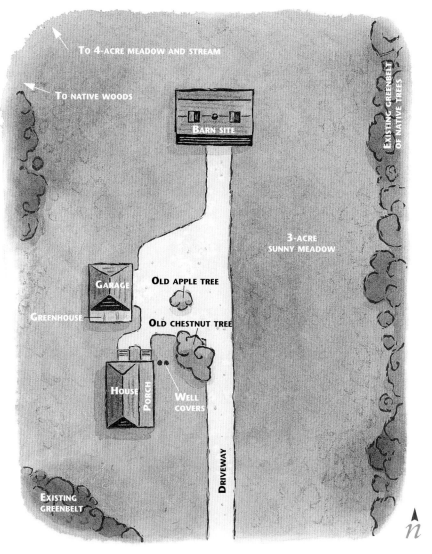

A 7-acre property, Wardwell Farm boasts a variety of habitats, from sunny upland fields to a shaded salmon stream. Surrounded by a dense greenbelt, the property presented exceptional opportunities for development as a naturalistic garden and productive organic farm.

Keen Observations

We had drawn an overall map locating trees and shrubs, as well as hardscape, but we still needed answers for a number of simple but important questions: What kind of soil do we have to work with? Is it the same everywhere? What about sun and shade patterns? Are there any drainage issues?

After exploring the site, we discovered mostly rocky clay soil with patches of sandy loam. The soil had few nutrients and was low in tilth (humus). The property around the house received full sun, except for a small area that was partially shaded in the morning by the old chestnut tree. We saw persistent puddling after a rain, and concluded that the overall drainage was average to poor.

Paths and Places

We noted that paths were one of the main problems with the existing site. The front entry to the house was not clear to visitors, and there wasn't a path to get from the house to the garden. We also needed to consider how the meter readers, kids, and family pets approached the house.

The house had a wonderful, deep front porch that just begged to be used, so we knew we should plan for lush gardens all around that area. It was important to tie together the entry, the porch, and the garden.

A rough meadow was transformed into curvaceous planting beds in a single day. Herbs, vegetables, and cut flowers share space and nutrients in these mounded beds.

The Best and the Worst

All sites have them—a few assets and a few drawbacks. I call them "The Best and the Worst." We asked ourselves two main questions about the property: First, what are the best features of the site, and second, what makes it difficult to use the site well?

At Wardwell Farm, the assets included: territorial views (some were only partial views, but still worth savoring), good light, shelter from wind, mature trees to serve as centerpieces or backdrops, great neighborhood trees we could "borrow," potential for good flow through the property, adequate storage and practical spaces (for composting, storing tools, and so on), and structurally sound porches.

We identified problems on this site that are common to many sites: a lack of privacy, street noise, poor drainage, narrow paths, and overgrown hedges. This house also sits very high on its foundation, so it needed to be anchored to the garden with tall foundation plantings. The key plant near the house, a large chestnut tree, was aging, but it still had enough character to possibly be a focal point.

The site offered both full sun and partial shade. We found room to create a sunny sitting area—the existing camellia and holly hedge provided privacy to the south, and the house and hedge offered shelter from the wind. All in all, we had good features to work with and a lot of room to make improvements.

Problem Solving by Design

ONCE WE HAD THOROUGHLY EXPLORED THE SITE AND made a list of assets and drawbacks to help us refine our garden ideas, we started work on a plan to solve the site's problems attractively and inexpensively. We identified several major problems with the site, then set our sights on tackling the most important ones first. We discussed several workable options, putting an emphasis on using space effectively. We reached solutions quickly in some cases and after much debate in others. As you read through the problem and solution examples, think about how you could apply some of the ideas we used at Wardwell Farm to improve areas of your own garden.

PROBLEM: Along the driveway, this site required privacy screening that would block sound and dust without sacrificing sunlight and air flow.

SOLUTION: We added a low berm the length of the driveway and planted 8-foot-tall hedge plants.

When we evaluated the 40 × 50-foot space between the house and the driveway, we realized that this area needed screening from the busy road. The area seemed cozy, but it would be even more intimate if we add a sense of enclosure. It would be very easy to link the planned gardens to the magnificent tree lines across the street and along the property edge, but the house was still visible to anyone who passed by. In order to create a sense of privacy, we added a small berm.

Privacy berms are long mounds of soil that buffer street noise and help screen out unwanted views. They may be almost any length or height, though a huge berm can look a bit odd on a small, flat lot.

At the farmhouse, we made a low mound just over 2 feet high that ran the length of the driveway. We chose shrubby dogwoods for our screening plants, setting them on 8-foot centers to filter out traffic dust and block the view of the road. These shrubs link the garden to the woodlands across the street, where native shrubby dogwoods line the edges of a large stand of alders and maples. By blocking out the driveway and connecting to the tree line, they make the garden feel like part of the greater woodland around it.

The garden space was already partially enclosed by a rough hedge of old hollies and camellias. Though not in great shape, we kept most of them for the protection they offered. Their eventual replacements are being planted on the outside of this informal hedge, and the ragged old trees and shrubs will be removed as their replacements come of age.

Behind the old chestnut tree, a 2-foot-high berm elevates garden plantings to help screen a neighbor's sheds and parking area. On the other side of the driveway, a natural mound was tidied up and planted to deepen the green screen.

Because the small house sits very high on its foundation, the site required unusually tall foundation plants to integrate the house with the garden. Layering plants in the surrounding beds helped "place" the house naturally in its garden setting.

PROBLEM: The house stood very high above the ground and looked disconnected from the garden.

SOLUTION: We planted foundation trees, shrubs, and perennials to connect the house to the garden.

The quaint farmhouse at Wardwell Farm was perfectly in character with the property, but it seemed disconnected from the earth because it sat high on its foundation. Our goal was to "lower" the house, reconnect it with the garden, and plant shrubs and perennials that would transcend the space between the soil and the house. We started by planting tall evergreen viburnums (*Viburnum odoratissimum*). They spread to about 8 feet wide, so we set the glossy-leaved shrubs on 8-foot centers, 7 feet out from the house wall. To create a more interesting look, we added an unusual 'Katsura' Japanese maple that grows to 15 feet high and offers great fall color. This choice little tree is set 7 feet out from the wall with the arch of its eccentric trunk pointing outward. As it grows, it will stretch away from, rather than back toward, the farmhouse and porch.

The bed would look quite empty for at least 2 or 3 years if we simply put in the tree and shrubs, so we added an understory of perennials and grasses for all-season interest. As the shrubs fill in, the frontline plants will be moved to other parts of the garden. The groundcover, a lacy, silvery form of our native beach wormwood called *Artemisia stelleriana* 'Broughton Silver', will probably remain across the sunny front of the bed, as will the groundcover planting of *Lamium maculatum* 'Cannon's Gold' across the bed's shady backside.

PROBLEM: The porch steps faced the driveway, not the garden.

SOLUTION: We created a wide, curving path from the driveway to the stairs, and we designed an attractive entry to lead visitors through a lush garden on their way to the house.

When designing a garden, it's always a good idea to start at the house and work outward, and it's important to create a handful of possible designs before making any final decisions. All traffic heads to or from that direction, so creating an inviting, usable path is always your best bet. When we began the garden, the front porch steps lacked a sidewalk, so we made a curving, 4-foot-wide path between the driveway and the house, using 6 inches of concrete that was brushed the morning after pouring to expose the aggregate and give it a nice texture. Now the path connects the front and back doors, providing visual unity as well as dry, safe footing.

This path widens to 5 feet at the front steps, emphasizing their importance to visitors. The generous curve looks graceful, and the bed it defines is large enough in scale to visually balance the mass of house and driveway. The curve of the path also created a moon-shape bed along the house, where we added foundation plants. Such strong, simple curves help counterbalance the overwhelming geometry that's often found in urban settings.

In front of the house, we made a courtyard garden, using a flowing, 5-foot-wide gravel path that widens to make a seating area before shrinking back to path width and winding behind the house and into the backyard. The sweeping, gently curved path links the main home entry to the garden and also ties the garden to its rural, woodsy setting far more effectively than straight lines could. The 5-foot width of the garden path allows two people to walk side-by-side and permits the passage of loaded wheelbarrows despite the spillers and sprawlers that creep into the path in summer. At midpoint, where the garden path ballooned out in a broad arch, it created a pleasingly irregularly oval graveled seating area in the sunniest part of the garden.

The path narrows again and continues around the south side of the house, widening slightly at the other end of the porch. We surrounded the porch and the entire house with a strip of gravel about 18 inches wide and 6 inches deep. This creates a plant-free zone, greatly simplifying house painting, window washing, and other maintenance chores. It also helps keep foundation plantings away from the house walls and out

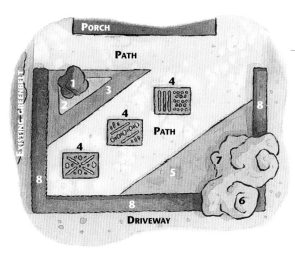

PLANT KEY

1. STEWARTIA
2. 'NANA' DROOPING LEUCOTHOE
3. BLACK LIRIOPE WITH BULBS
4. HERBS (PLANTED IN PATTERNS)
5. GREEN LIRIOPE WITH BULBS
6. OLD CHESTNUT TREE
7. WINTERGREEN (PLANTED UNDER CHESTNUT TREE)
8. COLUMNAR YEWS (8' HIGH)

POSSIBLE DESIGN: This formal design for the front garden at Wardwell Farm fits neatly into the rectangular shape, and it echoes the lines of the house. However rewarding to look at from the windows, though, this design does not create a place for people to be in the garden.

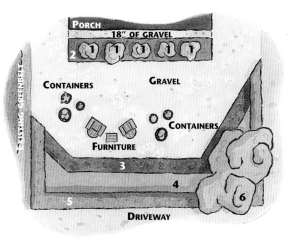

PLANT KEY

1. MEXICAN ORANGE BLOSSOMS
2. BULBS AND GROUNDCOVERS
3. BULBS AND HERBS
4. PERENNIALS
5. ARCTIC GRAY WILLOWS (8' HIGH)
6. OLD CHESTNUT TREE

POSSIBLE DESIGN: Geometric beds and pathways in the front garden look tidy but fight the existing lines of greenbelt and backdrop. This angular kind of garden works best where surroundings are equally linear.

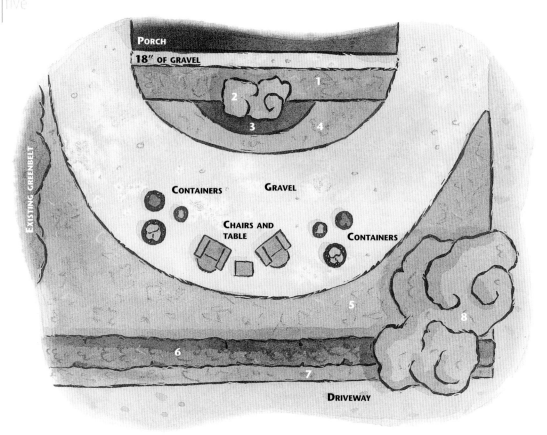

PORCH

18" OF GRAVEL

1

2

3

4

EXISTING GREENBELT

CONTAINERS   GRAVEL

CHAIRS AND
TABLE

CONTAINERS

5

8

6

7

DRIVEWAY

from under the eaves, where dry roots often require supplemental watering.

The shape of the seating area in the front garden is softly rounded and slightly irregular, yet has enough formality to match the trim look of the house. In front of the porch, a graceful half-moon–shape bed matches the curve of the seating area. We gave this bed and those surrounding the path a base of 8 inches of sandy loam, then topped them with 8 inches of organic topsoil. We topdressed the bed with 4 inches of aged compost to keep down weeds.

In this half-moon bed, we placed a small specimen tree and a number of foundation shrubs. The key tree is a young *Stewartia monadelpha*, chosen for its delicate branching pattern and pronounced upright habit. It leafs out in midspring, blooms in June, and burns like

ACTUAL DESIGN: We settled on this design for the front garden at Wardwell Farm. The smooth, simple curve of the path is powerful enough to balance the mass of the house and connect it visually with its woodsy backdrop. Softly shaped wrap-around beds incorporate the old chestnut tree and lead the eye around the back of the house.

PLANT KEY

1. 'MIDWINTER FIRE' BLOODTWIG DOGWOODS (5) AND EVERGREEN IRISES
2. STEWARTIA
3. 'NANA' DROOPING LEUCOTHOE
4. EVERGREEN GRASSES, DECIDUOUS SHRUBS, AND PERENNIALS
5. EVERGREEN GRASSES, HERBS, AND SHRUBS (2'–3' HIGH)
6. REDTWIG DOGWOOD AND ARCTIC GRAY WILLOW (8' HIGH)
7. COPPER-COLOR SEDGE AND EVERGREEN HERBS
8. OLD CHESTNUT TREE

a flame of hot reds, coppers, oranges, and yellows in fall. The tree was placed 12 feet out from the house so that even when it reaches its full girth of 18 to 20 feet, it won't brush against the porch or grow under the eaves. We flanked the tree with three bloodtwig dogwood shrubs (*Cornus sanguinea* 'Midwinter Fire') planted on 8-foot centers. These were planted 7 feet from the house, so that when they expand to their full width of 6 to 8 feet they, too, will have plenty of breathing room. The stewartia was also underplanted with groups of a small arching native shrub, *Leucothoe axillaris*, and fans of the fruiting evergreen *Iris foetidissima*. We clustered evergreen grasses, compact evergreen shrubs, and perennials throughout the bed so even in winter it will appear well-filled, maintaining its structure and interest all year-round.

PROBLEM: The driveway and parking area were uninviting. The owner wanted to create a garden to soften this entry to the property.
SOLUTION: We designed a vegetable, herb, and cut-flower garden in the turnabout to add a soft, natural look to this utilitarian area.

The owner expressed interest in growing herbs, vegetables, and flowers for cutting in gardens near the driveway, and wanted to center the gardens around an old apple tree with a wonderful, gnarled shape.

Along the driveway, we opened a section of meadow about 40 × 100 feet for the gardens. When we set out to design the beds, we knew we wanted to avoid the straight rows usually found in vegetable gardens and the quadrants found in traditional herb gardens. We did, however, want to make it easy to grow and gather the garden's bounty by making usable paths and manageable-size beds. We created a variety of designs for this area, some with straight lines and some with gentle curves, before settling on a design with interesting swoops.

The old 'Golden Transparent' apple tree along the driveway made the perfect centerpiece for the main bed closest to the house. We chose an elliptical shape for that bed (see page 97) to showcase the tree, sloping the new soil down in a smaller bed-within-a bed to avoid smothering its crown. By removing weeds and grass from its base, we were able to add several inches of fresh soil without altering the original soil level around the trunk. Under the tree, we planted a small shade garden with plants that have year-round interest,

Almost a year after planting, the front garden at Wardwell Farm is already beginning to knit back into the borrowed tree line across the street. The rays of morning sun and misty morning dew create a snapshot in time that is breathtaking.

POSSIBLE DESIGN: The rectangular area available for the organic vegetable and cut-flower beds at Wardwell Farm seemed to suggest traditional, linear designs. The straightforward paths simplify garden chores and harvest but lack a naturalistic style.

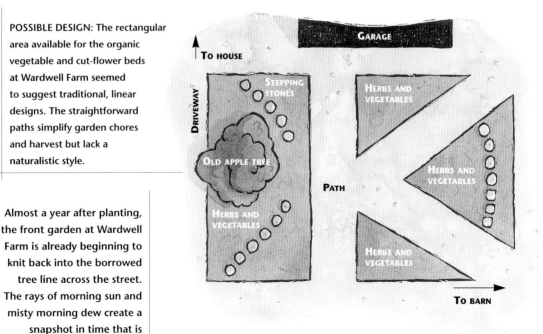

TO HOUSE

DRIVEWAY

GARAGE

STEPPING STONES

HERBS AND VEGETABLES

OLD APPLE TREE

PATH

HERBS AND VEGETABLES

HERBS AND VEGETABLES

HERBS AND VEGETABLES

TO BARN

and we provided plenty of space for herbs and vegetables. We created a narrow, curved access path through the bed to make harvesting easy.

We added a circular turnaround for the driveway that also defined the central bed. We flowed a 10-foot-wide circle of gravel around the bed and continued it around each subsequent bed, narrowing the path width to 5 or 6 feet, as needed. When first laid out, the rounded beds looked like floating islands above a meandering river. We created two other beds in this area, giving each gentle curved lines and rounded corners so they nested within each other. The smallest bed near the future paddock holds a Sargent crabapple tree that, in time, will mirror its elderly cousin across the herb beds. The herb and

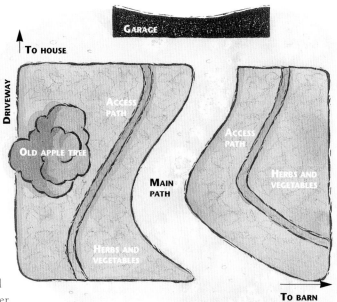

POSSIBLE DESIGN: As an alternative to strict geometry, we created a design with softer lines and sinuous shapes for the gardens. These beds offer the gardener more flexibility because the paths and beds can be reshaped effortlessly for crop rotation, but we decided we wanted a more free-floating design in the long run.

An elderly apple tree became the centerpiece for the raised bed gardens. When the beds are reshaped to allow for crop rotation, the paths can be remade by moving soil away from the gravel drainage layer. The old apple and the new crabapple trees lend an air of permanence to the garden, and within a few years, both trees will seem as naturally a part of the garden as the herbs and vegetables that thrive in the raised beds do now.

vegetable garden is attractive to look at and easy and pleasant to use, but looks far less linear than most vegetable patches.

The backyard meadow abuts the vegetable garden, but we decided to hold off on expanding the gardens too quickly. Since the owner was unsure about plans for the backyard, we simply tilled it and sowed winter rye as a cover crop. We wanted to take our time about developing this large area, so we planned a 3-year rotation of cover crops (rye, clover, and mustard) to build tilth and raise healthy soil bacteria levels. This simple program is being carried out seasonally while we work on the primary gardens. Instead of lying fallow or becoming a weedy mess, the degraded soil will be in better condition when the time comes to develop the back garden more fully.

One Step at a Time

Our step-by-step problem solving at Wardwell Farm allowed us to develop an overall plan for the site, yet enabled us to take our time making decisions and implementing plans. Since we needed to stay within a budget, it was an effective way of working because we prioritized our goals and worked on areas of the garden that would benefit most from a redesign.

If you're faced with a property that needs significant improvement, break the process down into manageable parts, solving design problems as you go. Most sites take years to overhaul, especially if you're starting from scratch. Set a goal of redoing one or two areas a year. You'll find that you'll change your mind about what you want (and I'll bet you'll often discover that your new ideas are better!), so time is really on your side when designing a garden.

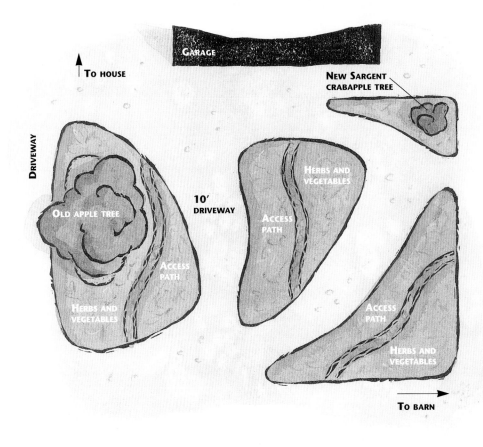

ACTUAL DESIGN: This is the design we chose for the Wardwell Farm production gardens. Its flowing lines and inflated wing-shaped beds were more in keeping with the setting. From the house, the beds seem to float like islands in a sinuous river of black gravel.

Creating a Natural Backdrop

Layering is perhaps the most vital principle behind organic garden design, one that governs the design at every level. The challenge is to apply the principle of layering to your actual site, which may have very little in the way of natural layering. Whether you choose **patterns drawn from habitat** and wilderness or you simply want to employ the open-centered "golden bowl" design pattern (see page 74), you need to know how to create layers that really work. This means putting plants together in **ways that look natural and attractive** and that also satisfy the cultural needs of the plants. The goal is for plantings to look inevitable rather than contrived and to remain healthy, visually appealing, and **ever-changing throughout the seasons.**

As I've mentioned in previous chapters, at its simplest, layering can be broken down into the patterns of the natural woods. The canopy or tree line seen against the sky is the top layer. Next come high and medium understory, the intermediate plantings that **visually connect** the largest plants to the ground level. In these layers, low understory shrubs mingle with a **floral carpet of perennials, annuals, bulbs, and groundcover.**

These stepped plant layers are ecologically united. In a young forest, every ecological niche is full. The forest is dense with underbrush, and shrubs of many sizes make physical and visual ladders to link the trees to the ground level. In **old-growth forests,** the scene is quite different. Here, mature trees create such dense shade and underground root mats that very little can compete successfully. The **open, spare understory** of the old-growth forest is the model for certain kinds of Zen gardens in which moss, stones, and a few ferns become the main ornamentation, with drought-tolerant rhododendrons and azaleas **filling in the edges of the garden,** just as they do in real old-growth woodlands.

Harnessing the Layers of Nature

WHETHER YOU PREFER LUXURIOUS GARDENS OR LEAN ones, you can use many of the techniques discussed in the previous chapters to create layers in your garden. You can "borrow" trees and distant views by framing them with plants. You can cluster important plants (usually trees and shrubs) where they will screen views, create privacy, and carry the eye up to larger plants that are on or are visible from the property. The "golden bowl" garden style, with an open central area rimmed with gently layered plants, may be generously planted or may have the understated look of the old-growth patterns important to Zen garden design, where each element (whether it be a rock or a shrub) is treated as a structural one.

In most layered gardens, the largest plants (again, generally trees and shrubs) create a ruffled, irregularly tiered backdrop for garden plantings. These living walls create a sense of enclosure, making us feel cozy and welcome in our green havens. The sheltering plant layers also provide a habitat for birds, butterflies, and native pollinators of many kinds. In any climate zone, abundantly layered gardens tend to be full of life and to feel furnished in every season of the year.

> The way to make layering look natural in nonwooded settings is to study the places where layering actually occurs.

These basic layering patterns and planting techniques work well for wooded gardens, and even for gardens in parts of the country where woodlands are an important feature of the landscape. But what about mountain, prairie, plains, and high desert settings? What about rocky seaside gardens where constant wind keeps plants low? Do these layering principles and visual patterns still apply?

Looking to the Wild

The way to make layering look natural in nonwooded settings is to study the places where layering naturally occurs. In dryland regions, plants tend to follow water. In dry mountain and desert settings, willows and cottonwoods grow along the rivers, and aspens are tucked into the narrow channels cut by small streams. In the high desert, pockets of plants—often shrubs and small trees—reveal little seeps where water oozes from the ground and nourishes life. In prairies and on plains, the presence of water also changes the nature of the plants.

Even in wet thickets or swamps there will be small trees, low scrub, and a perennial base layer. In the high desert, the tallest plants may be dwarfed by drought and wind, yet they are still surrounded by colonies and clusters of lower and smaller plants. In the driest regions, these plant communities are far more spread out than they are in lusher settings. In the foothills beyond El Paso, Texas, or outside of Reno, Nevada, you can read the water table by noting the spacing of the sagebrush and mesquite. Where water is more plentiful, the bushes are more closely grouped. When the distances between them stretch for yards, water is rare indeed. Even in such places, lone junipers stand tall and mighty above the lower mass of scrub, and the ground itself holds an astonishing array of seasonal perennials.

All of the natural plant communities that form around water sources emulate to some degree the layering patterns of the woods and forests. However small the scale and however limited the palette, plants tend to organize themselves into the same general hierarchies. Thus, when we organize our plants into those same layers in our gardens, the result tends to look more appropriate, more comfortable, and less artificial than when we use formal or arbitrary plant placements.

Virtually all natural communities exhibit layering patterns, but the layers in a high desert garden may look very different from those in a typical woodland.

Layering to Link with Nature

Swept by wind, this dry, sunny California hillside supports a complex community of drought-tolerant plants. Here the natural layers are more compact and less differentiated than those in the standard woodland.

ALTHOUGH EVERY NATURAL LAYERING PATTERN HAS ITS own beauty, not all are directly applicable to garden design. However, organic garden design does not copy nature so much as draw lessons from it. If you garden in or near natural settings, the most important places to create layers that reflect native plant communities will be in the transition zones between your gardens and the surrounding or adjacent natural area. The traditional solution is to make the gardens near the house more formal, and then, as they approach the wild, to allow the look and feel of the gardens to grow less regulated and more natural. If

you have a small property, these transition zones will have fewer stages than if you have an acre or more to work with. However, even small transition areas will help to visually integrate the garden into the natural setting around you.

Many traditional gardens have wilder parts that offer good models for transitional areas. One example is the gardens at Hidcote Manor in Gloucestershire, England. Here Lawrence Johnston, an expatriate American, created a highly influential garden during the early 1900s that started several significant design trends. First, he created a series of hedged and walled garden rooms, giving each a specific character and flavor. One, for instance, holds nothing but a circular pool so large that it almost fills the entire space. Others are filled with intricately planted beds and borders. The concept of garden rooms is as old as the idea of gardens themselves (the Persian word 'paradise' means "an enclosed garden"), but Johnston gave this ancient idea a fresh interpretation that is still inspiring modern designs today.

Hedges are also as old as the hills, but Johnston again broke with tradition by creating tapestry hedges, mixing the plants in them to make patterns of foliage color. (His combination of plain and copper beech with holly is especially famous.) Near the house at Hidcote, the tapestry hedges are sheared tightly, but farther from the house, the hedges are left loose, unsheared, and are even more mixed. Within the wild garden itself, the hedges are spinelike

backbones made up of trees and shrubs that serve as the anchor points for the perennial-based borders that run on either side.

Johnston also used woody plants to add structure throughout the garden. While the garden contains some traditional hardscape elements, the overall design relies significantly more on the architectural lines of plants than on man-made materials. Important shrubs are trimmed, more often than not, and in many places, specimen trees are placed or framed with great distinction and regard. In addition, the contrast between sheared and natural forms is dramatically emphasized in many parts of the garden.

Growing Wilder

The wild garden at Hidcote provides several practical examples of how to transition from a formal garden into a more naturally layered one. For example, the beds and garden rooms nearest to the house at Hidcote are regularly shaped and formally filled. Farther from the house, both beds and plants take on more natural shapes. As the garden becomes less formal, the contrasts between the controlled and the natural are used to create a dramatic visual tension.

Following this concept, you might opt to leave plantings near your house fairly formal, but change the strict geometric shape of your vegetable garden to a softly curving one. It will be just as easy to tend, yet it will also help ease the eye gently into nearby woods,

an unsheared hedge, or whatever natural scene borders your property. Instead of presenting jarring contrasts of form and line where the garden proper meets the wild, this design modification would create a simple but effective transition area. Behind the vegetable beds, you could plant a row of unpruned shrubs such as blueberries, flowering currant, wild sand cherry, and twiggy dogwoods to create a buffer between the wild area (or your neighbors) and the garden proper. This wild garden will also double as a bird sanctuary. As shrubs and trees mature, they will grow together and create a sheltered habitat.

This Massachusetts garden echoes a familiar woodland pattern—the relatively open understory of a middle-age eastern forest.

Setting Shrubs Free

Working with the existing shrubs or hedges in your yard is a good place to start creating the framework for a naturalistic layered garden. You can "unshear" both freestanding clipped shrubs and mature sheared hedges. A yard full of shrubs shaped like bowling balls, gumdrops, and pincushions will always look contrived, so try allowing these artificial shapes to relax into natural plant forms. After you figure out what your yard might look like when the sheared forms are released, you may opt to remove some shrubs and repair others. You may also elect to remove them all in favor of smaller, more appropriate plants.

Tightly sheared plants tend to become stressed over time because their dense growth restricts the amount of light and air that can reach their cores. Once they have been opened up a bit, the plants can return to their normal, healthy growth patterns. It may take several years of unshearing to fully restore a sheared plant to its authentic shape. Most, however, will respond to the initial unshearing session with a flush of healthy new growth that will produce a more natural appearance in just a few seasons.

If you have shorn forsythias, weigelas, or other cane-producing shrubs, the best method for restoring natural plant form is simply to cut these poor creatures to the ground. Good-natured cane-throwing shrubs will respond quickly with a flush of new growth from the roots. To keep them from becoming overly crowded again, thin the new shoots, removing the smallest and most crowded and leaving a sturdy framework of the largest and strongest-looking canes. Other types of shrubs need a more involved thinning process, which I explain in detail in "Thinning Large Shrubs" on the opposite page.

When you're working with a hedge, you may decide to transition the whole hedge to a natural form. Or it may be necessary to continue shearing portions of hedges that would otherwise take up too much

Sheared weigelas recover their natural shape quickly if they are cut back to the ground soon after bloom or in late winter. You'll be rewarded with a flush of vigorous growth during the next growing season.

room and only unshear those portions of the hedge that can be set free without hogging the whole yard. In either case, unshearing means using a remedial pruning technique to restore congested plants to their natural state (as explained in "Unshearing a Shrub" on page 258).

If your hedge plants are too big to let loose, you can reduce the formality of their appearance and keep them healthy by adapting this unshearing technique: Each year, you clip tight older growth and also reduce bulky new growth. This method can be used to control the overall size of any hedge plant, which should then be given extra attention and care to make up for removing its foliage. Ideally, however, you should replace unsuitable plants with others of a more appropriate mature size, rather than perpetuating the endless chore cycle required by oversize hedges.

Thinning Large Shrubs

Overgrown freestanding shrubs may need major thinning as well as unshearing of the surface layers. When you thin your shrubs is less important than how you do it. Be sure to use sharp pruning tools that make clean cuts without tearing bark or mashing stems. Scissor-action or bypass pruners are better in this respect than anvil pruners, which are sometimes called "the nurseryman's best friend" for their ability to kill off plants through damage and resulting disease (thus necessitating another trip to the nursery for replacement plants).

When you remove twigs and small branches, make clean cuts that leave no stubs. This does not necessarily mean that you make a flush cut that is perfectly flat against the main branch or trunk. Before making

your initial cut, touch the branch and feel for the branch collar, a slight swelling that marks the place where a twig comes off a branch or a branch comes off the trunk. Most trees and all shrubs with a main trunk and interior branching have this kind of collar. Make your cut just outside it, rather than cutting flush with the trunk or branch. An exception would be in plants (like pine trees) that don't have any collar. If you can't see or feel any collar swelling at any twig or branch bases on your plant, you can make flush cuts. Either way, after you've finished pruning, you should be able to run your hand smoothly over pruned areas without catching it on anything.

Getting started. When it's possible, the best way to start the thinning process is to work from within the shrub. Climb right inside it, or get as close as you can to its center. Try to get a sense of its natural growth pattern, and evaluate which are the most important structural branches.

Prune away dead, damaged, and misshapen branches. For your first cuts, remove all deadwood, large and small. Next, look for broken branches, branches with wounds, and misshapen branches; remove these, too. Start with the worst-looking, and work slowly. Ask yourself what each piece contributes before removing it. In many cases, if you were to prune off every misshapen branch, you'd be left with very little.

Undercut large branches before removal. If a branch is so large that you can't remove it with loppers, you'll have to use a pruning saw. In these cases, make a small preliminary upward cut from the underside of the branch before cutting into it from above. Otherwise, heavy branches can break downward, tearing bark and creating a wound that extends into the main branch or trunk.

When you thin a large shrub, don't be timid. You'll have to prune away some large branches (shown in black) to open the shrub to light and air. The shrub will respond by regrowing with a more irregular, natural form.

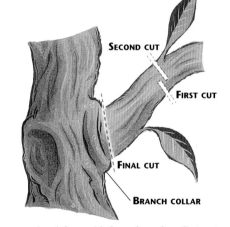

To remove a tree's large side branch, make a first cut up from the underside of the branch to prevent tearing when the limb falls. Make a second cut to remove the bulk of the limb, then make a final cut just above the branch collar.

If your rhododendron has one main trunk, consider transforming it from a shrub into a small tree by removing the lower branches and pruning out small, twiggy branches. A new "tree" in a mixed shrub border can transform a quiet garden area into one filled with visual variety.

Evaluate progress. Once the dead and damaged branches are gone, reevaluate the shrub from the outside. If the plant looks great, stop. If it still looks congested (it probably will), you'll need to remove more wood. Try pruning all downward-curving twigs that grow off the bottom of a large branch. Also remove all watersprouts (twigs that sprout straight upward from a larger branch) for a more natural look.

You may need to reevaluate thinned shrubs after a year to decide whether they need more wood removed. When shrubs have a natural form, they're much easier to integrate into a fully layered planting that includes groundcovers, perennials, annuals, bulbs and other plants. Intermingling this variety of plant types in the layers near ground level is what I call "sandwich gardening," which I'll discuss in depth in "Sandwich Gardening" on page 112.

Turning Sheared Shrubs into Trees

If your yard includes shrubs that are really small trees (such as English laurel, yew, holly, and certain boxwoods), you have the option of transforming a large sheared shrub into an attractive small tree through careful pruning (previously unsheared shrubs usually make this transition easily). This kind of pruning is done by look and feel, first by studying the natural form of the plant, and then by revealing it snip by snip. Good candidates for this treatment include pieris (*Pieris* spp.), mountain laurel, rhododendrons, privet, boxwoods, and camellias, among many others.

To figure out whether your shrub can be converted into an attractive small tree, take a look at how it's put together. Cane-throwing or thicketing shrubs

are not good candidates for treehood, because they lack a main trunk. If, however, your sheared shrub has a main trunk (or several) with a lot of interior branching, it may well make a charming small tree.

The conversion involves taking a shrub that is clothed to the ground and cutting back the lower branches to a main trunk. When the trunk (which may have several leaders) is then cleaned up by removing small twigs, you get a very small tree with a low canopy.

1. Start at ground level. The first step in converting a shrub to a tree is to remove the lowest of the shrub's smaller branches, those that brush the ground. Don't remove any larger branches yet. Once you've removed some branches, you'll be able to see into the interior of the shrub, and you may even be able to climb inside. Either way, evaluate whether the shrub would look most attractive with a single trunk or multiple trunks.

2. Mark the trunk(s). Once you've decided whether to create a single- or multi-trunked tree, mark the trunk(s) at several points along their length with brightly colored surveyor's tape. This is to remind you what *not* to cut.

3. Cut away clutter first. Before you remove any large side branches, prune away any downward-curving twigs that grow off the bottoms of the branches. Sometimes this alone is enough to lift the remaining branches to the desired height. Also remove all watersprouts (twigs that sprout straight upward from a larger branch).

4. Raise the canopy bit by bit. If you decide you want to expose even more trunk, start removing larger side branches. Carefully follow the lowest-hanging branches to their sources rather than simply cutting branches off starting at the bottom of the shrub. The lowest hanging branches may well stem from branches

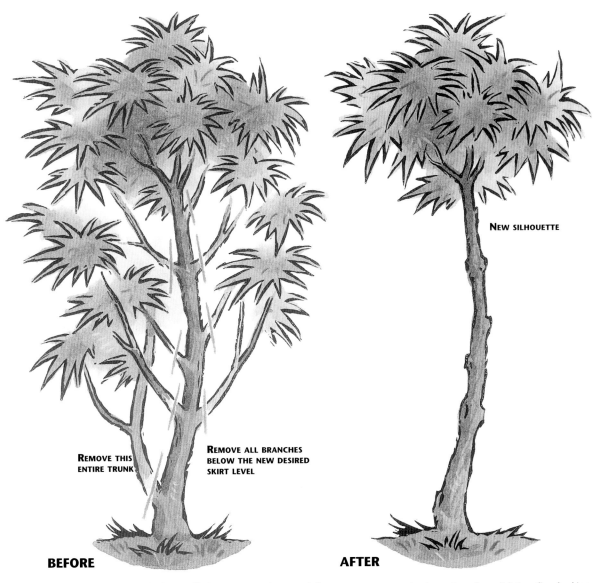

REMOVE THIS ENTIRE TRUNK

REMOVE ALL BRANCHES BELOW THE NEW DESIRED SKIRT LEVEL

NEW SILHOUETTE

BEFORE

AFTER

Selectively removing the lowest limbs or a secondary trunk from an overgrown shrub can transform it into a fine-looking small tree. If you want a higher canopy on your new "tree," you can also remove some of the larger, upper branches to create your new tree shape and allow room to plant taller understory plants underneath.

that begin high up on the main trunk, and branches that begin lower down may well end high up in the shrub. Before removing any large branch, gently move it around to be sure it does not leave an awkward gap in your desired skirt, or lower line.

If the shrub is very large and it's hard to keep climbing in and out to check on your progress, work with a partner who can observe from the outside and guide your cuts. When you aren't sure which branches to remove, wiggle each candidate or lower it a bit (gently, to avoid breakage) so your partner can see how the shrub might look without it. Should you make a mistake and remove a branch that leaves an unsightly gap, you can minimize the goof by removing any small hanging twigs from branches below the gap and by ruffling the surrounding foliage.

You can shape the final canopy level of your new tree as high or low as you like. The optimal height for each plant will reflect both the appearance of the newly revealed trunk(s), the bulk of the plant, and the scale of your garden as a whole.

For your first experiment with converting a shrub to a tree, choose a shrub whose looks you're not crazy about, or that is not performing an essential function. That way, if you don't like the end result, you won't have lost anything.

Where the plant in question *is* providing an important service, such as screening an unpleasant view, and you're not sure that your pruning attempt will be successful, consider planting its replacement as close to its spot as possible. If you need to prune the old plant severely to make room for the new, go ahead and do it. You may also want to use a small section of fence or trellis screen to create immediate shelter and privacy while your replacement shrub comes of age.

Editing the Woods

In woodland gardens, stumps and fallen logs provide habitat for birds and wildlife. Rotting logs will also act as nursery beds for seedlings of many forest plants, including young trees.

IF YOUR PROPERTY ABUTS A WOODED AREA, YOU'LL HAVE the task of editing your part of the woods to create effective transitions between your gardens and the wild. This is most important where woods have been newly cleared to make room for new houses. In such settings, gardeners often find themselves with an artificial woodland edge that lacks its natural transitional layers. Initially, you'll work toward the woods by making your garden layers intersect gracefully with the natural layers under the woodland canopy. Next, you may work from within the woods themselves to connect the transition area from inside the natural habitat.

Where tall trees loom skyward, you may want to restore the native understory layers, perhaps supplementing native plants with suitable ornamental ones. You may also want to tidy up the woods a bit, in order to create more pleasing views into them. This does not mean you should "park out" the woods. (This deplorable phrase refers to the practice of replacing native habitat with lawn, thus destroying the natural ecosystem entirely.)

Editing the woods is a much simpler process, one that requires a light hand and a thoughtful eye. Begin by deadwooding, clearing tree trunks of dead lower branches that impede walking or visual enjoyment. But leave whole dead trunks, whether standing or fallen, in place. They provide homes and shelter for a wide range of small wild creatures.

Fallen logs are often called "nurse logs" because they become nurseries for many forms of life. In a few years, they may support thick coats of mosses and ferns. Next come young perennials and shrubs, followed by seedling trees that will draw nourishment from the mother log for many years. Nurse logs may be considered garden sculptures—beautiful, natural forms that remain powerful in any season. Old stumps are also valuable as living sculptures, especially when they're trimmed with native mosses, ferns, and shrubs.

Native shrubs can also benefit from deadwooding, just as garden plants do. Some may also require light, restorative pruning to repair storm damage or reduce congested growth caused by overbrowsing deer and other herbivores.

The forest floor may be improved by a bit of tidying, as well. Again, this does not mean imposing garden standards on a wild setting. However, in areas where you often walk or places you see daily, mild editing can give a great deal of visual pleasure. Before beginning this delicate process, take a long, careful look at what you see. It may be that the view is essentially perfect and requires no assistance at all.

It may also be that just by picking up a few sticks you can uncover hidden plants, mossy rocks, and lovely old stumps that were obscured by fallen deadwood. It's important not to let any prissy instincts take over during this stage. Wild settings are not gardens, and they should not be treated as mere extensions of our gardens. However, a little judicious caretaking can result in a great deal of pleasure without any subsequent degradation of the natural environment.

Dealing with Weeds

Editing natural environments can also involve clearing away troublesome weeds. In my part of the world, we do battle daily with English ivy that threatens to turn parts of the wild into ivy deserts where natives lose ground to this relentless invader. We also struggle with Scotch broom and Himalayan blackberries, both deliberate imports that ran amok, causing enormous loss of native plants. In other parts of the country, bittersweet vine, kudzu, and purple loosestrife are rampant killers that choke out native plants.

Even if you know your native flora quite well, it's a good idea to contact your local county extension agent to find out which weeds (and garden plants) are on your regional hit list. The USDA also maintains a list of noxious weeds for each state. These include ornamental plants (such as loosestrife and English ivy), as well as pests like Canadian thistles. Sometimes cousins of native plants such as euphorbias and St. John's worts are hard to recognize when they're small because of their resemblance to harmless native forms. By familiarizing yourself with the appearance of the young plants—and diligently weeding them out when you spot them—you can help stop the spread of dangerous weeds into the wild, where they do irreparable damage.

There are also friendly weeds that are less aggressive than they are just opportunistic. Queen Anne's lace, foxgloves, and chicory are common roadside weeds that often appear where woods have been logged. Sometimes called "seeds of disturbance," the seedlings follow

human activity faithfully. When you know pretty much how a given weed is likely to behave, you can make better decisions about which should be pulled on sight and which may be left to flower in peace.

Protecting Native Plants

When you're making changes to the appearance of a natural area, it's also wise to get to know as much as you can about your native plants. That way, you can identify any that may be endangered and in need of special protection. You can also make decisions about which seedlings to keep and which to remove. This process, too,

Editing the woods with a light hand means leaving moss in place and allowing leaves to accumulate. Leaf mold (natural compost made from decaying foliage) adds beneficial nutrients to the soil. Many native plants, including mosses, can be used as groundcovers in a woodland.

A woodland garden can be created where once only a tangled understory grew. You can give the woods a light editing by clearing out dead twigs and branches, tidying up shrubs, removing invasive plants and seedlings, and pruning low-hanging branches to make room for a pathway.

may be considered part of the editing process and can greatly influence what happens to the land in your care over time. For instance, in my backyard, I found seedlings of a native dogwood, a native madroña, and a native bigleaf maple within a few feet of each other.

All are desirable trees in their place, but they most certainly can't share ground. The dogwood is the most uncommon of these and in extreme youth is not averse to travel. I replanted this one in a sheltered but open corner of the woods near a wild cherry that is nearing the end of its lifespan. As the dogwood matures, the cherry will decay and die, leaving plenty of room for the dogwood to expand.

Madroñas don't transplant well, and throughout their natural habitat, many of these elegant, tawny-barked trees are now diseased and dying (mainly from water stress caused by lawn watering). Therefore I left the madroña seedling in place, and a nearby vine maple will be pruned back a bit to give it plenty of room. The bigleaf maple is a lovely thing, but hardly endangered. Since I don't have room for another huge tree with massive leaves, I recycled this seedling into the compost heap.

Good stewardship does not mean allowing wild plants to fight their own battles while we ignore their plight. Especially where foreign weeds are energetic and pervasive, gardeners need to be vigilant in caring for our native plants. Keeping the woods—or any natural environment—clean of invasive non-native weeds is perhaps the single most important service we can offer. The best way to do this is to set up a regular schedule for patrolling the natural areas near you. A few hours invested each month can mean the difference between a degraded habitat and a thriving one. It's also a great excuse to get outside and experience natural environments.

Gardening for Habitat

THESE DAYS, MANY OF US ARE INTERESTED IN WELCOMING a wide range of living creatures into our gardens. Happily, gardens designed according to organic design principles such as layering are by their very nature attractive to birds, butterflies, and other critters. They often go beyond seasonal attractions (such as feeders) to include more lasting lures; they're not just a short-term food source, but a place to live all year-round. If that's what you're after, you can easily devise layered gardens that offer homes to any creatures you want to keep around. Layering your plants creates the shelter that many small creatures need in order to feel safe and protected.

How much shelter you can offer will depend on the size of your site, but even a small garden can become a refuge for wildlife when we take their needs into consideration. Like us, birds, bees, butterflies, and animals have three primary needs: food, water, and shelter. Well-planted gardens can provide food and shelter with very little effort from the gardener (beyond the initial planning and plantings). Those important transitional layers can be made up of plants that offer a harvest of fruits, berries, foliage, and bark, as well as protection and a place to live. Freestanding shrubs and trees are less attractive than those that are layered. The connectedness of layered plants creates a kind of hidden trail system for small creatures, offering good cover as they forage for food or travel through the yard.

To make the freestanding shrubs and trees in your yard a better habitat for wildlife, you can link them by planting a running ruffle of compact shrubs and perennials between and in front of them. If you only have shrubs, you can add a small tree to offer birds a resting place that's safe from cats. If you choose a crabapple or ornamental plum, you'll also be providing another food source. My style of sandwich gardening is perfect for creating the kind of complex, multilayer habitat that shelters and feeds birds, butterflies, and a variety of other wildlife.

Monarch butterflies swarm on purple coneflowers (*Echinacea purpurea*), a good source of nourishing pollen and nectar. While sipping nectar, butterflies often help to pollinate the wildflowers that feed them.

Water in the Garden

Thanks to new technologies, you can provide a year-round water source (or several) in your yard that will stay unfrozen, even in freezing weather. Garden supply catalogs offer water bowls with misters, sprayers, and heating coils that keep ice at bay. The best have sensors that shut off the units when water is absent. New materials for water containers resist cracking or breaking at low temperatures. Larger water features can mimic natural streams and ponds and will be highly attractive to wildlife.

If you don't have a natural pond, pool, or stream, you may want to explore the option of adding at least a small water feature of some kind. Again, new technology and improved materials make water feature construction far simpler and less expensive than in the past.

Sandwich Gardening

When you climb a mountain, walk the wild plains, or make your way through undeveloped woods, you'll find a community of plants happily cohabitating in each natural environment. If you visit those same natural settings every month or so over the course of the growing season, you'll notice **seasonal changes:** Deciduous trees and shrubs leaf out in spring, mature in summer, color in fall, and then lose leaves in winter. Evergreens grow, too, and shed old needles. Flowers are often followed by fruit, and **seedheads and cones ripen** and fall to the ground.

While the most noticeable changes take place at eye level, you may be surprised to know that change happens faster and far more **dramatically** at ground level. Spring enlivens meadows, prairies, and woodlands with bulbs, annuals, and early perennials. Each habitat is home to a host of plants that share ground with one another. **Each species in turn rises and blooms,** sets seed, and retreats into dormancy. The garden is alive year-round, yet individual plants may only have a moment or two in the sun.

You can mimic the changes that take place in natural habitats in your own garden by using a practice I call **"sandwich planting."** When several kinds of plants in the same piece of ground have compatible life cycles, **they'll intermingle just as they do in their native homes**—one plant begins to bloom while another is going dormant and another is pushing its way to soil level for its turn to shine.

If you want to try sandwich planting in your beds and borders to bring this naturalistic planting pattern home to your garden, **you need to do your homework first.** Anybody who has ever enthusiastically overplanted a garden will immediately realize that it's not enough to simply jam a bunch of plants together and hope for the best—the best is exactly what you *won't* get. The result will almost surely be a jumble of stressed plants duking it out for nutrients and space, and it's not a pretty sight. But if you're careful about plant selection and if you prepare your soil properly, your sandwich plantings will be **successful and rewarding.**

Adaptability Preferred

THE IDEA BEHIND SANDWICH PLANTING IS TO CHOOSE A combination of plants that can be intermingled in the soil, will get along well, and don't need very much help from you. In the wild, sandwich plantings are generally made up of site-adaptive plants; these plants are easygoing rather than fussy, and they can make themselves at home in a wide range of situations. For instance, here in the Pacific Northwest, monkeyflowers and lupines are common sights in open meadows and damp woodlands. You'll find different species of these two plants growing in many diverse microclimates, from dry parking lots, shady woods, and high mountain meadows to damp streamsides and spots near small seeps that keep the ground moist year-round.

Moving Plants from Site to Site

There are two kinds of sandwich plants. The first group is called site-adaptive, because they can make themselves comfortable almost anywhere. True, these plants tend to look healthier where conditions are lush than they do when they're grown in challenging situations. Site-adaptive plants, however, are likely to succeed in a wide variety of garden settings. Site-adaptive species are the easygoing workhorses that chug along year after year, flowering well with little care, rarely needing division, and contentedly growing in ordinary conditions. These undemanding plants are a boon to the busy gardener, pouring out their plentiful good looks without much help.

The second group of sandwich plants, which are only found when particular conditions are present, is called site-specific plants. These are the fusspot types that would rather die than grow in an unfamiliar environment. Site-specific plants rarely make the transition from the wild to the garden. Even in the hands of experts, they are apt to be sulky and hard to please. This makes them poor bets for gardens of any kind and especially dubious for partnering in a sandwich planting.

The difference between site-adaptive and site-specific is an important distinction to draw when you're choosing native plants for garden settings. With the new interest in using native plants, many less-familiar native plants are becoming available. Wild-collected plants may look great initially, but they'll fail to grow well once you transplant them into the garden. Often, the problem is that garden beds and borders are too well fed and too-often watered to please wildlings that need leaner conditions to thrive. Or, you are simply dealing with plants that don't enjoy change or

Pinyon pine and autumn sage (*Salvia greggii*) are site-adaptive natives that grow readily in gardens. These plants are tough as nails, contentedly adapting to whatever conditions they're offered.

don't transplant well. Most garden soil lacks the wild flora and soil organisms (called biota) that are found in native soils, so even though the soil is nutritionally sound and has great tilth, it still cannot supply what a wild plant requires in order to thrive.

You may find site-specific plants offered through small specialty nurseries or native plant societies. It can be tempting to try these shy beauties, especially when their genus or species is prized in horticultural circles. Lady's slippers and ground orchids are always sought after, for instance, but very few of them persist in the garden for more than a few seasons at best. It's worth keeping in mind that rare plants are rare for a reason. Even when given the best of care, many of these difficult-to-please plants will die when taken from their natural habitat. If you do decide to try growing rare plants, re-create their natural setting as best as you can. Don't try to make them fit in with others in a sandwich planting, even if they successfully intermingle in the wild.

Looking for Plants in All the Right Places

When you choose plants for sandwich plantings, you want to pick site-adaptive plants, no matter what their provenance. To make a healthy sandwich planting that works lastingly well in a specific place, you'll need to experiment. Here's what you'll need to do: Start by assembling a group of adaptable plants that have similar cultural needs. Ideally, each will have fairly low nutritional requirements and will share available resources readily with companion plants. You also want to find plants that tolerate drought once established, because root competition can reduce the amount of water in the soil even where summer rains are common. You'll want plants that will enjoy the conditions you can offer and will appreciate the rigors of the local climate.

You're probably thinking that all of this makes sense, but you're wondering how you could possibly learn so much about each possible plant candidate.

Look to nature when selecting plants for sites with specific requirements. At our local library, my "Friday Tidy" volunteer group is planting a bioswale that filters parking lot runoff before it enters the storm drains. The soil along the little "stream" stays moist for most of the year, providing places for native filtration grasses, reeds, and rushes, as well as ornamental water-loving plants.

The drier upper banks of the bioswale at the library garden offer perfect spots for many kinds of ferns. In this newly planted Hardy Fern Society demonstration garden, thousands of bulbs such as bluebells, crocus, and lilies are sandwich layered between the ferns. Our next step will be to add mannerly groundcovers of many kinds to weave a weed-suppressing carpet throughout the garden.

Some of the information is obvious and can be found on most plant tags or in any good gardening reference books. Gathering plants that enjoy similar conditions is relatively simple (though it is surprising how few of us are really careful about this). The broadest categories will be plants that like sun or shade, and that prefer moist or dry soils.

You can obtain even more information about plants just by keeping your eyes and ears open. For instance, if you want to find plants that will tolerate a sunny bed with damp soil, seek out plants from sunny swamps, open meadow streamsides, and damp prairies. And don't forget to be creative in your search for information about plants. Nurseries that specialize in aquatic plants will also sell hardy marginals—plants that inhabit the banks of ponds, rivers, and streams. Investigate more specific kinds of habitat by seeking out nurseries that specialize in prairie plants and that categorize them according to the situations in which they thrive (such as wet or dry soil and clay or sand). Books about water gardens may also include information on these marginal plants, as well as on aquatic plants.

There are only a handful of nurseries or garden books that categorize or organize plants in terms of their natural habitat, so if you come across obvious sources of information, refer to them again and again. Until habitat and site information are widely available at garden centers, look for books about specific sites and settings, pamphlets and handouts from native plant societies, articles from gardening magazines, or catalogs from specialty gardens and nurseries. If you find a great book, be sure to buy a copy so you'll have it on your shelf when you need it.

Rescuing Native Plants

If you live in a community where native plants are threatened by development, you may have the opportunity to buy site-adaptive plants for your garden. Some communities have salvage programs that rescue wild plants and sell them to the public for a nominal fee. These programs help to protect and maintain a stock of native plants.

It's important to remember that native creatures are also displaced when development threatens their habitat; these rescued plants will help sustain native animal species whose territory is quickly disappearing. Plants distributed through salvage programs are usually reliable, adaptive plants that will thrive in gardens settings. Contact your local extension office to see if your community runs a plant-rescue program.

Learning by Trial and Error

MY FIRST SANDWICHING ATTEMPTS WERE MADE MANY years ago. In Seattle, our tiny urban yard spurred me to do some creative thinking about layering underground, since every obvious available garden space was soon full of plants. By combining sequences of bulbs with groundcovers, I was able to enjoy many plants in a single space. These first bulb-and-groundcover sandwiches were easy to coordinate and care for, and they became the models for the more complex sandwich plantings that followed.

When we left Seattle for an old farm on a nearby island, I found myself with acres to cover. Even so, I was still intrigued by the idea of making independent, self-supporting garden plantings that would mimic the effortless plantings in natural settings. Much of the farm site was wooded, so I began to study the woods, seeing what came up in company and how the intermingled plants got along.

Planning Native, Natural Sandwiches

I wanted to make gardens that were as autonomous, healthy, and beautiful as the native woods and meadows. The gardens that came with the farmhouse had been wonderful once, but had fallen into disarray. I decided to plant my first complex sandwich beds in a neglected corner of the overgrown garden where a large, elderly quince occupied a central position in the raggedy lawn. I looked for plants that grew well in dry

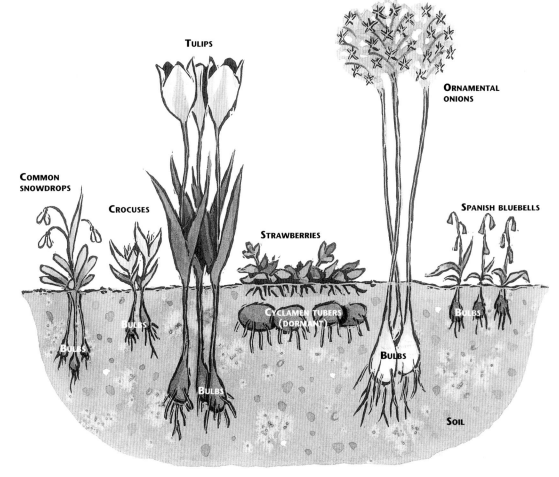

If you could see underground, a cross-section of a sandwich planting of bulbs and perennials might look like this. As bulbs emerge, bloom, and retreat into dormancy, their perennial companions provide cover for their fading foliage and shelter for the bulb itself.

I experimented with growing plants in the kinds of seasonal sequences I admired in the wild.

Don't forget to include old-time favorites like Western bleeding heart (*Dicentra formosa*) in your sandwich garden. This native is about as easy-care as they get, and it combines beautifully with ferns, hostas, epimediums, and lungworts.

shade and intractable clay soil by consulting plant tags, reference books, and nursery catalogs. Then I made extensive notes when I visited local gardens or walked through native woods, taking care to observe what was doing well in dry, shady places and in our heavy native soils. In this region, the ground may be saturated for half the year, but when summer arrives, the ground dries out deeply almost overnight. Thus it made sense for me to look first at our own native flora and then at plants from other parts of the world that have a similar wet-winter and dry-summer climate.

I experimented with growing plants in the kinds of seasonal sequences I admired in the wild. Back in those days, native plants were rare in nurseries, and few gardeners had yet learned to appreciate them. I loved many of the native plants and grew some in my garden, but it had not yet occurred to me (or to most other garden writers) that the natives represented a huge and neglected resource. Even though my first sandwich plantings were based on wild plant patterns, my beds held relatively few native plants.

As cooperative weeds popped up in my garden, I kept them because I thought they were pretty; I didn't recognize then that they were terrific plants in their own

rights. These days I know better, and I use a native plant sandwich in every garden I make. Back then, I accepted the western bleeding heart (*Dicentra formosa*), wild coral bells (*Heuchera cylindrica*), false Solomon's seal (*Smilacina racemosa*), and yellow stream violets (*Viola glabella*) that crept into the scene as serendipitous accidents.

My goal was to choose plants that would "sequence" effortlessly through the year, so I didn't want to limit the sandwich plantings to bulbs and groundcovers. After making big lists of possible perennial candidates, I refined the lists by selecting plants that had small root systems and that either went dormant quickly and gracefully or left small rosette crowns that would look attractive in wintertime. The large perennials filled the garden beds in summer, taking over when the early bulbs were fading. I chose a few large summer onions (*Allium* spp.) for the sandwich planting because their lovely and long-lasting seedheads stick around well into fall, when the late-blooming bulbs are coming into force.

My mild Zone 8 climate made it easier for me to choose plants that provided color and change over the whole year. In more challenging climates, a more practical cycle might run from early spring into midfall. In an intermediate climate, you may be able to extend the season at both ends to include plants that look great in both very early and very late winter. You can also extend the seasonal color in sandwiches by including plants with two seasons of beauty, such as wintergreen (*Gaultheria procumbens*), which has spring flowers and autumnal red berries, or Italian arum (*Arum italicum*), which also blooms in spring and produces showy berries in fall.

Long-Term Success

My first sandwich plantings are still going strong after some 15 years, despite very little care and the fact that new owners care for the farmhouse gardens now. The trick to creating this successful sandwich was choosing a series of easygoing, adaptable plants that had similar needs and were more cooperative than greedy. I credit the hardworking plants I chose and the time I invested in doing my homework before I purchased plants. I'm sharing my plant choices here to illustrate how I sequenced plants through the year and to explain why I made the choices I did.

This large sandwich combined popular perennials, such as brief-but-beautiful Virginia bluebells (*Mertensia pulmonarioides*) and double columbines (*Aquilegia vulgaris*), that bloomed as the bluebells browned out and went dormant. By midsummer, the columbine foliage was usually riddled with leaf miner tracks and needed to be sheared back. To cover the gap, I used a selection of easygoing hostas such as *Hosta* 'Undulata' and the unstoppable *Hosta* 'Honeybells'. These took over effortlessly from the passing columbines and displayed pewtery, blue-green growth that persisted throughout the winter months.

In early fall, the hostas turned sunset shades of gold and copper, then faded rapidly. To relieve them, I mixed in *Arum italicum* 'Marmoratum', whose stout stems were always studded with fat, tomato-red berries by late summer. The snowflakelike new leaves of *Geranium tuberosum* appeared next—this tuberous hardy geranium makes fresh leaves in fall, then overwinters and opens with soft blue flowers in spring, going dormant along with the bluebells.

I don't like to see bare earth in a garden bed, so I added some dusky-leaved black Labrador violets (*Viola labradorica*), which made an almost evergreen

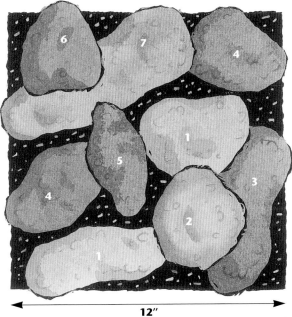

12"

12"

PLANT KEY

(Number in parentheses indicates number of plants)

1. COLUMBINE (1)
2. HELLEBORE (1)
3. ARUM (1)
4. VIRGINIA BLUEBELL (1)
5. ORNAMENTAL ONIONS (5)
6. HOSTA (1)
7. LABRADOR VIOLETS (4)

This sample 1-square-foot sandwich demonstrates how I group compatible plants. The key is to think cubically because a sandwich planting involves much more than flat ground. In the month of April, the bloom of Virginia bluebells is front and center, but will soon be followed by the drooping flowers of columbines, the broad leaves of a hosta, and the glorious flower globes of ornamental onions in a steady sequence from early spring to fall. Evergreen companions such as winter-blooming hellebore and arum and a groundcover of dark-leaved Labrador violets fill the yearlong cycle with aplomb.

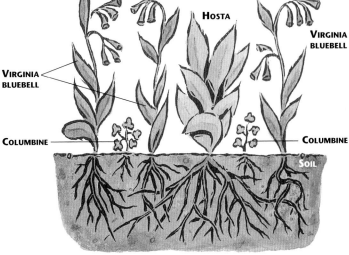

HOSTA

VIRGINIA BLUEBELL

VIRGINIA BLUEBELL

COLUMBINE

COLUMBINE

SOIL

Large alliums look like fireworks in a mixed border, with their sphere of star-shape flowers towering high on slender stalks. Plant 'Purple Sensation' onions (*Allium aflatunense* 'Purple Sensation') near a walkway where passersby can appreciate the intricacy of the flower heads.

groundcover between the resting crowns of the larger perennials. A mix of snow crocus and later-blooming species (such as *Crocus kotschyanus*) created bright carpets both early and late in the season, while a few clumps of late-flowering lenten rose (*Helleborus orientalis* subsp. *abchasicus*) brightened November and December with deep red flowers.

There were several kinds of bulbs in this planting, too, including the showy *Crocus ancyrensis*, an early bloomer with shining golden goblets that can attract bees even in late winter. Next came a species tulip, *Tulipa tarda*, whose ivory petals and deep golden throat make it look something like a floral fried egg. These bulbs were nested in swaths of blue and white Grecian windflower (*Anemone blanda*), with parsleylike foliage and starry, fine-textured flowers.

In summer, clumps of rosy little nodding onion (*Allium cernuum*) decorated the edge of the bed between clumps of black Labrador violets, while taller 'Purple Sensation' onions came up between the hostas. Their deep purple flowers were vivid in May and June, but faded to a handsome chamois color by late summer. Throughout autumn and winter, the skeletal seedheads retained their architectural good looks effortlessly.

The overall balance between the plants remained stable as the seasons ticked by, so I intervened very little. The plants required some supplemental water in dry years, but they grew well when given a single annual feeding mulch (see page 209) each spring. In many parts of the country, an inch or two would be plenty of compost. Here in the Northwest, however, our stubborn, often soggy soils mean that too much is barely enough, and deep annual mulches are a constant chore. Keep your plants happy, and they'll reward you for years; mine have almost made the 2-decade mark!

There's one very important thing to remember with sandwich plantings—don't use thugs (plants that grow all too well). Thugs tend to take over a space, competing with neighbors rather than sharing resources gracefully. Though thugs vary by region (soil and climate can make a huge difference in how plants behave), a good rule of thumb is to avoid plants offered for free by gardening "friends." Here in the maritime Northwest, plants such as bishop's weed (*Aegopodium podagraria*), yellow archangel (*Lamium galeobdolon*), snow-in-summer (*Cerastium tomentosum*), and purple-leaved loosestrife (*Lysimachia ciliata* 'Purpurea') are all dreadful thugs. Elsewhere, however, these same plants may be considered choice and even hard to grow. To learn which plants to avoid in your region, consult your local extension office or talk to experienced local gardeners. It's also smart to look at overgrown, out-of-control gardens to see what's flourishing despite a lack of care. Those that thrive better than expected are rarely good mixers in a naturalistic garden.

Sandwich Plantings Made to Order

WITH A BIT OF PLANNING AND RESEARCH, SANDWICH gardening can be adapted to suit almost any site or situation. When faced with a wet, sunny spot or a patch of dry, root-infested shade, refer back to the native plants and groupings observed on nature walks. In every region, appropriate plantings can be developed by starting with a base of adaptable natives. From there, branch out by adding relatives or like-minded species that appreciate similar conditions.

There is one important exception—when planting sensitive areas of any kind, such as along a stream or river, it's especially important not to use invasive non-native plants. In these situations, human disturbance can enable wandering exotics to displace native plants.

Beginning with Bulb Sandwiches

The very easiest way to make a long-lasting sandwich planting is to layer several kinds of bulbs in a patch of soil, then cover the top with a carpet of one or more kinds of groundcovers. Depending on your climate (and on the site you choose for your first trial run), you can arrange a selection of bulbs that bloom in sequence from late winter through fall. Tough little plants like snowdrops and snow crocuses really will bloom right through the snow, appearing from the first early thaws into midspring. Others, like hardy cyclamen, autumn

crocus, and true late-blooming crocus (such as *Crocus kotschyanus*), will spangle the fall garden with their bright blossoms.

In mild-winter areas, use an evergreen groundcover as a "carpet" for a sandwich planting. This carpeting role is an important one—groundcovers not only hide bare earth, but they also help to hide browning foliage. A long-blooming collection of bulbs is bound to display

ABOVE: In my former garden, orange parrot tulips celebrated the arrival of spring.

LEFT: During summer, the tulip bulbs are enveloped in a sea of leafy companions. The sunny site, gritty soil, and reflected heat from the basalt rock wall combine to make this spot hot and dry enough that the tulips return each spring.

121

both blooms and spent foliage at any given time. Try using several compatible groundcovers that offer two or three seasons of beauty to hide any fading bulb foliage.

In order to persist, bulbs need to ripen their foliage properly, transferring stored sugars and complex carbohydrates from the leaves to the bulbs. This can't happen when leaves are removed before they are completely limp and yellow, or when leaves are braided, twisted into ties, or similarly made "tidy." The best way to hide the fading leaves is to smooth them gently under a carpet of groundcover. There they can rot away in peace without disturbing the carefully orchestrated display above.

One way to disguise the passing of bulb foliage is to partner each patch of bulbs with perennials as well as groundcovers. Remember that most bulbs dislike summer water; you must select perennial partners that are drought tolerant so the bulbs don't fall prey to rots or diseases. For instance, snow crocus can be given a carpet of leadwort or creeping veronica, then matched with clumps of drought-tolerant ornamental herbs like Lebanese oregano (*Origanum libanoticum*). Taller tulips and daffodils can be interplanted with compatible wildflowers such as orange false mallow (*Sphaeralcea munroana*). As the bulb leaves brown off, the rising perennial foliage will help to minimize the aftereffects of your spring display and will keep the garden full.

Summer bulbs such as ornamental onions, gladiolas, and lilies present fewer problems. These late risers can be placed between clumps of grasses and sturdy perennials. Most of these summer bloomers remain attractive into fall and some offer modest fall color of their own. Alliums, for instance, turn a lovely biscuit brown that looks especially handsome with the swaying branches of ornamental grasses.

Bulbs for Simple Sandwiches

One great way to experiment with unfamiliar bulbs is to grow them in containers. Try them for a season, then select your favorites for sandwiching in beds and borders.

COMMON NAME (BOTANICAL NAME)	BLOOM TIME	HARDINESS ZONES
Autumn crocus (*Colchicum autumnale*)	Fall	4–9
Blue camass (*Camassia quamash*)	Spring and summer	4–10
Bulgarian garlic lily (*Nectaroscordum siculum*)	Summer	6–10
Checkered lily (*Fritillaria meleagris*)	Spring	3–8
Common snowdrop (*Galanthus nivalis*)	Winter and spring	3–9
Dog's-tooth violet (*Erythronium* spp.)	Spring	4–9, varies with species
Fall crocus (*Crocus kotschyanus*)	Fall	3–8
Geranium (*Geranium tuberosum*)	Spring and summer	8–9
Gladiolus (*Gladiolus* spp. and cultivars)	Summer	8–10
Golden bunch (*Crocus ancyrensis*)	Winter and spring	5–8
Grecian windflower (*Anemone blanda*)	Midspring	4–8
Italian arum (*Arum italicum*)	Spring bloom and fall fruit	6–9
Lily leek (*Allium moly*)	Spring and summer	3–9
Nodding onion (*Allium cernuum*)	Late spring	4–10
Poppy anemone (*Anemone coronaria*)	Spring and summer	8–10
'Purple Sensation' onion (*Allium aflatunense* 'Purple Sensation')	Summer	4–8
Resurrection lily (*Lycoris squamigera*)	Fall	6–10
Showy fall crocus (*Crocus speciosus*)	Fall	3–8
Snow crocus (*Crocus chrysanthus*)	Winter and spring	3–8
Stars of Persia (*Allium christophii*)	Summer	5–8

Groundcovers for Bulb Sandwiches

Truly great groundcovers grow well, but are not at all invasive. Grow a sampler of several kinds in a nursery bed before you begin introducing them into your garden.

COMMON NAME (BOTANICAL NAME)	BLOOM TIME	HARDINESS ZONES
Barren strawberry (*Waldsteinia fragariodes*)	Spring	5–9
Creeping thyme (*Thymus* spp.)	Summer	4–9
'Georgia Blue' veronica (*Veronica peduncularis* 'Georgia Blue')	Spring to fall	6–8
Ground ivy (*Glechoma hederacea*)	Summer	3–9
'Jekyll's White' periwinkle (*Vinca minor* 'Jekyll's White')	Spring and summer	4–9
Leadwort (*Ceratostigma plumbaginoides*)	Spring to fall	6–9
'Metallica Crispa' pyramidal bugleweed (*Ajuga pyramidalis* 'Metallica Crispa')	Spring	3–8
'Pink Panda' strawberry (*Fragaria* 'Pink Panda')	Spring and summer	5–9
Prostrate speedwell (*Veronica prostrata*)	Spring to fall	5–8
Selfheal summer (*Prunella vulgaris*)	Summer and fall	3–9
Sheep's burr (*Acaena* spp.)	Summer	6–9
'White Nancy' spotted dead nettle (*Lamium maculatum* 'White Nancy')	Spring and summer	4–8
Wintergreen (*Gaultheria procumbens*)	Spring	3–8

'Pink Panda' strawberries (*Fragaria* 'Pink Panda') make great groundcovers. Just pinch off the excess runners and push the roots into the soil, tamping the soil with your hand. This strawberry looks exceptionally natural along curbs and walls where it can sprawl and spill over the hard edges.

Shady Sandwiches for Dry Soil

Dry shade is traditionally seen as a major gardening challenge. However, if dry shade seems like a problem, you can often find the solution in the very things that create the situation. For instance, most sites are dry and shady because of tree roots and shadows. To find plants that can tolerate and even thrive in competition with mature trees, start by visiting native woodlands. There you'll see groundcovers, wildflowers, shrubs, and foliage plants that coexist happily with large trees.

Site-adaptive woodlanders from similar climate regions can often be persuaded to join your natives in garden settings. Hostas, ferns, hellebores, and toad lilies are good examples of plants that can rise to a challenge without taking over the garden.

It is always vital to improve the soil before trying to introduce new plants to a difficult site. Where tree roots fill the undersoil, adding 2 to 4 inches of soil, including a ½- to 1-inch layer of compost, will give newcomers a chance to get established before greedy tree roots penetrate their soil. But be sure to keep soil well away (2 to 3 feet) from tree and shrub crowns to avoid smothering mature plants. Trees and shrubs grow best when you keep fallen leaves in place and allow lichens and twigs to rot where they fall. Annual mulches of shredded leaves will help to keep woodland soil in balance.

In urban settings, dry shade may come from walls and buildings. Without root competition, all you need to do is renew the depleted soil in order for plants to grow well. Just create mounded beds of fresh soil to give new plants the best start.

Sandwich Plants for Dry, Shady Spots

Native woodlanders are a great resource when we need to find plants that grow happily in dry conditions. Noninvasive exotic shade plants like hostas and toad lilies are excellent choices, too.

COMMON NAME (BOTANICAL NAME)	GARDEN NOTES	HARDINESS ZONES
Bleeding heart (*Dicentra* spp.)	Spring bloomer; does best in clay or loamy soil	2–9
Bloodroot (*Sanguinaria canadensis*)	Spring ephemeral	3–9
Blue wood aster (*Aster cordifolius*)	Late-summer bloom	5–8
'Catlin's Giant' carpet bugleweed (*Ajuga reptans* 'Catlin's Giant')	Use a root barrier to keep inbounds	3–9
Columbine (*Aquilegia* spp.)	Self-sows obligingly	4–8, varies by species
Ferns (many kinds)	Ideal for naturalizing	Varies by species
Fringe cups (*Tellima grandiflora*)	Self-sows freely; best in clay or loamy soil	4–8
Grecian windflower (*Anemone blanda*)	Dies back after spring bloom	4–8
Hosta (many cultivars)	Very attractive to slugs and deer	3–8
Jacob's ladder (*Polemonium* spp.)	Intolerant of hot, humid conditions	4–8, varies by species
Small Solomon's seal (*Polygonatum biflorum*)	Will tolerate dry, stony soil	3–9
Sweet cicely (*Myrrhis odorata*)	Anise-flavored foliage	3–7
Toad lily (*Tricyrtis hirta*)	Flowers in fall	4–9
Wood anemone (*Anemone nemorosa*)	Dies back after spring bloom	4–8
Yellow corydalis (*Corydalis lutea*)	Self-sows readily	5–8

Sandwich Plants for Damp, Shady Spots

Seasonally soggy soil pleases a nice variety of shade plants, both native and imported. In permanently wet places, bog plants and hardy marginals are top choices.

COMMON NAME (BOTANICAL NAME)	GARDEN NOTES	HARDINESS ZONES
Blue corydalis (*Corydalis flexuosa*)	Goes dormant in summer	6–8
Blue-eyed Mary (*Omphalodes verna*)	Spring-blooming groundcover	6–9
Great Solomon's seal (*Polygonatum biflorum*)	Can form large colonies	3–7
Hepatica (*Hepatica americana*)	Buy only nursery-propagated plants	3–8
Hosta (many kinds)	Susceptible to slug and snail damage	3–8
Japanese primula (*Primula japonica*)	Good in a mass planting	3–8
Lungwort (*Pulmonaria* spp.)	Best in well-drained soil	5–8, varies by species
Ragged robin (*Lychnis flos-cuculi*)	Grows easily from seed	6–9
Rodgersia (*Rodgersia* spp.)	Large, textured foliage	5–8
Swamp spurge (*Euphorbia palustris*)	Robust plant can reach 3' tall and wide	5–8
Umbrella plant (*Darmera peltata*)	Suitable for pond or stream bank	5–9
'Variegata' water betony (*Scrophularia auriculata* 'Variegata')	Good foliage plant; does not come true from seed	5–9
Water forget-me-not (*Myosotis scorpioides*)	Self-sows readily	5–9
Welsh poppy (*Meconopsis cambrica*)	Self-sows readily	6–8
Wild ginger (*Asarum* spp.)	Attractive groundcover	Varies by species

Damp Sandwiches Can Be Delightful

I've had the opportunity to experiment with sandwich layering in damp, shady spots in several kinds of soils. I made a very successful (and simple) sandwich planting on a base of hardpan mixed with heavy clay. This was not a promising combination, so I used a foot of sandy loam as a base, then created raised mound beds and topped them with another foot of good garden soil (brought from a former cow pasture where grass was quickly being replaced by new houses). The loamy new soil was full of natural peat, so it retained moisture nicely, yet it drained far better than the native clay we started with at the site.

The beds had graceful, curving sides so the plants could spill into the gravel paths. Japanese maples flourished here, and a flock of dainty native vine maples made the colorful Japanese hybrids look right at home. A number of small species rhododendrons also grew well here (native rhododendrons had flourished here once but were lost to clearcutting many years ago). Clusters of native evergreen huckleberries in the bordering woods had rusty new growth that exactly matched the rust-color scales on the backsides of the rhododendron foliage, making a pleasant color echo. To give this area a comfortably clothed look year-round, I carpeted the beds with evergreen native groundcovers. These included wood sorrel (*Oxalis oregana* 'Wintergreen') and fringe cups (*Tellima grandiflora*), as well as piggyback plant (*Tolmiea menziesii*) in plain and golden forms.

Sandwich plantings of all kinds work best when you combine plants that are cooperators rather than competitors. Avoid groundcovers that deplete soil, strangle small shrubs, or smother dormant perennials.

Carpeting groundcovers, by contrast, are cooperative creepers that thread companionably between larger plants without crowding them out.

In spring, sheets of blue-eyed Mary (*Omphalodes verna*), a deceptively delicate-looking early bloomer with blue forget-me-not flowers, popped through the evergreen groundcovers. Hostas in many shades rose in spring and carried on until late autumn, bringing tints of blue, green, and gold to the shady beds. I added a number of ferns, both evergreen and deciduous, to the mix. Between the hostas and the deciduous ferns,

clumps of lesser celandines (*Ranunculus ficaria*) brightened the beds with their golden yellow buttercups from late winter into early summer.

For greater contrast, I used several shade-loving streamside plants such as 'Superba' featherleaf rodgersia (*Rodgersia pinnata* 'Superba'), whose huge, boldly shaped leaves look utterly dramatic from early spring into autumn, and native umbrella plant (*Darmera peltata*), whose leaves look like giant circular plates. I also planted 'Variegata' water betony (*Scrophularia auriculata* 'Variegata'), which puts on a striking show all

summer long. In mild climates, this eager grower retains an evergreen basal rosette, but in cold situations, it vanishes completely from winter into spring.

This four-season sandwich thrived in its damp, shady home. In winter, the sandwiched beds were dappled with green and cream evergreen ferns and hellebores. Spring brought sheets of buttercups and masses of blue-eyed Mary. In summer, bold foliage took over the display and carried on well into fall. This large planting required about 3 hours of maintenance work each season, most of which consisted of clearing away faded foliage, removing wind-blown twigs, and pulling the few weeds that could penetrate the solid carpets of groundcovers.

Sunny, Soggy Sandwiches

If your garden has damp areas, whether persistently wet sections of lawn or boggy borders, you might consider converting the trouble spots into sandwich meadows. To avoid problems with root rots, seek out sun lovers of all kinds that don't mind moist soil. Damp prairies make an excellent model for this sort of

The dampest areas in my shade garden hold a host of closely sandwiched plants, including many natives. Here, umbrella plant (*Darmera peltata*), variegated fleeceflower (*Persicaria virginiana* 'Painter's Palette'), and swamp spurge (*Euphorbia palustris*) mingle with astilbes and ferns.

Natural woodlands offer planting pockets with varying mixtures of light and shade and damp and dry. Finding the right plant for each place takes some experimentation, which is very likely to succeed when based on nature's own layering patterns and plant choices.

sandwiching. Bergamot, bottle gentian, cardinal flower, coneflower, Culver's root, and cup plant will all thrive, as will dozens of other noteworthy natives.

To find more candidates, take a look at what's growing well along open meadow streams, on sunny riverbanks, and at the edges of sunny bogs. In every part of the country, the native flora on these sites will give valuable clues as to what may succeed in your homemade soggy sandwich; use these handsome natives in your planting. Quite often, these plants will have ornamental border "relatives" that are also adaptable to damp, sunny situations.

To reduce your maintenance needs, you may decide to create a main planting of shrubs that enjoy wet feet (such as twiggy dogwoods and small willows), leaving the spaces between the shrubs for sandwiching. Select wetland perennials with small root systems (and that go dormant with dignity or leave handsome resting rosettes in winter). Between these main characters, there will be plenty of room to layer in smaller plants such as shooting stars (*Dodecatheon meadia*) and creeping water forget-me-nots (*Myosotis scorpioides*), as well as wetland bulbs.

Bulbs are not famous for tolerating wet conditions, and most border beauties will rot away quickly in permanently damp conditions. Fortunately, there is a large group of wetland bulbs, both native and exotic, that will take to soggy spots with aplomb. Bog lilies (true lilies that grow in wet places) are common across the country and are often found in company with attractive native grasses, rushes, and sedges. Spreading or invasive grasses are not good choices for sandwiching because they soon choke out their neighbors.

There is also a delightful group of European buttercups called lesser celandines (*Ranunculus ficaria*) that occur naturally in damp woods and soggy meadows. There are several dozen forms of this variable species, all of which are charming and extremely easy to grow.

Checkered lily (*Fritillaria meleagris*) is common in damp meadows, where it threads amiably through grasses and perennials. Featuring nodding bell flowers, checkered lily comes in solid pure white, deep purple, rose, or lavender, and the more-familiar checkered pattern comes in heathery shades of lavender, plum, and rose.

Softly yellow and sweetly scented *Tulipa sylvestris* grows well in most garden situations, but in the wild, it is most common in moist meadows. It is the only tulip I know of that can tolerate damp situations without rotting and dying. Don't plant it in an outright bog, though; try it in an open, sunny spot, where it would happily keep company with checkered lily and buttercups.

Naturalistic sandwich plantings of adaptable prairie wildflowers knit seamlessly into a floral carpet that performs over many months. Several species of purple coneflowers (*Echinacea* spp.), black-eyed Susans (*Rudbeckia* spp.), and bee balm (*Monarda* spp.) combine in a dazzling display that requires relatively little care and rewards the gardener generously and abundantly.

Prairie Plants for Moist, Sunny Spots

Hummingbirds and bees love the streamside and sunny bog plants that thrive in damp soil and open sites. Moist prairie plants, such as blazing star and cup plant, are also good candidates for such places.

COMMON NAME (BOTANICAL NAME)	GARDEN NOTES	HARDINESS ZONES
Blazing star (*Liatris spicata*)	Prefers poor soil	4–9
Blue cardinal flower (*Lobelia siphilitica*)	Divide every 2 to 3 years to rejuvenate the plant	5–9
Boneset (*Eupatorium perfoliatum*)	Late-season bloom	3–9
Bottle gentian (*Gentiana andrewsii*)	Requires cool nights and good drainage	4–9
Cardinal flower (*Lobelia cardinalis*)	Attracts hummingbirds	4–8
Culver's root (*Veronicastrum virginicum*)	Can grow to 6'	3–9
Cup plant (*Silphium perfoliatum*)	Can reach 8' to 10' high	5–9
Cutleaf coneflower (*Rudbeckia laciniata*)	Deadhead for repeat bloom	3–9
Daisy rosinplant (*Silphium integrifolium*)	Great for naturalistic settings	4–7
Golden alexander (*Zizia aurea*)	Great for naturalistic settings	3–9
Joe-Pye weed (*Eupatorium fistulosum*)	Attracts butterflies	3–8
Mexican hat (*Ratibida columnifera*)	Great for naturalistic settings	3–10
Prairie dock (*Silphium terebinthinaceum*)	Grows to 10' high; prefers loamy soil	3–7
Queen-of-the-prairie (*Filipendula rubra*)	Self-sows readily	3–9
Shooting star (*Dodecatheon meadia*)	Goes dormant in summer	4–8
Wild bee balm (*Monarda fistulosa*)	Divide regularly	3–9

Prairie Plants for Dry, Sunny Spots

Dry prairies are a wonderful resource for gardeners in sunny, dry climates. You should also check with local plant societies for advice on planting regional natives.

COMMON NAME (BOTANICAL NAME)	GARDEN NOTES	HARDINESS ZONES
Ashy sunflower (*Helianthus mollis*)	Grows to 6' high	4–9
Bird's-foot violet (*Viola pedata*)	Buy nursery-propagated plants only	4–8
Black-eyed Susan (*Rudbeckia hirta*)	Self-sows readily	3–7
Butterfly weed (*Asclepias tuberosa*)	Prefers sandy, well-drained soil; does not transplant well	4–9
Canada milk vetch (*Astragalus canadensis*)	Can reach 4' high	8–9
Eastern pasque flower (*Pulsatilla patens*)	Suitable for a rock garden	5–7
Goldenrod (*Solidago* spp.)	Choose hybrids that won't self-sow readily	5–9
Lanceleaf coreopsis (*Coreopsis lanceolata*)	Deadhead for all-season bloom	4–9
Large beard-tongue (*Penstemon grandiflorus*)	Needs sandy, well drained soil; intolerant of winter moisture	3–9
Narrow leaf blazing star (*Liatris microcephala*)	Prefers sandy, well-drained soil; drought-tolerant	6–10
Pale purple coneflower (*Echinacea pallida*)	Generally not long-lived	4–8
Prairie poppy mallow (*Callirhoe involucrata*)	Prefers cool summers; protect from winter moisture	4–6
Prairie smoke (*Geum triflorum*)	Ornamental seedhead	1–5
Rough gayfeather (*Liatris aspera*)	Taller and later-blooming than other *Liatris* species	4–9
Silky aster (*Aster sericeus*)	Mostly available as seed	4–8
Snakeroot (*Liatris punctata*)	Prefers sandy soil	3–7
Spiderwort (*Tradescantia virginiana*)	Cut back ragged foliage to encourage new growth	4–9

Sandwiching in Dry, Sunny Spots

If your chosen sandwich spot is dry and sunny, with a sandy soil base and quick drainage, begin your search by looking at dryland prairie plants. Black-eyed Susans, blazing stars, butterfly weed, pale purple coneflowers, and pasque flowers are a few of the treasures that thrive in dry, well-drained soils.

Depending on where you live, you may also want to consider plants that inhabit the high desert of the West and the dry plains of the Southwest. Sages, salvias, gaillardias, and globe mallows will flourish in tough spots where ordinary border beauties flag. These adaptable plants also coexist peacefully with small bulbs and early bloomers, making them excellent sandwiching candidates.

Remember that these drylanders will need to be watered through their first season in the garden. (Even very adaptable plants must have a solid year of new root growth behind them before being asked to face summer heat and drought unassisted.) And mulching with compost, dried grass clippings, chopped straw, shredded leaves, or similar materials will help to conserve moisture as well as build soil tilth.

It's also important to add compost to the nursery beds you've created for dryland plants, even though you've chosen plants based on their toughness and adaptability. In my experience, plants that are given a good start will grow better than those that have to tough it out in lean native soil. Rest assured: Before long, the plants' roots will be in that lean native soil. In any case, small, young plants are far more vulnerable than well-established, mature ones. So by offering new plants decent soil and adequate moisture during their youth, you are simply protecting your investment.

Combinations and Vignettes

Vegetables are usually grown in neat, tidy rows, so many new flower gardeners assume that perfectly manicured beds and borders are the way to go. Collectors of irises, daylilies, and roses often grow them in precise, long rows, as if they were a crop to be harvested. Many gardeners pass through this stage, but many also remain there indefinitely; after all, what else can you do with 600 daylilies but row or mass them? In recent years, however, magazines and books have started featuring more photos of **beautiful naturalistic gardens** and information about how to garden without battling nature. Face it: clipping, tidying, and keeping everything uniform is a never-ending job. The relentless perfectionism of our culture urges us to do everything "right." **Relax!**

Creating pleasing garden combinations is a long, happy, and fulfilling process that includes **experimenting, making mistakes, learning, and editing.** Once you dip your toes in the water, you'll discover that creating artful combinations of flowers and foliage is an exciting and deeply rewarding practice. It's also a **completely personal art form.** When you start to doubt your own taste, remember this—in your own garden, you don't need to follow anyone else's rules about what constitutes "good taste." You reign supreme. Begin with what you like, and **learn as you go.**

In this chapter, I'll offer advice on choosing contrasting colors and tonal values that will help you understand why **some combinations have strength and conviction** while others don't quite work. There are also several interesting considerations to explore about color relationships and the play of **light and shadow** in a garden; these considerations can help you place plants to their best advantage and can assist you in creating lastingly attractive combinations and expanded vignettes.

Don't worry, though—I'm not going to prescribe a "guaranteed tasteful" color palette. And I'm not going to tell you to never use lowly, common annuals like marigolds. **I love marigolds** and all kinds of "ordinary" plants, and I often place them right alongside the most sophisticated plant treasures. No plant is really ordinary, and almost anything grown well has beauty. If you love a color combination and the plants in it are happy, **then it's exactly right.**

Rooting in Reality

YOU MAY ADORE THE LOOK OF A BOLD-LEAVED HELLEBORE next to a silvery lavender cotton (*Santolina* spp.), but it's a sure bet that at least one partner in this combination will be unhappy before long in any imaginable site. Sun-loving santolinas can't tolerate the shade and moisture that hellebores crave, so this partnership is doomed from the start. Similarly, if you fall for the way velvety, burgundy-leaved coleus contrasts with coppery dahlias, choose your coleus with care. Unless you pick one of the new 'Sunfast' coleus cultivars that tolerate a lot of direct sunlight, those lovely leaves will soon look sad instead of sumptuous. Instead of a win-lose relationship with combinations, you want to create win-win partners.

The Right Site

The simplest factor in determining whether a combination will work is knowing each partner's preference for sun or shade. It seems quite obvious that you would accommodate the needs of your plants, but I've found that logic can fly out the window when artistic impulses arise. You may have unhappy combinations in your own garden that illustrate basic cultural incompatibility, but don't think you're alone. Even professional designers can fail to take this vital principle into consideration.

I was recently asked to consult on a young garden where many plants had died after a wet winter. The garden had been designed by a professional and the plants were installed by a trained crew. Even so, there had been terrible losses in the shade garden. I spied the santolina and hellebore combination I mentioned earlier. This bed of shade-loving ferns, hostas, and hellebores was edged in sun-loving santolina, all of which was dead. Similar combinations had met with the same fate. The wet winter probably contributed to the demise of the sun lovers because of the limited

Coleus have long been considered strictly shade plants. But many of the newest hybrids, including the luscious 'Sunfast' series, take a lot of light and heat in stride. At the garden school, a new coleus called 'Storm' is underplanted with a chartreuse skirt of ornamental sweet potato, *Ipomoea batatas* 'Marguarite'.

drainage and heavy clay soil in this shade garden, but the santolina plants were clearly unhappy in their dank, dark conditions—and they died to prove it.

All these points underline what is perhaps the most important principle in garden making, let alone in creating combinations: Put plants where they want to be, meet their genetically programmed needs, and they will do their best to grow well. No matter how well you prepare the soil, a position in full sun will not please an understory plant that thrives in shade. No matter how much fertilizer you offer them, sun lovers will grow lank and flopsy in shade. When you discover a wonderful combination of color, form, and texture, but you realize that the plants won't be happy in the same site, seek out culturally compatible substitutes that re-create the look of that original inspiration. But don't try to force plants to overcome their true nature; it simply won't work.

There are other things to consider when combining plants with various colors, forms, and textures. Most golden foliage will scorch in full sun, even when the plant's roots are kept moist. If you want a touch of gold or yellow in a sunny site, use flowers instead of foliage to get the color you want. If you really want to use golden leaves in a sunny spot, seek out plants with predominately green leaves that have a moderate amount of golden variegation, which is often more sun tolerant than solidly yellow foliage.

Conversely, many deep reds and oranges won't fully develop in low-light situations. If your red daylilies fade in full sun yet remain pale in shade, try putting them where they get a great deal of reflected light, perhaps from house walls or a nearby pool of water. Purple-leaved foliage may green out in deep shade and scorch in sun. Again, a situation in which the plant receives plenty of reflected, filtered, or dappled light will allow the leaves to develop their best color, particularly where summers are hot.

Meeting the Challenge

Most gardens have a few challenging conditions that make it hard for plants to grow well. For example, few plants will be really luxuriant under the skirt of a large, mature tree. Scouring wind can stunt every plant it hits. Walls may cast a "drought shadow," and walls made of concrete can also shed lime into nearby soils (not all plants appreciate lime). Houses with deep eaves may prove difficult to clothe with foundation plantings. Playful kids may wreak havoc on your cherished border beauties. Bored dogs may trample out a runway for themselves, and cats may prefer to sprawl in the heart of your favorite border.

In each case, the solution is to start by being utterly realistic about what will and won't grow in that particular place. For instance, hungry surface roots will generally devour any fresh soil you place under the skirts of mature trees and shrubs, quickly stressing out any new plants you try to establish. If you have a deep urge to create a lush combination for such a trouble spot, put the plants in a large container instead of the unyielding ground.

Where winds prevail, seek out seaside, desert, and prairie plants that take sweeping winds in stride. Rugosa roses, hardy brooms, desert sages, and dryland grasses can all manage nicely in a windblown spot. In mild climates, Mediterranean herbs like rosemary, lavender, and cooking sage appreciate sunny, windy spots, as do heaths and heathers. Create windbreaks with slim trees (poplars are traditional, but upright junipers also work well) to give plants a break, providing enough protection so a wide range of plants can live together in peace.

Layering the garden with trees and shrubs will also create a shelter "belt" that makes an inner oasis of calm in a windy site. Often, tough native shrubs can be

Put plants where they want to be, meet their genetically programmed needs, and they will do their best to grow well.

Guidelines for Good Combinations

When you are ready to consider how to fill your beds and borders with delightful combinations, the best place to start is in your own backyard. To be successful, you have to know your territory. Every yard has a variety of conditions, even if the difference is only that there is more shade on the north side of the house than on the south. The kinds of questions you need answers to are: What kind of soil do you have? Where will your plants be coolest, warmest, dampest, or driest? Where is the best wind protection or shelter from frost?

Know your site like the back of your hand so you'll know what conditions you have to work with when you start selecting plants. Here's a brief list of guidelines that can help you make great decisions:

1. Pick plants that like what you have to offer in terms of site and soil.

2. Use a high percentage of proven performers for your region.

3. Seek out long bloomers or plants that reliably rebloom.

4. Choose plants with more than one strength (flowers, foliage, fruit, and seedheads).

5. Look for plants with more than one season of beauty.

6. Give preference to plants with strong natural architecture.

7. Choose plants with a variety of shapes (arching, spiky, sprawling, mounding, and fanning).

8. Select plants with contrasting textures (fine, medium, and bold).

9. Think in terms of layers (canopy; tall, medium, and low understory; and groundcover), and consider where each plant may be used in the garden.

10. Decide on a color palette for each bed or border, and use only plants that fit your parameters.

woven into a tapestry hedge that provides visual screening and privacy while filtering fierce wind. Screens of native shrubs make a great backdrop for garden beds and borders, and they offer several seasons of beauty, including spring flowers and fall foliage color.

Walls present another challenging planting problem. The ground at the base of a wall is apt to be persistently dry. Plants placed too close to any wall, whether it's freestanding or part of a structure, can develop fungal and mildew diseases from poor air circulation. The solution here is the same as for houses with deep eaves: Keep plants 18 inches out from the wall base, and they'll receive plenty of natural rainfall and good air circulation. (You may want to add an 18-inch-wide skirt of gravel at the base of the wall to keep plants away from the tough conditions.)

Where pets play or spend a lot of time, it's best to stick with plants they can't hurt (and that can't hurt them). An organic eco-lawn of short, clumping grasses, clovers, daisies, and herbs won't need mowing and will support an amazing amount of roughhousing from kids and pets. Keep all poisonous plants (and skin irritants like tulips and daffodils) out of play areas for kids and pets. There are a surprising number of attractive, tough plants that take stress in stride, as I learned when I made my soccer border; none of the plants were easily damaged by my sons' straying soccer balls. I used easygoing, cane-throwing shrubs such as forsythia and hydrangeas, as well as hardy perennials that would resprout if cut down. The result was pleasing, even if it lacked horticultural finesse. I developed a simple rule of thumb over the years: Don't plant fancy combinations—or anything that would be painful to lose—in a vulnerable spot. It's best to keep expectations of dazzling beauty low for rough-and-tumble spots.

Compatible Combinations

Be deliberate and highly selective when choosing plants. It's fine to gather up an armload of whatever looks pretty the day you visit the nursery, but don't assume that all such spur-of-the-moment picks will be equally steady performers. Because you have a terrific range of plants to choose from these days, it's worthwhile to put some effort into making judicious and attractive choices. A decade ago, the range of perennials and border shrubs was quite limited. Most of us settled for whatever we could find, because making do was a lot easier than tracking down our ideal first choices.

Today, garden centers all over the country have expanded their offerings dramatically. There are also hundreds of specialty nurseries with mail-order catalogs that will ship plants almost anywhere. Every region now boasts nurseries that specialize in plants for warm or cold climates, or that offer plants for specific conditions, such as acid or alkaline soils. This means that most of us can pick and choose, making sure the plants we choose for our garden are worthy and long lasting.

CLOCKWISE FROM TOP LEFT: Long-blooming, easygoing daylilies make an excellent base for developing lasting partnerships. This one, 'Artist', offers a wide range of colors. Prairie blanket flower (*Gaillardia × grandiflora* 'Goblin') brings variety to the mix with its fringed texture and enriches the color palette with its deep, red-brown eye. The third flower in the combination is firecracker vine (*Ipomoea lobata*). Its flowers change color as they mature, refreshing the planting time and time again. The indefinite billows of the vine foliage soften and unite the three potent flower forms.

Put Perennials to Work

Combining plants that will work well together for a full season or longer means you need to seek out hard-working perennials that bloom for many weeks or several months, instead of just a few glorious days. Next, you need to look for companions that will help each other shine. Finding these great plants requires some research—the most pleasant kind of research, though! Spend time browsing in local garden centers, specialty nurseries, and public gardens (as well as any private ones you have access to). These are not buying trips, but investigations into what's available, what persists well, and what consistently draws your attention.

Finding plants that appeal to you is as important as finding solid performers. There is little point in accumulating a lot of hardworking, long-blooming plants that you don't particularly like. However, when you see certain plants looking great despite adversity, don't be too surprised if those plants start looking pretty attractive to you, even if you weren't initially drawn to them. There are certainly sillier reasons to buy plants than because they have great endurance, terrific manners, and are utterly reliable. Plants that carry beds and borders through bad times and good allow you the luxury of doting on a few special (but impractical) plants that may or may not come through for you.

Plants that rebloom reliably (such as yarrows and daylilies) are generally great candidates for long-lasting combinations. (Although if they have wandering ways or require division almost every year, they may not prove so worthy over time.) Plants with extended periods of bloom that come and go over several or many months should also be at the top of your list. Big clans, such as the asters, the hardy geraniums, and the tickseeds (*Coreopsis*), are good starting places in most parts of the country.

Be on the lookout for plants with lastingly attractive foliage, particularly if it undergoes seasonal changes. For example, the tough yellow loosestrife, *Lysimachia punctata*, has a dazzling form called 'Alexander', whose new shoots are shrimp pink and very cold tolerant. They glow at ground level in the winter garden (even in Minnesota) and emerge in full brilliance in spring. By summer, the shoots elongate and turn soft green with large patches of butter and cream, studded liberally with clear yellow flowers. In fall, they turn a gentle shade of gold (with a rosy tint) before finally fading to brown. Providing that kind of contribution over a very long season earns a plant high horticultural status, even if it comes from a "common" family.

You'll also want to find plants with a good growth habit. This means both that they have an attractive

"New and Better" Is a Judgment Call

The trend these days is to try almost anything new just because it's new. With inexpensive plants, this isn't a problem. If you try it and it works, great. If it doesn't, you're just out a few bucks and a season of pleasure. However, many fancy catalogs are selling expensive new plants that don't have a long performance history. This alone makes them poor choices for an important combination position, simply because you don't really know how these plants may behave over time. You also have to remember that catalog descriptions are often written by smitten plantaholics who may have had success with these new plants (in the ideal growing conditions of their greenhouses, of course). You need to be realistic about your site conditions before spending precious dollars on unproven plants.

I must admit that I have spent far too much money on highly touted new plants whose performance and habits were far from proven. Many times I've either been sadly disappointed by a poor showing (and even the plant's demise) or horrified as a new plant proved lustier than suspected and took over a bed. My advice is hard-won: When you want to make long-lasting combinations, stick with plants that have a proven track record.

Workhorse Perennials

Workhorse perennials are time-proven winners, not finicky fusspots. Old favorites like these earn their status by providing a solid, reliable performance year after year.

COMMON NAME (BOTANICAL NAME)	HARDINESS ZONES
Aster (*Aster* spp.)	4–8, varies by species
Black-eyed Susan (*Rudbeckia fulgida*)	4–9
Blanketflower (*Gaillardia* × *grandiflora*)	3–8
Butterfly weed (*Asclepias tuberosa*)	4–9
Catmint (*Nepeta* spp.)	3–8, varies by species
Columbine (*Aquilegia* spp.)	4–8, varies by species
Daylily (*Hemerocallis* spp.)	3–10
Evening primrose (*Oenothera* spp.)	5–8, varies by species
False sunflower (*Heliopsis helianthoides*)	4–9
Feverfew (*Tanacetum parthenium*)	4–9
Geum (*Geum* spp.)	4–9, varies by species
Globe thistle (*Echinops* spp.)	3–9, varies by species
Hellebore (*Helleborus* spp.)	5–9, varies by species
Iris (*Iris* spp.)	4–9, varies by species
Meadow rue (*Thalictrum* spp.)	5–9
Penstemon (*Penstemon* spp.)	Varies by species
Phlox (*Phlox* spp.)	3–9, varies by species
Purple coneflower (*Echinacea purpurea*)	3–9
Sage (*Salvia* spp.)	5–10, varies by species
Sea holly (*Eryngium* spp.)	3–8, varies by species
Shasta daisy (*Leucanthemum* × *superbum*)	5–8
Tickseed (*Coreopsis* spp.)	4–8
Verbena (*Verbena* spp.)	Varies by species
Veronica (*Veronica* spp.)	Varies by species
Yarrow (*Achillea* spp.)	4–8, varies by species

Jewel blue sea holly (*Eryngium alpinum* 'Blue Star') is vividly set off by hot orange calendulas and African marigolds in my butterfly garden. Sea holly holds its distinctive shape long after the color drains from its petals and bracts, creating a strong silhouette that holds into winter.

Easygoing and trouble-free, blue star flower (*Amsonia tabernaemontana*) thrives in most gardens with little care. Growing to 3 feet tall, this native is dense enough to use as a low screen or hedge, and it offers splendid fall color.

natural shape and that they hold that shape well over time. Some plants begin life with a lovely form, arching or upright, but wind or rain causes them to tumble or sprawl. The zebra-striped maiden grass, *Miscanthus sinensis* 'Zebrinus', is a perfect example of an exciting plant that doesn't fulfill its promise to remain upright over the long haul. The best border plants remain upright without staking, even in windy and wet conditions. A very similar grass, *Miscanthus sinensis* 'Strictus', often called porcupine grass, offers both the creamy horizontal stripes and reliably upright form, despite reaching as much as 9 or 10 feet tall in favored spots. Tall plants of all kinds tend to have both floppy and sturdy forms, so learning which is which before bringing them into the garden is an excellent idea. You can find this information in books and magazines.

Even lower-growing plants such as daylilies have forms that hold their shape well or poorly. Whatever their flowering abilities, those that flop over their neighbors and smother out smaller plants by summer's end are less worthy than those that dwindle away without taking other plants with them. Tour gardens in late summer and fall to see which plants hold their own without staking and which fade at season's end with grace instead of disgrace. It's a good idea to get in the habit of appraising the overall looks of your own garden (as well as others) in autumn, noting which plants hold their shape and which are sloppy finishers. In practical terms, those with lax late-season manners should be removed, or else partnered with upright plants that won't be smothered by their neighbors' floppy foliage.

By tracking performance over several seasons, you can give preference to plants that keep their looks after they flower. Plants that age well are a visual asset to the garden through their entire life cycle. You should avoid plants that look terrific in bloom but that turn shabby

after flowering. If you find a few sloppy plants that you simply must grow, be sure to place them along a pathway or border edge so that you can give them the frequent grooming they require without continually beating a path through the other plants in the bed.

The same plant can behave differently in different settings, so it's smart to create a master list of regionally appropriate plants. You'll need to be observant whenever you visit gardens, and you'll need to get recommendations from regional experts as often as possible. Your main goal is to select plants with the most positive attributes—this means looking for plants with several strings to their bows. You may find early-blooming plants that stay tidy all summer. Or you may find a plant that will reflower in the fall, or that offers a foliage color all through winter. Blue star flower (*Amsonia tabernaemontana*), for example, is a native plant that's truly a star in its own right. In spring, the slim, delicate foliage bursts up in a lovely, hazy mass. In summer, the soft blue flowers reflect the cloudless sky. In fall, the leaves turn warm gold and shimmer with every breeze. It's pretty hard to beat that kind of season-long contribution to a planting combination.

You need to ask the tough questions when auditioning plants: Which last the longest? Which are the least needy and stay healthy and happy in many settings and conditions? Which seem to require lots of care or look sorry after a hard winter or a dry summer? Which look great no matter what happens? By answering these questions and selecting plants with great qualities, you can create a palette of beautiful, hardworking plants that are almost guaranteed to thrive in your backyard. I have a stable of plants that I use time and again when I create new beds. They are dependable and sturdy, not to mention attractive, and I'm sure you'll come to depend on them for your gardens, too.

A Flurry of Ferns, Foliage, and Grasses

A few years ago, foliage was rarely even mentioned when people talked about plant combinations. These days, you can find whole books on foliage. This is great because foliage is as important to the overall look of the garden as the more-fleeting flowers are. When you look for solid performers for combinations, you should consider plants that offer handsome foliage. In recent years, many excellent foliage perennials such as hostas, heucheras, and verbascums have become widely available. There are also a lot of long-flowering plants such as yarrows, penstemons, and salvias that combine attractive foliage with a steady supply of flowers. This

Foliage perennials look great massed in groups. Golden sage (*Salvia officinalis* 'Icterina') offers gray-green and gold marbled foliage while its neighbor 'Chocolate Candy' hardy geranium brings grey-brown foliage to the mix. Dusky-leaved *Aster lateriflorus* 'Lady in Black' contributes soft cloud of nearly black leaves.

Hardworking Foliage Perennials

Flowers fade fast but foliage lasts for months on end. Foliage plants with color, character, and strong architectural form make long-lasting contributions to beds and borders.

COMMON NAME (BOTANICAL NAME)	HARDINESS ZONES
Artemisia (*Artemisia* spp.)	Varies by species
Barrenwort (*Epimedium* spp.)	4–9
Bugbane (*Cimicifuga* spp.)	3–9, varies by species
Coral bells (*Heuchera* spp.)	Most are 4–8
Dead nettle (*Lamium* spp.)	4–8
Elephant's ear (*Bergenia* spp.)	4–8
Fleeceflower (*Persicaria* spp.)	Varies by species
Hosta (*Hosta* spp.)	3–8
Jack-in-the-pulpit (*Arisaema triphyllum*)	4–9
Lady's mantle (*Alchemilla mollis*)	4–7
Lambs'-ears (*Stachys byzantina*)	4–8
Lavender cotton (*Santolina* spp.)	6–9
Lungwort (*Pulmonaria* spp.)	4–8, varies by species
Mallow (*Lavatera* spp.)	7–10, varies by species
Mullein (*Verbascum* spp.)	Varies by species
Oregano (*Origanum* spp.)	5–9, varies by species
Rodgersia (*Rodgersia* spp.)	5–8
Rue (*Ruta graveolens*)	5–9
Sage (*Salvia* spp.)	Varies by species
Sedum (*Sedum* spp.)	Varies by species
Spurge (*Euphorbia* spp.)	Varies by species
Trillium (*Trillium* spp.)	Varies by species
Violet (*Viola* spp.)	Varies by species
Wild ginger (*Asarum* spp.)	Varies by species
Yucca (*Yucca* spp.)	5–10, varies by species

Great Garden Ferns

Ferns are underrated, probably because they don't offer showy flowers. However they do offer structure, contrasting textures, and years of reliable good looks in exchange for very little care.

COMMON NAME (BOTANICAL NAME)	HARDINESS ZONES
Button fern (*Pellaea rotundifolia*)	8–10
Flowering fern (*Osmunda reaglis*)	4–9
Hard fern (*Blechnum* spp.)	9–11, varies by species
Holly fern (*Cyrtomium* spp.)	6–10, varies by species
Holly fern (*Polystichum* spp.)	Varies by species
Lady fern (*Athyrium filix-femina*)	4–9
Lip fern (*Cheilanthes* spp.)	8–10
Maidenhair fern (*Adiantum* spp.)	Varies by species
Ostrich fern (*Matteuccia struthiopteris*)	3–8
Polypody (*Polypodium* spp.)	Varies by species
Spleenwort (*Asplenium* spp.)	Varies by species
Wood fern (*Dryopteris* spp.)	Varies by species

The graceful, arching fronds of ferns conjure up images of shaded retreats and cool walks by woodland streams, so you may be surprised to know there are numerous ferns that love full sun! Since foliage is often a fern's major asset, consider the color and texture of the fronds before you make your selection at the garden center.

abundance means that when you begin choosing perennials, you can be quite demanding about their attributes. Not only should they be pretty in leaf or flower, but they should also be long-lasting, mannerly, and good-looking in or out of bloom.

It's always wise to start by selecting a basic palette of plants that thrive in your region. For instance, in the Southeast, where fancy-leaved coral bells (*Heuchera* spp.) may scorch in sandy soils, selections of the native *Heuchera americana* may persist better than European species crosses do. In the hot, dry Southwest, gray-leaved yarrows such as buttery *Achillea* 'Taygetea' generally outperform those with kelly green leaves. Similarly, the verbascums with large, thickly felted foliage succeed better in drier climates than in damp ones, where disfiguring mildews and molds are common.

Quite a number of hardworking perennial families offer forms that make as significant a contribution with foliage as with flowers. The tough little golden feverfew (*Tanacetum parthenium* 'Aureum') sparks up a shady spot or sings in a sunnier one, only flagging in exposed, dry places where its leaves get tattered from sun and wind. True, it seeds itself with utmost generosity, but the offspring are very easy to pull and will often be welcome gifts for gardening friends. Similarly, the golden lemon balm (*Melissa officinalis* 'All Gold') makes a shimmering mound of dappled gold and green that smells as refreshing as lemonade on a hot day. It thrives under all kinds of conditions, and if it reproduces itself too well, simply cut this generous creature back before the small flowers have time to set seed.

Less aggressive are dark-leaved forms of bugbane (*Cimicifuga* spp.), which range from velvety near-black to rich plum or bronzed green. The native bugbanes

At the Garden School, palomino tresses of feather grass (*Stipa tenuissima*) stay tidy well into winter. Small structural evergreens, such as *Hebe* 'McKean' and *Euphorbia characias* keep the silky grass company year-round.

are easygoing plants in much of the country, but they don't flower well in the deep South, perhaps because hot nights discourage them. Even so, the dusky-leaved forms such as 'Brunette' are worth growing anywhere, because the dramatic foliage more than makes up for their scanty flowers. In most areas, this willing creature provides both showy leaves and white, sweet-scented flowers in late summer.

I turn to a wide variety of ferns, foliage perennials, and grasses when I want to make a dramatic impact in a combination. These unwavering good-lookers generally have leaves that stay fresh all season and that aren't susceptible to leaf diseases. The foliage is often distinctive, whether it's color, size, shape, or texture you're after. And taking care of foliage plants is relatively simple—just cut off leaves and foliage that lose color or look battle-weary. Or, let nature take its course and allow withering foliage to age on the stem.

Great Garden Grasses

Grasses bring flow, softness, and fabulous texture to shrub borders that might otherwise look static. Small grasses also blend into floral combinations, partnering with a whole season of flowers.

COMMON NAME (BOTANICAL NAME)	HARDINESS ZONES
'Aurea' Bowles' golden sedge (*Carex elata* 'Aurea')	5–9
'Aureola' golden hakone grass (*Hakonechloa macra* 'Aureola')	5–9
Blue oat grass (*Helictotrichon sempervirens*)	4–9
Blue wheat grass (*Elymus magellanicus*)	7–8
Buffalo grass (*Buchloe dactyloides*)	3–9
Common quaking grass (*Briza media*)	4–10
Crinkled hair grass (*Deschampsia flexuosa*)	4–9
Feather reed grass (*Calamagrostis × acutiflora*)	5–9
Glaucous hair grass (*Koeleria glauca*)	6–9
Gray's sedge (*Carex grayi*)	3–8
Leatherleaf sedge (*Carex buchananii*)	6–9
Maiden grass (*Miscanthus sinensis*)	5–9
Mexican feather grass (*Stipa tenuissima*)	7–10
Northern sea oats (*Chasmanthium latifolium*)	5–9
Orange-colored sedge (*Carex testacea*)	8–9
Palm branch sedge (*Carex muskingumensis*)	3–8
'Red Baron' Japanese blood grass (*Imperata cylindrica* 'Red Baron')	4–9
'Red Rays' red switch grass (*Panicum virgatum* 'Red Rays')	5–9
'Snowbird' snowy wood rush (*Luzula nivea* 'Snowbird')	4–9
'Spiralis' corkscrew rush (*Juncus effusus* 'Spiralis')	6–9
Squirrel-tail grass (*Hordeum jubatum*)	4–8
Toe toe (*Cortaderia richardii*)	7–10
Tufted hair grass (*Deschampsia cespitosa*)	5–9
'Variegata' creeping broadleaf sedge (*Carex siderosticha* 'Variegata')	6–9
'Variegata' silver variegated Japanese sedge (*Carex morrowii* 'Variegata')	5–9

Using Color-Filled Shrubs in Combinations

You should also consider compact shrubs to be important players in color borders. The best candidates are smaller shrubs with distinctive foliage that contribute over several seasons and may increase steadily in beauty from spring into fall. If your yard is quite small, select very compact shrubs that won't grow larger than 2 to 4 feet in height and spread. If your borders are deep and wide, you can consider larger ones as well and weave them into the border back as part of the visual ladder.

Among my particular favorites are the charming border spireas; there are a multitude of distinctive named forms. My particular pet is 'Goldflame' Japanese spirea (*Spiraea japonica* 'Goldflame'). This medium shrub (it grows to 4 feet high) is a color changer that starts off in spring with rusty, cinnamon red leaves, which then turn chartreuse. In fall, the fireworks begin as the foliage takes on sunset tints, then turns rich pumpkin orange. Coppery-bronze 'Magic Carpet' spirea (*Spiraea × bumalda* 'Magic Carpet') is very similar, but it gets only about 18 inches tall, instead of 3 to 4 feet tall.

Silver-leaved cinquefoils (*Potentilla* spp.) offer lovely leaves and a heavy crop of flowers over a long season, in a range of sizes and colors. There are small willows galore, from fine-textured purple osier willow (*Salix purpurea*) to the velvety carpeter silver creeping willow (*Salix repens* var. *argentea*). The palette of shrub possibilities is extensive, and almost every genus has a member or two tough enough to live happily in the coldest or warmest parts of the country. A good regional shrub guide will be a great help, as will experienced gardeners and nursery folks.

Colorful Border Shrubs

Compact border shrubs link flowers to trees and large shrubs that frame the property. The best choices combine an attractive form with spring or summer flowers and seasonally colorful foliage.

COMMON NAME (BOTANICAL NAME)	HARDINESS ZONES
Azalea (*Rhododendron* spp.)	Varies by species
Beautyberry (*Callicarpa* spp.)	Varies by species
Butterfly bush (*Buddleia lindleyana*)	8–9
California lilac (*Ceanothus* spp.)	8–10, varies by species
Cinquefoil (*Potentilla* spp.)	5–8, varies by species
Dogwood (*Cornus* spp.)	Varies by species
Dwarf fothergilla (*Fothergilla gardenii*)	5–9
Elder (*Sambucus* spp.)	Varies by species
Flowering currant (*Ribes sanguineum*)	6–8
Holly (*Ilex* spp.)	Varies by species
Hydrangea (*Hydrangea* spp.)	4–9, varies by species
Japanese spirea (*Spiraea japonica*)	4–9
Leucothoe (*Leucothoe* spp.)	Varies by species
Mahonia (*Mahonia* spp.)	Varies by species
Mock orange (*Philadelphus* spp.)	Most are 5–8
Osmanthus (*Osmanthus* spp.)	Most are 7–9
Rhododendron (*Rhododendron* spp.)	Varies by species
Rockrose (*Cistus* spp.)	8–10
Smokebush (*Cotinus coggygria*)	5–8
St. John's wort (*Hypericum* spp.)	Varies by species
'Sungold' butterfly bush (*Buddleia × weyeriana* 'Sungold')	6–8
Viburnum (*Viburnum* spp.)	Varies by species
Virginia sweetspire (*Itea virginica*)	6–9
Willow (*Salix* spp.)	Varies by species
Winter daphne (*Daphne odora*)	7–9

Natural Architecture

MANY COMBINATIONS ARE PRETTY WITHOUT BEING striking or memorable. To create a compelling combination, you need to look past color to other attributes. The easiest way to assemble powerful combinations is to employ potent contrasts of form and tonal value. Most plant shapes fall into loose categories of mounds and balls; spills and sprawls; cones and columns; spires and spikes; fans, fountains, and arches; and eccentrics. All plants have a natural shape, but some are certainly more distinctive than others.

A common yucca, for instance, has strong, clean lines and a definite fan shape. A tall New England aster (*Aster novae-angliae*) may be vaguely columnar, but its tendency to flop blurs the strength of the upward lines. By comparison, a Frikart's aster such as 'Mönch' (*Aster × frikartii* 'Mönch') makes a clean arch (at least it will do so if pinched). Catmints are smooth, almost solid mounds, while oriental poppies past their prime look like the aftermath of a cat confrontation. Most asters make neatly shaped soft billows, while their cousin boltonias look airy and tangled (but certainly lovely) in a bed.

Dwarf Alberta spruce makes a perfect upside-down ice cream cone that looks clipped, while lupines send up tapering, almost conical spires that seem softly inflated and puffy. Slim South American (or Brazilian) verbena (*Verbena bonariensis*) rises like an exclamation mark, while a broader sheaf of Culver's root (*Veronicastrum virginicum*) makes a massy column with slender, spiked tips.

And there are some plants that have plenty of natural architecture, but it's difficult to characterize their form into any neat category. These potent shapes are generally lumped as eccentrics or simply as structural plants. Eccentrics include plants like globe thistles, cardoons, and sinuous verbascums. They often display complex forms that incorporate several kinds of shapes within a unifying framework. For instance, a cardoon (*Cynara cardunculus*) consists of a bulky, mounded mass with several inflated, spirelike arms, each tipped with spiky flowering shoots that end in ball-like flowerheads. This combination cone-shape, spired, mounded, and ball-shape plant makes for rhythmically interesting natural architecture in the garden, very unlike the blobbiness of, say, your average bachelor's button (*Centaurea cyanus*).

By pairing potent shapes, you can create instantly powerful contrasts of form. These can and will supply all the drama missing from pretty but tame combinations

Swordlike yucca makes a powerful impression in beds and borders. As structural as any shrub, yucca's dramatic leaves and showy flowers help balance fluffier neighbors.

that rely on color alone. Picture a fan of pale yellow variegated water iris behind a smooth billow of dusky purple sage. That simple combination has considerable and immediate impact. To expand it into a more complex vignette, add a compact conifer with a natural columnar shape behind the iris fan, and tuck a spill of silvery, prostrate artemisia at the base of the sage. To soften these sculptural shapes, add a small, arching grass that will sway and ripple in any breeze.

You'll notice that none of these plants depend on their flowers for effect. There will be blossoms at various times and they will enhance the overall picture. However, this combination is what I call plant-driven, rather than the more typical florally driven combinations seen in most amateur gardens. Here's what the pros know that can make professional work so potent: To be fully appreciated, flowers need strong architectural support. By creating a combination of solid, distinctive shapes, you can anchor the garden for much or even most of the year. You can then proceed to embroider and amplify the borders with as many flowers as you like, sandwiching them in between the more structural border plants.

Texture Counts, Too

For many gardeners, the idea of plant textures is mildly puzzling. What difference can using small- or large-leaved plants possibly make to a floral combination? In design terms, the use of texture is extremely important. Texture is what makes a cat fluffy or a piece of beautiful fabric soft and cushiony. Plants like woolly lamb's-ears or velvety sages invite your touch, as do swaying grasses, whose threadlike leaves shimmer *en masse*.

The texture of a leaf (as well as its shape and color) determines how light is absorbed or reflected by

> The glimpsed scene has a deliciously secret quality, as if you are seeing something marvelous and hidden from other eyes.

it, which in turn affects the way it looks to human eyes. Matte or glossy, rugged or smooth, and pleated or veined foliage can be used to create powerful visual contrasts between otherwise-similar forms and colors. Most folks focus on color, whether matching or contrasting, when they make plant or floral combinations. However, contrasting textures are equally valuable in blending colors, visually differentiating plant shapes, adding dramatic structure, and creating a powerful flow of form and color.

Layering from the Ground Up

Many gardeners begin combination work by mixing and matching a few flowers and enjoying the result, which is generally planted right at the front of their beds and borders. When you expand the concept, you find that combinations can involve trees and shrubs as well as a few perennials or annuals. Your layered

Light-textured plants weave through solid-looking ones in eye-pleasing layers. Arching wands of tussock grass (*Cortaderia fulvida*), an evergreen grass from New Zealand, and sheaves of South American verbena (*Verbena bonariensis*) preside over the scene. Colorful shrubs include red-berried *Hypericum androsaemum* 'Albury Purple' and 'Goldflame' spirea, with feather grass (*Stipa tenuissima*) softening the line of the path.

backdrop stands ready to frame and support your floral effusions, but you still need to create intermediate visual ladders to integrate the floral combination layer with the taller ones behind the flowers.

Accenting perennials and annuals with compact border shrubs will help to weave your flowers back into the shrubby layer. Small shrubs anchor the seasonal flow of perennials and annuals and can act as rungs on the visual ladder that carries the eye to the tree line and back. The issue here is greater than the standard advice to stair-step plants from back to front. Nearly all garden books urge you to put tall plants at the back of the border and shorter ones up front. This seemingly obvious size-ordering principle is only part of the picture, and as a rule, can certainly be broken when your artistic instinct suggests a more interesting placement.

Clearly it makes sense to arrange plants so they can all be seen, but you can also create a tantalizing sense of mystery by placing a few taller plants near the border front so that you must move past them to see what lies beyond. In a small garden, this kind of scrim (a light, see-through veil) helps create the illusion that the space is larger than it really is. You can also create a sense of intimacy by placing low plants around a taller one near the back of the border, then masking the vignette with taller plants so it can only be seen from certain angles. The glimpsed scene has a deliciously secret quality, as if you are seeing something marvelous and hidden from other eyes.

Color Work, Color Play

COLOR IS A COMPLICATED SUBJECT AND MANY BOOKS have been written about it, but, to my eyes, this is what it comes down to: Do what you want, and you'll be successful. That's really all there is to it. For intuitive artists, color work is effortless and doesn't even require much thought. Plants are assembled, edited by eye, and planted without angst. However, problems may arise when you're not satisfied with your plantings or when you hope for art in the garden but have to settle for artlessness. If you want to educate your eye, a few simple exercises will quickly clarify the mechanics of your own taste.

Start your training by taking a notebook with you everywhere you go. When you see something visually pleasing, make a simple sketch (even if you can't draw). If what catches your eye is a single object, ask yourself what's great about it. Is it beautifully shaped, colored, or textured? Is it lighted intriguingly? Make some notes about what you feel and think when you look at this object. Don't worry if your responses seem simple. The point is to find out what you like to look at and why you find it appealing.

Perhaps you see an apple and love its roundness, its redness, or the shine of light on its sleek, glossy side. You can assume you like round things, red things, and shiny things, but you can also ask more questions. Is the apple perfectly round? Probably not. Would you like it better if it were? Would an artificial "perfect" apple look better than this real one? Could it be that the slight imperfections underline its "realness?" If so, you might be able to make the leap from your apple observations to your garden, realizing that a softer, more natural curve in a garden path or garden bed will please your artist's eye more than a strictly "perfect" one.

Now look at the redness of the apple. Is the apple all one color? Are there contrasting flecks of gold or green? Is one rosy cheek more deeply blushed than another? Does the gloss or matte finish alter the way the color looks in various lights? Perhaps you love the sight of a clear, singing red emerging from shadow. If so, you may want to plant some strongly colored red astilbes such as 'Fanal' in a spot where light will strike them while leaving the backdrop dim. If you like the shading of cream and gold and green on the apple because it sets off the red so well, you may want to add some creamy variegated hostas to the astilbe planting, as well as some gold and chartreuse ones. Fresh green ferns will complete the color run you saw in the apple.

> Color does not necessarily come last in terms of choosing plants, but if you want to make balanced designs, color can only be as important as the other considerations.

If the scene you noticed and noted in your notebook has more than one part or is a group of objects, try to see the spatial relationships between the pieces more clearly. Are the shapes distinct or blurred? Do you like clean definition and strong contrast, or do you prefer the softness of the overall image? Are the components the same size? Asking yourself these questions will help you identify distinguishing characteristics in the things that bring you visual pleasure.

The next time you visit a garden, use your visual senses to identify what you like about the plants and combinations that draw your eye. Examine each group in terms of the primary elements—the main players—and then expand your view to take in their neighbors and supportive backdrop. You can also do this with glossy garden books. Instead of simply reveling in the pretty pictures, let your imagination go deeply into them. Ask yourself what it is about each picture that you find compelling, and think of as many factors as you can, including color, contrast, form, texture, mass, structure, and balance, as well as light and shade.

It's equally useful to ask yourself why you don't like a particular combination or picture. What would need to be changed in order to please you? If it's too complicated, would adding strong, simple shapes calm it down? If it's too dull, would more color, more texture, or more interesting forms work best? By taking the time to understand the way your own taste works, you will find it increasingly easier to assemble plants into relationships that make you happy.

Color as an Organizer

Color is glorious, enticing, and joyful, but it also gets you into trouble if it's the only thing you think about. Gardens where color is king can look chaotic and unruly. Even when plants are coaxed into combinations, combinations based solely on flower color tend to be short-lived and lacking in interest once the flowers have faded. Combinations based on foliage color will clearly last longer, especially if you are also employing contrasts of plant form, leaf shape, and texture. Color does not necessarily come last in terms of choosing plants, but if you want to make balanced designs, color can only be as important as the other considerations. Remember, design is about space, not about plants.

Making combinations is all about plants, but they will certainly be more pleasing when you consider the

Yellows dominate this bright border of prairie wildflowers. Color themes do not need to be rigidly exclusive; a touch of coral, salmon, or peachy pink can add just the right contrast to an otherwise predictable color scheme.

big picture as well as the details. When I am asked to consult in gardens where combinations are stubbornly unsuccessful, the most common problem is a lack of organization. Many gardens look chaotic because they are put together without any organizing principles. Creating a geometric layout and framing everything in little boxwood hedges gives an immediate effect of organization, but unless the plantings within those frames make sense, they just look like a jumble with a tidy edge. Layered gardens provide a natural hierarchy of plants that looks right to the eye and feels right to the plant (which gets to live in its true ecological niche). By placing your combinations into the established layers, the plants will look as if they belong, instead of as if they were dropped out of the sky.

The second most common problem I see in gardens is a lack of discipline. Many of us are fairly indiscriminate in our tastes—I personally have yet to meet a plant I can't admire in some context or other. It's fine to like a wide variety of plants, but you can't necessarily bring them all home to live with you. If you must, you'll need to create a framework that helps integrate them with each other and the layered backdrop. If your garden simply looks gay and cheerful and makes you happy, then you don't need to worry. If, however, you are aware that your plants don't look their best and you want to make some changes, consider adopting a color palette for each part of the garden.

Color Themes

Developing a deliberate color palette involves choosing either a main color theme or a series of related colors that designers and textile artists refer to as a "color run." Color-theme gardens, like the Red Garden at Hidcote Manor in Gloucestershire, England, are a popular way to integrate plants into a common scheme. You can design a palette for each bed or border, deciding to group all of your pink plants in one area, while keeping the yellow ones to themselves.

Bright white can easily outshine other colors, throwing off the balance in a delicately colored composition. Creamy pastel yellows, blues, and pinks would work better than clean whites to keep the tonal values all in the same range.

Generally, the predominate color in every section will be green, and since there are as many shades of green as any other color, this needs to be considered as much as the focus color.

Many white gardens don't work very well because not enough attention is given to the blending power of green. Massed whites often make each other look dim or dirty because of their ill-matched undertones, which are usually pale pink, blue, or yellow. Putting a yellow-white near a blue-white won't do justice to either flower. White is actually one of the most difficult colors to work with, in large part because of the often-unrecognized undertones.

To make a terrific white garden, you really need to make a terrific green garden, using a full range of tints and tones of green. Seek out gray-greens and blue-greens. Look for olive and duff and as many other shades as you can find, from fresh kelly green down to chartreuse. Creamy variegated plants will look great in white gardens, as long as they are set off by the right greens. Thinking as much about foliage as about flowers will make success far more likely.

Theme gardens based on primary colors—red, yellow, or blue—will look best if all the important color elements used are of the same tonal value. Tonal value refers to the intensity or saturation of a color. If you put a fire-engine red rose next to a pale pink 'Barnsley' lavatera, you have an imbalance of color. Hot, heavy red is very saturated, while a chalky pink is cool and light. Visually, the pale color floats while the heavy color sinks.

When the focus color in your theme garden is a saturated one, all plant partners need to match its intensity. If they don't, some parts will float and others will sink. And even though individual combinations

may look great, the composition as a whole will stubbornly refuse to integrate. This kind of imbalance can sometimes be fixed by using your greens very well. Strong, saturated colors tend to make softer ones looked washed out or dirty, but the greens (and other colors) of foliage plants can balance and refocus the overall composition by making transitions between colors.

The role of foliage is important, both on its own and as a buffer between more dramatic and colorful flowers. Just as you can use various sizes of understory plants to create transitions between a canopy and groundcovers, you can use color to transition the eye from one color or intensity to another. Using shades and gradations of foliage is the easiest and longest-lasting way to do this.

This warm color run looks rich because it involves both bright colors and muted ones. The vivid colors are set off nicely by silvery gray-greens, which also help to integrate the shock of gold at the border back. Where the harsh tonal value of clean white would break the color run, gentle grays and silvers softly knit more potent colors together.

Color Runs

By using (or running) a single color from its lowest to its highest saturation, you create a complex, disciplined palette that is rich, full, and sumptuous, instead of simple and boring. For example, pastel-theme gardens will look best if you choose plants that feature both shades (darker versions) and tints (lighter versions) of the main color. If you are making a pink garden, you'll want to extend the range from palest shell pink up past clear rose to murky ruby. You'll need to use both bright pastels that are cooled with white as well as the grayed French pastels that are warmed with black. You can use warm or cool tones for your color palette: For a warmer look, add some peachy and bronzed pinks, as well as some yellowish pinks. For a cooler look, keep all your colors on the pink-purple side, and stay away from the yellows.

Full color runs in the garden are more sophisticated and larger versions of a single-color theme. Like the expanded pink palette, these may be accented by tints, tones (grayed versions), and shades of each color in the run. In lectures, I always explain this concept by showing students fabric swatches. To see what I mean, stroll through a fabric shop and look at a book of swatches. Look for a series of related prints in which the same pattern is available in a variety of colors. Usually, they will all match

in tonal value, so you could use several versions in the same room with ease. A pretty chintz pattern may have a pink background with green and blue flowers in one sample, and in another sample, the background may be yellow with blue and pink flowers. The same tonally related colors are found in each sample, but their role switches from primary to secondary.

To learn which color runs attract you most, take a look at your wardrobe and study the pictures on your walls. If you favor seascapes, you will probably love blue, cream, and buff in the garden. If your pictures are mostly outdoor scenes and forests, a symphony in green may be most suitable for your garden. If your home looks like a rainbow, you have many options, including that of simply growing everything you like and not worrying about its artistic merit.

Color runs make an excellent organizing principle when building borders. For one thing, developing color runs helps you to place all of those miscellaneous plants that somehow find their way into your garden. Giving each bed a broad color theme simplifies decision making. Are the flowers creamy yellow? Pop that plant into the morning mist bed. Plants with flame orange flowers go in the hot sunset bed. This concept works with foliage as well: Plants with blue, purple, or silvery foliage can be grouped just as floral plants might be.

Hot Sunset

Bronze, Copper, Salmon, Coral, Peach, and Apricot

This warm-toned palette looks great under the cloudy, northwestern skies, particularly in winter. In a region with stronger sunlight, I'd probably "up" the intensity of the colors, using warmer and more saturated tones of each main color. The greens in this palette tend to be on the gray side, which adds a dramatic contrast. In this color run, white is not welcome because it would look glaring and harsh. Use grays and blues as blenders for these warm, delicate colors.

Autumn Mist

BUFF, BUTTER, BISCUIT, CREAMY YELLOWS, AND CHARTREUSE

This very gentle palette glows softly in a shady setting. All of these colors are excellent blenders for more powerful tones, and this range can easily be played up to include fully saturated citrus and sunset colors. The greens here are mainly fresh, light, and clear, and often have soft variegation in cream or butter.

Thundercloud

PURPLE, DEEP BLUES, PLUM, BURGUNDY, DEEP RED, MIDNIGHT ANYTHING, AND BLACK

Dramatic, punchy, and full of high contrasts, this palette stands up to the lean, clean lines of modern architecture very well. With a palette this bold, it's important to select deep-toned foliage plants in many colors, using lots of burgundy and blue, as well as murky and dark greens. Avoid soft, pale colors because they would create an imbalance that would throw off the color values in this run.

Lavender Smoke

BLUE, LAVENDER, GRAY-GREEN, BLUE-GRAY, SMOKE, PEWTER, SILVERY BLUE, AND SLATE

Softer than the previous palette, this is a moody, evocative range of colors that recalls the Maquis region of southern France. Not surprisingly, this palette works best in full sun and dry conditions. To make this color run successful, concentrate on plants with blue, silver, and gray foliage, nearly all of which are designed by nature to thrive in warm, dry places.

Blending Colors

IF YOUR TASTE IS VERY ECLECTIC, THEN DISCIPLINED approaches like using color runs may not be for you. You can still have a gorgeous garden full of enticing combinations if you choose a few overall integrating principles. This can be as simple as excluding one color, or as complex as using almost every color. My friend Margaret (who's now in her nineties) had a showplace garden that was the delight of our island for many years. She was fond of all kinds of plants and all kinds of colors, and her garden always looked harmonic. Her secret was to avoid clear, soft pinks, but to use everything else with abandon.

Orange is perhaps the least popular color in plants, so for most people, eliminating any and all shades of orange would achieve the same goal from a different color standpoint. If you like orange but find it hard to work with, try surrounding it with sunset colors such as reds and yellows, and with clean, strong greens. You can also partner oranges with complementary blues and greens, making for high contrast and lots of dramatic character. Playing around with color partnerships you would not ordinarily consider can help you see both plants and colors with a fresh eye.

The role of blenders is also worth emphasizing—blenders are the neutrals and in-between shades that you may easily overlook. Green is, of course, the great garden neutral, functioning like a basic black dress to set off anything and everything we partner it with. Greens play the blending role beautifully, creating transitions between colors that need help to find common ground.

A whole host of other colors will do this, too, including many that may not seem attractive at the outset. Many gardeners shy away from deep, dark colors like burgundy and brownish reds, but these murky colors are excellent transition colors, setting off all kinds of brighter tones with panache. Put a pale pink against a warm, chocolate brown and you have both drama and snap. The new geranium called 'Pink Spice', which combines milk chocolate foliage and soft pink flowers, has been selling out at nurseries across the country, so I must not be alone in liking the effect. Bronze and copper are also excellent blenders and transition colors for reds, golds, and oranges, and they also look great with blues and purples.

White is often suggested as a good blender, but in truth, white is the worst possible blender. Instead of integrating colors, it makes them stand apart. White only works well with pale pastels and with high, clean colors such as lemon yellow and ocean blue.

Integration means knitting disparate things together into what appears to be a seamless whole. To make gentle transitions between strongly contrasting colors, you can use both flowers and foliage plants. Subtle tints of blue, purple, gray, and silver are splendid soothers and softeners. Plants with maroon or purple stems, leaf petioles, and buds can also be used to strengthen these understated contrasts.

In my own gardens, I tend to combine plants of all kinds and all colors. To avoid the jumbled look common to so many collectors' gardens, I adopt several

integrating color principles. For starters, I avoid primary colors, concentrating on shades that are muted with gray or warmed with black. This may sound dull and dim, but in fact, it creates a powerful, sophisticated palette, even if you are using tame pink and blue for your color theme. It works by setting up what plantswoman Pamela Harper calls "color echoes." In her gorgeous book of the same name, Pam shows dozens of examples of this kind of planting. Even minor amounts of similar colors throughout the garden (in my case, the dusky parts of each plant) add up quickly to the eye, giving a concerted look to the garden as a whole.

I also pick plants as much for their details as for their main colors. For instance, in my texture garden, nearly all the plants have some trace or touch of rust, cinnamon, bronze, or black. In the herb garden, everything is touched with gray, green, bronze, or gold. In the more florally dominated borders, I tend to use plants that have burgundy stems and leaf veins, and often a trace of burgundy in the flower, as well (sometimes found in the throat or on the back of the petals).

The goal is to create a coherent composition that encompasses a wide palette of plants. In natural settings, certain species will be dominant, but most habitats are very mixed. In your garden, the goal of biodiversity is easily achieved when you integrate as many plants as you want into clusters of plants requiring similar conditions. To avoid the hodgepodge effect, you can use color themes and themed combinations or you can repeat certain colors at set intervals.

Seasonal Flow

Most gardens have a relatively static base of screening evergreens and key structural plants, and the changes in color and texture that enliven a garden are usually provided by less structural and more **ephemeral plants**. "Seasonal flow" is the term garden designers use to indicate these changes during the cycle of the year. Annuals and perennials, bulbs and grasses, and vines and groundcovers are the **key ingredients of change** in a naturalistically layered garden.

If you make smart choices, at least some of your screening and structural plants will also supply **periodic boosts of color** from fresh leaves and flower buds in spring; flowers and fruit in summer; foliage color in fall; and twigs, bark, and berries in winter. When you begin to plant a new garden area or to amplify an older section of your garden, you can make sure this happens just by keeping in mind the rule of thirds that I introduced earlier in the book (see page 64).

Following that informal rule to create a **well-clothed garden space**, about two-thirds of the plants should be structural (one-third evergreen and another third deciduous). The final third can then consist of plants that offer seasonal color, such as bulbs, perennials, and annuals. The simplest way to significantly expand your garden's seasonal flow is to **choose plants of every kind** with a seasonal category in mind, as well as whatever other function (groundcover, backdrop, and so on) they will serve. Just how you divide up your choices among the seasons will depend on when you want your gardens to peak.

In most gardens, the seasonal color display begins in spring, when **bright bulbs mingle** with flowering shrubs such as forsythia and quince. Flowering trees like dogwoods and crabapples carry gardens into early summer, when **roses and peonies light up** the garden. Lilies and sunflowers take us into high summer, and fall-bloomers like asters and 'Autumn Joy' sedum finish off the season with **panache**. If the winter garden is dull, many gardeners hardly notice, for their expectations for this season are extremely low or nonexistent.

Extending Seasonal Flow

Establishing a smooth flow of color from late winter into autumn will enormously enrich most gardens and the pleasures they bring to gardeners. It can be fairly simple to push a garden's seasons of interest past the usual timeframe. Add a few spring-blooming shrubs that also offer fall color, some early- and late-blooming bulbs and perennials, and a selection of evergreen groundcovers, and you'll notice a real difference. In this chapter, I'll suggest techniques and plants that will help you extend the flow of seasonal color at the beginning and end of the garden year.

Start Early in Spring

The trick to encouraging early-blooming plants to flower extra-early is to place them in the warmest corners of your yard. The best possible setting would be a sunny, sheltered corner with both some protection from wind and warmth from reflected heat off house or garage walls. Such a microclimate will provide favorable conditions for all kinds of plants that wouldn't thrive in more open places.

To find microclimates like this, watch your pets when they're out in your yard. They know all about

Early-Flowering Perennials for Sun

In late winter and early spring, the first flowers that appear are deeply appreciated. Early bulbs look less artificial when partnered with spring-blooming perennials like these.

COMMON NAME (BOTANICAL NAME)	HARDINESS ZONES
Basket of gold (*Aurinia saxatilis*)	4–8
Cushion spurge (*Euphorbia polychroma*)	4–9
Globeflower (*Trollius* × *cultorum*)	5–8
Horned violet (*Viola cornuta*)	7–9
Leatherleaf (*Bergenia cordifolia*)	3–8
Marsh marigold (*Caltha palustris*)	3–7
'Miss Mason' leopard's bane (*Doronicum columnae* 'Miss Mason')	4–8
Pasque flower (*Pulsatilla vulgaris*)	5–7
Sweet violet (*Viola odorata*)	8–9

Early-Flowering Perennials for Shade

Shady woodland gardens generally offer more light in late winter and spring, before deciduous trees have leafed out. Here are some easygoing early bloomers for such a setting.

COMMON NAME (BOTANICAL NAME)	HARDINESS ZONES
Bleeding heart (*Dicentra eximia* and other species)	4–8
Blue corydalis (*Corydalis flexuosa*)	6–8
Fairy bells (*Disporum smithii*)	4–9
Labrador violet (*Viola labradorica*)	2–8
Longspur barrenwort (*Epimedium grandiflorum*)	5–8
Red wood spurge (*Euphorbia amygdaloides* 'Purpurea', also sold as 'Rubra')	6–9
Spotted lungwort (*Pulmonaria saccharata*)	4–8
'Wester Flisk' stinking hellebore (*Helleborus foetidus* 'Wester Flisk')	6–9
Wood anemone (*Anemone nemorosa*)	4–8
Yellow corydalis (*Corydalis lutea*)	5–8

Spring-Blooming Shrubs with Fall Color

Selecting shrubs that offer multiple-season beauty can dramatically extend the garden year. Visit nurseries and gardens in both spring and fall to look for dual-season performers.

COMMON NAME (BOTANICAL NAME)	HARDINESS ZONES
Azalea (*Rhododendron* spp.)	4–9, varies by species
Barberry (*Berberis julianae, B. koreana, B. × stenophylla,* and other species)	6–9
Deutzia (*Deutzia* spp.)	5–8, varies by species
Dwarf fothergilla (*Fothergilla gardenii*)	5–9
Enkianthus (*Enkianthus* spp.)	6–8, varies by species
Forsythia (*Forsythia suspensa* and hybrids)	6–9
Japanese flowering quince (*Chaenomeles japonica*)	5–9
Rhododendron (*Rhododendron* spp.)	5–8
Summersweet (*Clethra alnifolia*)	3–9
Witch hazel (*Hamamelis vernalis* and some hybrids)	4–8

Early-Blooming Bulbs

Regional climate differences spread bloom dates for these cheerful early-bird bulbs over a period of many weeks. However, all of these bulbs are reliable in their preferred zones.

COMMON NAME (BOTANICAL NAME)	HARDINESS ZONES
Common snowdrop (*Galanthus nivalis*)	3–9
Cyclamen (*Cyclamen repandum* and other species)	7–9
Daffodil (*Narcissus* spp.)	3–9
European dog's-tooth violet (*Erythronium dens-canis*)	3–9
Golden bunch crocus (*Crocus ancyrensis*)	5–8
Grecian windflower (*Anemone blanda*)	4–8
Reticulated iris (*Iris reticulata*)	5–8
Siberian squill (*Scilla siberica*)	5–8
Tomasini's crocus (*Crocus tommasinianus*)	3–8
Winter aconite (*Eranthis hyemalis*)	4–9

finding comfortable, cozy corners to snuggle up in. These are nearly always places where early-blooming plants will do well. (You may need to use some low fencing around the plants to convince pets that giving up their favorite basking spots is a good idea—at least for you!)

Cluster early bloomers in small groups or islands, where they can shine against the dim backdrop of mulch or dormant plants. One clump of violets won't have much impact, but a ribbon of violets and primroses surrounding ruffled clumps of windflower and snowdrops is going to be an exciting sight in early spring (they bloom as early as February in my garden). Play around with your additions, using them in combination with what you already have, and before long you'll find yourself making room for as many early flowers as possible.

Feed spring bloomers a light (1-inch) mulch of compost just as they come into bloom. The mulch will help keep spring rains from splashing mud on your first flowers. Compost also provides a steady supply of nutrients when roots are in active growth, even during cold spells.

Groom early bloomers lightly, shearing them back just enough to promote bushiness rather than cutting them hard. That way, new growth will appear in time to make a lovely backdrop for summer flowers.

The Late, Late Show

Let's skip past summer (because there are plenty of summer-flowering plants that are well known and reliable) and turn our attention to adding fall interest. If you want the garden to put on a lively show in autumn, you'll need to set aside a reasonable percentage of garden space for late-season performers. You don't need to allot them as much room as you give to the summer show, because if even 10 or 20 percent of your plants offer strong flower or foliage fall color in fall, they can carry the day. For one thing, many late performers are strapping plants with robust character. For another, they boast bold colors. Tuck these big beauties in with reliable rebloomers such as daylilies, daisies, and yarrows, and their concerted efforts will produce a stronger display.

Many fall flowers have striking foliage that adds texture and fullness to your beds while the late-arriving flowers are on their way up. These fall bloomers, which make an ongoing contribution from the time they break ground in spring until they peak in fall, are the ones you want to be sure to include. For example, common asters can be splendid in fall, but may look homely in summer, when their lanky stems flop and their foliage mildews. The solution is to seek out superior forms, such as bushy Aster × frikartii 'Mönch', which makes a fine backdrop for summery penstemons before creating its own long-lasting cascade of periwinkle stars. Black calico aster, A. lateriflorus 'Prince', has a marvelously tiered structure that makes it outstanding on its own or mixed in a border, where its lavender flowers glow against its dusky, purple-black leaves.

'Autumn Joy' sedum is a border classic precisely because it offers so many periods of interest. In spring,

Perennial Late Performers for Sun

Late bloomers abound, once you start looking for them. Native asters are an obvious first choice, but many other sturdy perennials contribute a last gasp of glory as well.

COMMON NAME (BOTANICAL NAME)	HARDINESS ZONES
Black-eyed Susan (Rudbeckia fulgida)	4–9
Blanket flower (Gaillardia × grandiflora)	3–8
Blue star flower (Amsonia tabernaemontana)	3–9
Boltonia (Boltonia asteroides)	4–9
Calico aster (Aster lateriflorus 'Horizontalis' and other cultivars)	4–8
Goldenrod (Solidago rugosa 'Fireworks' and other cultivars)	5–9
Helenium (Helenium autumnale)	4–8
Leadwort (Ceratostigma plumbaginoides)	6–9
Mountain fleeceflower (Persicaria amplexicaulis)	4–7
New England aster (Aster novae-angliae)	4–8
Tall sedum (Sedum telephium)	4–9

Perennial Late Performers for Shade

Our handsome native white wood aster is a classic fall bloomer for shade. Asian woodlanders like toad lilies and Japanese anemones also expand the possibilities excitingly.

COMMON NAME (BOTANICAL NAME)	HARDINESS ZONES
'Amethystina' purple toad lily (Tricyrtis formosana 'Amethystina')	6–9
Autumn fern (Dryopteris erythrosora)	6–9
Bugbane (Cimicifuga spp.)	4–8
Cardinal flower (Lobelia cardinalis)	4–8
Japanese anemone (Anemone hupehensis var. japonica)	5–9
Monkshood (Aconitum spp.)	5–8
'Robustissima' grapeleaf anemone (Anemone tomentosa 'Robustissima')	4–8
Stinking iris (Iris foetidissima)	7–9
'White Towers' white toad lily (Tricyrtis hirta 'White Towers')	4–9
White wood aster (Aster divaricatus)	4–8

At the garden school, golden globeflower (*Trollius* × *cultorum*) first flowers in midspring, when its perennial companions are low-growing tufts and rosettes. In good garden soil, it often repeats in late summer, just as the tall 'Autumn Joy' sedum in the front of the bed is entering the "green broccoli" stage.

its fat stems pierce the ground when the early bulbs emerge. In summer, the plump stems are packed with green buds with the texture and color of broccoli. In fall, these buds burst into clouds of rusty rose that are followed by tarnished seedheads that persist until spring. The seeds may attract birds such as black-capped chickadees, dark-eye juncos, house sparrows, and white-breasted nuthatches all winter. The good news is that 'Autumn Joy' has dozens of equally garden-worthy relatives, such as sizzling pink 'Brilliant', dusky 'Indian Chief', and frosty 'Stardust'. All are equally easy to grow, and it's fascinating to watch them develop and change through the seasons.

Late-Blooming Bulbs

Most late-blooming bulbs are summer dormant, so it's important to mark their spots with small stones or golf tees. That way you won't uproot them when you're planting perennials and grasses, thinking that garden space is available.

COMMON NAME (BOTANICAL NAME)	HARDINESS ZONES
Algerian iris (*Iris unguicularis*)	7–9
Autumn crocus (*Colchicum autumnale*)	4–9
Fall-blooming crocus (*Crocus medius, C. pulchellus,* and other species)	3–8
Fall snowflake (*Leucojum autumnale*)	5–9
Golden-rayed lily (*Lilium auratum*)	4–8
Hardy cyclamen (*Cyclamen hederifolium* and others)	5–9
Magic lily (*Lycoris squamigera*)	5–9
Saffron crocus (*Crocus sativus*)	5–8
Showy Japanese lily (*Lilium speciosum*)	4–8
Zephyr lily (*Zephyranthes candida*)	9–10

The Winter Garden Palette

IF YOU'RE LIKE ME (AND I'VE BEEN RELIEVED TO DISCOVER that many gardeners are just as plant-smitten as I am), you are always interested in finding out about plants that will boldly go where few plants have gone before. For us, continually increasing the garden's season of liveliness also continually increases our active enjoyment of the garden year. This does not necessarily mean that everybody everywhere can garden outdoors all year long: Where winters are mild, it is perfectly possible to plant all (or nearly all) year long; in regions where the ground freezes hard for months at a stretch, it's not at all possible.

In southern and western parts of North America, the palette of possible season-extending plants is a lot bigger than the selection available to northern and midwestern gardeners. However, even in the coldest and harshest environments, you can draw upon literally hundreds of beautiful, adaptable plants that can extend the garden's period of visual excitement for many months. It's quite possible to have a garden that remains attractive and even exciting in the depths of a cold, long winter.

Extend the season with plants that produce showy berries or fruit in gray-weather months. Roses that produce colorful hips put on a spectacular display when the first snows of winter fall.

Those of us who grew up thinking that native plants were weeds and that only exotic plants like dahlias and zinnias were "pretty" have a big treat in store.

In most cases, the plants that provide off-season interest are natives and their allies, because these plants will be genetically adapted to the local conditions. Those of us who grew up thinking that native plants were weeds and that only exotic plants like dahlias and zinnias were "pretty" have a big treat in store. As you learn to reevaluate your preferences, to look with wonder at adaptive natives and to appreciate their attractions and strengths, you quite often surprise yourself into finding hidden beauty everywhere. Not all local beauties are subtle, and scores of North American natives have won awards from England's Royal Horticultural Society. Once the cultural blinders are off, you can recognize "the plant next door" as the garden-worthy beauty it really is. With local flora for a solid base, any non-native allies and hardy companions you plant will shine all the brighter against the supportive backdrop of natives.

Stay Open, Stay Flexible

Seasonal flow also depends in part on what you think of as beautiful. No matter where you live, the garden in January is never going to look like the garden in June (or if it does, saying so is hardly a compliment). Spring's floral effusions and summer's billowing bounty provide one kind of standard, but there are other garden styles with at least equal beauty if less-immediate impact. Most people are comfortable with the idea that woods and meadows are beautiful, but not everyone finds as much delight in looking at rolling plains and prairies, which may seem bleak, empty, or even intimidating. When you train your eye to see the beauty in many kinds of natural environments (particularly those of your own region), you become better able to appreciate the entire range of natural beauty that surrounds you.

If your goal is to stretch the garden's glory beyond the usual time limits, it's very helpful if you learn to stretch your idea of what kinds of plants belong in a garden. As your main garden goal gradually shifts, your plant palette must change as well. Because the typical garden palette is quite limited, so too are the benefits you get from gardens where nothing out of the ordinary is employed. Very simple gardens offer very simple pleasures and a very limited range of experiences. If that feels right to you, then you have achieved just the right balance for you and your garden. If you find yourself wanting more, but you're not clear how to get there, a few pointers can help you to create seamless sequences of colorful events that never really stop.

One of the easiest ways to achieve seasonal flow is to go shopping during your garden's flat periods. When nothing looks very exciting at home, taking a trip to several nurseries can spark your creative impulses. For instance, in late fall I often cruise nurseries looking for plants with fall color. The perennial aisles will draw my attention first, with their billowing asters, boltonias, and Japanese anemones. However, I also check out the

Lettuce leaf poppy seedheads remain ornamental for months, often lasting well into winter. If plants seem to promise good winter structure or interest, experiment by leaving a few stalks standing this fall, and see what happens.

ornamental grass department to see which grasses are showing attractive color from leaf blades or seedheads. Next, I'll stroll through the shrub department, looking for flaming foliage. I'll look at broad-leaved evergreens and conifers, especially the dwarf and compact ones. Finally, I'll walk through the ranks of rhododendrons, paying special attention to compact border shrubs with interesting fall color (of which there are many, including *Rhododendron mucronulatum, R. 'P.J.M.' hybrids, and R. prinophyllum*).

Also, try visiting private and public gardens, nurseries, parks, and arboretums in fall and winter. After viewing several sites, you'll develop a clear idea about the kinds of visual effects that will work well in your own backyard garden.

If deep snow falls in your region in winter, visit natural settings like woods and prairies for vivid ideas of what kinds of natural beauties are available to take home. On the plains and prairies you'll see skeletal plants, structural stems and seedheads, and gilded grasses emerging from the snow. In the north woods you'll see how dim evergreens create a powerfully dramatic backdrop for the silvered tracery of bare stems and naked branches. To talk about the beauty of bark and berries is to risk cliché, yet there's truth at the heart of many a cliché. No matter what you have heard, no matter where you live, you truly can enjoy plants of all shapes and sizes that retain presence, dignity, and beauty in any season.

Winter Perennials for Cold Climates

Leave these perennials standing for their enticing winter foliage and seedheads.

COMMON NAME (BOTANICAL NAME)	HARDINESS ZONES
Anise hyssop (*Agastache foeniculum*)	6–10
'Atropurpureum' sedum (*Sedum telephium* subsp. *maximum* 'Atropurpureum')	4–9
'Autumn Sun' rudbeckia (*Rudbeckia* 'Autumn Sun', also sold as 'Herbstsonne')	3–9
Big bluestem (*Andropogon gerardii*)	2–7
'Gateway' Joe-Pye weed (*Eupatorium fistulosum* 'Gateway')	3–8
Little bluestem (*Schizachyrium scoparium*)	5–9
Prairie cord grass (*Spartina pectinata*)	3–9
Russian sage (*Perovskia atriplicifolia*)	6–9
'Superbum' sea holly (*Eryngium alpinum* 'Superbum')	5–8
Western white false indigo (*Baptisia lactea*, also called *B. leucantha*)	4–8

Quiet-Season Color

If you want your garden to have a living presence even in the depths of winter, start by thinking in terms of expanding upon what is already there. What can you add that will decorate your winter garden with a captivating collection of colors, shapes, and textures? Perhaps the real beginning point lies deeper within your visual imagination. For many gardeners, the first step in discovering how to create off-season interest is to stop being obsessed with tidiness and to simply let the garden alone in fall. As you learn to admire the slumping grace of the autumn garden, plants arching elegantly earthward as they slide down fall's path to winter slumber, you'll start to appreciate the subdued delights of winter beauties.

This isn't just the lazy way to do things (though laissez-faire gardening clearly has its advantages over

This section of the garden looks great in winter as well as in summer (shown here). During the colder months, burgundy swords of New Zealand flax (*Phormium tenax* 'Atropurpureum') look great in winter, as do the white skeletal stems of Russian blue sage that remain after the blue flowers fade. Other winter players include ornamental grasses and spurges (*Euphorbia* spp.) and several shrubby hebes, rosemaries, and lavenders.

pouring hours of work into each bed in cold or wet fall weather). You can certainly tidy up anything that looks awful, but leave standing any plants that retain grace and dignity as they approach dormancy. When you leave the strongest and most structural perennials to face winter's wind and snow, you'll get to watch the same kind of transformation that turns meadow or prairie stubble into sculpture. Winter offers subtle beauties of line and form and gentle gradations of delicate color. Red berries, green conifers, satin gray bark, and bronze stems take on added importance when more colorful competition is lacking. You can appreciate the beauty of all the tones of brown (the most neglected of colors), from tints of toast and biscuit to dark chocolate and rich molasses.

There are many subtle sounds and forms to appreciate in the winter garden, too. Grasses whisper in every wind, and the hollow stems of the taller grasses clack softly. The architectural stems of coneflowers penetrate the blanket of snow, which also sets off the shapes and colors of false indigo and bush clover. Skeletal teasel, angular rattlesnake master, seed-studded cup plant, and plumed goldenrod cast long, purple shadows on the white ground. Burnished and bronzed seedheads of prairie grasses and perennials nourish birds in deep winter, when other food is scarce. The flutter of their search for food brings new liveliness to the quiet scene.

To learn which perennials will remain dramatic instead of disastrous in your winter garden, try leaving likely candidates untrimmed, then evaluating their response (as well as your own). Leggy asters, bushy Russian sages, agastaches, and late-blooming salvias are all good plants to experiment with when seeking interesting off-season performance. So, too, are the many border versions of those native coneflowers and rudbeckias, Joe-Pye weeds, and goldenrods.

Keep track of their performances in your garden journal so next year you will remember which plants turn sloppy and which look lastingly lovely. Visit the garden on frosty mornings to see how plants look when rimmed with silver and in the afternoons to see which plants are most popular with seed-seeking birds. Observe which plants provide shelter for small birds. Through this ongoing editing process, you create your own regionally appropriate palette of plants to keep the winter garden lively and attractive.

Cultivating Color in Mild Winter Areas

Wherever winters tend to be mild (USDA Hardiness Zones 8 to 10), it is much easier to assemble a plentiful palette of colorful winter performers. Structural evergreens and clustered islands of border shrubs, such as dwarf conifers and compact rhododendrons, create a supportive backdrop for companionable groups of winter bloomers like hellebores, snowdrops, and snow crocus. Given such good company, even subtle winter flowers can make a cheerful show of color against the quiet browns and grays of the slumbering beds.

In shady places, red wood spurge (*Euphorbia amygdaloides* 'Rubra', also sold as 'Purpurea') offers stiff stems ruffled with whorls of leaves in holiday reds and greens. Stinking hellebores (*Helleborus foetidus*)—which don't stink at all, by the way—produce clusters of icy green bell flowers above dramatic leaves that look like spoke wheels without rims. At their feet, spotted lungworts (*Pulmonaria* spp.) are lush with new foliage that may be not just spotted but also marbled, striped, or spattered with silver. Red-flowered *Pulmonaria* 'Christmas Cheer' may be joined by pink and blue cousins anytime after the New Year.

Some of winter's flowers are even fragrant. Those so-called stinking hellebores, for example, may have perfumed flowers ('Miss Jekyll' is one that does). Sweet violets may start to open in midwinter, including those like 'Blue Remington', a rebloomer that flowers both early and late in the year. Common primroses, which often begin to bloom around the winter solstice, have their own distinctive fragrance that smells like the breath of spring.

Winter Perennials for Mild Climates

Winter-blooming perennials are an integral part of the garden in mild-winter regions. Consider amplifying the winter interest in your existing beds and borders with some of these striking plants.

COMMON NAME (BOTANICAL NAME)	HARDINESS ZONES
Algerian iris (*Iris unguicularis*)	7–9
Christmas rose (*Helleborus niger*)	4–8
'Golden Sword' yucca (*Yucca filamentosa* 'Golden Sword')	5–10
Heartleaf bergenia (*Bergenia cordifolia*)	3–8
Japanese sedge (*Carex morrowii*)	5–9
New Zealand flax (*Phormium tenax*)	9–10
Primrose (*Primula* spp.)	4–8
'Variegata' stinking iris (*Iris foetidissima* 'Variegata')	6–9
Winter hellebore (*Helleborus atrorubens*)	5–9

Winter-Blooming Bulbs for Mild Climates

Given a favorable microclimate, these earliest-of-the-early bulbs may brighten the garden in midwinter. Most are summer dormant, so mark their resting places with small stones.

COMMON NAME (BOTANICAL NAME)	HARDINESS ZONES
Cyclamen daffodil (*Narcissus cyclaminius*)	5–7
Greek crocus (*Crocus sieberii*)	3–8
'Guinea Gold' winter aconite (*Eranthis* × *tubergenii* 'Guinea Gold')	4–9
'Pictum' Italian arum (*Arum italicum* 'Pictum')	6–9
Snowdrop (*Galanthus caucasicus*)	5–9
Tubergen squill (*Scilla mischtschenkoana*)	4–7
Winter crocus (*Crocus laevigatus*)	5–8
Winter cyclamen (*Cyclamen coum*)	5–9

Getting the Most from Seasonal Effects

The palette of fall foliage color in the Pacific Northwest runs from crimson red to striking chartreuse. As the season draws to a close, the ornamental drumstick onions (*Allium sphaerocephalum*) and the sedums are more skeletal. Barberries and vine maples flame in hot reds and oranges and are offset by blue-green spurges and hebes.

GERTRUDE JEKYLL, THE FAMOUS ENGLISH COLORIST AND designer (1843–1932), accurately observed that when you cluster plants that bloom at the same time you greatly increase their visual impact. This doesn't have to mean lumping all the spring bloomers in one corner and filling another area just with fall flowers, as is often done in those charming English models. If you have a huge garden, you can afford to create whole gardens for each season. If not, everything you grow must share ground. Still, sweeps and runs of seasonal bloom will always look most effective when they have ample backup. You should strive to arrange partnered plantings that bloom together, interwoven with supportive plantings that provide interesting form, handsome foliage, and attractive textures (as well as their own season of color earlier or later).

As many gardeners quickly discover, rigidly dividing plants into seasonal groups can give beds a gappy look, especially if the spring bloomers are types that go dormant in early summer. To avoid awkward blank spots, try to interweave seasonal clusters with each other rather than planting in discrete chunks. That way, the color does not seem to "clump" in one spot each month, but is instead constantly running through the entire planting.

This advice may seem contradictory. The secret is not to make solid blocks of seasonal plants, but instead

> ## The secret is not to make solid blocks of seasonal plants, but instead to arrange them in thinner, more sinuous ribbons that weave through the bed.

to arrange them in thinner, more sinuous ribbons that weave through the bed. Gertrude Jekyll felt that the most vital concern was to avoid having the fading flowers of early bloomers detract from the flower display of later bloomers. Jekyll experimented with several kinds of planting patterns, settling on the winding ribbon as the most practical and natural looking. When you use similar planting patterns today, you'll find—as she did—that healthy, productive neighboring plants help to disguise the passing of fading seasonal flowers.

For instance, you'll want to plant clusters of plants that are of most visual interest during the winter, such as dwarf conifers, hellebores, and evergreen groundcovers. In a larger bed, you might have several groups making islands of winter interest through the border, perhaps with a running theme. Each cluster may include the same groundcover, or each may feature evergreen ferns and hellebores (even if the forms and species are different). Winter plants are the most isolated visually, since many of the bed's summer inhabitants will be in dormancy. By creating unified islands or cluster plantings of evergreens, you can ensure that the winter performers will have the fullest possible impact.

In spring, rising perennials knit a garden together in greenery so that the earliest bloomers are less lonely looking. Even so, it remains far more effective to group early bloomers near each other than to dot them about

the border. Just as a generous clump of 10 daffodils will look more powerful than a wandering row of 10 singletons, clusters of similarly colored primroses will "read" better than the same number of plants scattered randomly about the bed. Clusters of primroses that surround clumps of bulbs and are flanked by emerging coral bells and grasses will look even more significant. To further emphasize these flowering clusters, back them with compact rhododendrons or deciduous shrubs that are attractive even when leafless.

To gain the most amplified impact from the autumn garden, group late bloomers so that they reinforce each other. Fall performers can look forlorn and unconnected if they are simply dotted aimlessly about the garden. Usually this happens because they are added in as afterthoughts, with no real plan for how they will relate to the rest of the garden. However, if you can remember to set late bloomers in clusters and ribbons, and if you position them where they are backed up by supportive companions (such as backdrop evergreens and those reliable rebloomers), they will immediately gain significant visual impact.

Perky and punctual, primroses are among the earliest risers in springtime, preferring cool, overcast climates. Primroses fold their leaves after flowering and all but disappear by July or August where summers are hot.

Fine-Tuning
the Flow of Color

When you decide how you want your color sequences to change with the seasons, you need to consider how the plants you're considering will behave, not in general, but in your own yard. Both the starting and ending of bloom time take on new importance. When the delicate pinks and yellows of spring refuse to give way to summer's smoldering purples and reds, the result can be dismaying. If just a few scattered blossoms are off-cycle, the scissors become the gardener's best friend. Persistent flowers can always be snipped for the table, but if the problem persists through several seasons, it's probably best to move the uncooperative plant to a less-obtrusive location. Your journal will be your best guide here. Although general gardening books can give you an idea of when each plant is likely to bloom, specifics like soil, light, plant maturity, and temperatures can and will affect flower timing from year to year as well as from place to place.

That's why the most effective way to keep track of each plant's schedule is to record annual performance in a garden notebook or journal. Journals that compare several years at a glance—3 or 5 years would do—are the most efficient. It isn't necessary to record every detail or every last blossom, but do make note of how all your visually important plants perform. In general, this means recording when the first flowers appeared and the last ones faded each year. (Tracking weather can also help; if you often get fall storms that knock down tall plants, you will be wise to seek out shorter ones.) Over time, patterns will emerge to help you fine-tune your floral color schemes.

Fine-tuning seasonal flow largely consists of choosing your peak periods. If you always spend the month of August at a vacation home, it makes little sense to stock the garden with flowers that appear in

The garden school's courtyard holds plants with interest in every season, including the lovely coral bell called 'Plum Pudding'. It's flanked by dark-leaved 'Johanna' azalea and our native bog rosemary, *Andromeda polifolia* 'Blue Ice'. The near-black groundcover is *Ajuga reptans* 'Catlin's Giant'.

August. If you adore spring and summer but haven't yet discovered the richness of fall, investigate the many early bloomers that also offer fall color. Also, try perennials such as 'Fireworks' goldenrod, pale yellow *Bidens heterophylla,* and boltonia (*Boltonia asteroides*), all of which have attractive spring foliage and then bloom hard from late summer into fall.

Several families of shrubs have many gorgeous members that can enrich your garden with color in exchange for very little care. For instance, the witch hazel family includes winter- and spring-bloomers that boast spectacular fall foliage color. In small gardens, blue-leaved *Fothergilla gardenii* 'Blue Mist' and fragrant 'Jane Platt' combine honey-scented spring flowers with flashy fall foliage. Where space permits, try sweet-scented *Hamamelis* × *intermedia* 'Pallida' or any of the colorful, hardy witch hazels, all of which become good-size shrubs (to 15 feet tall) in time.

Many other plant families make similar contributions. Consider, for instance, the sumacs, whose fall foliage looks like a fern in party clothing. Sumacs come in every size, from the sprawling fragrant sumac (*Rhus aromatica* 'Gro-low', 2 to 6 feet high) to lustrous shining sumac (*Rhus copallina,* 15 to 30 feet high). Smoke bushes (*Cotinus coggygria,* to 15 feet high) can bring purple, burgundy, or pinky green foliage into the garden from early spring on, followed by plumes of deliciously textured "smoke" from their fizzy flowers. Their fall color is extraordinary, particularly in 'Grace', a copper-bronze form with extra-large foliage and particularly long-lasting foliage color in autumn.

Spireas are similarly blessed, for all bloom in spring or summer in shades of pink and white. Spireas come in a large range of colors, from rusty red or cinnamon to bronze and copper and lemon or lime.

Sequencing the Year

WHEN YOU THINK OF THE CONCEPT OF LAYERING IN THE garden, the most familiar model to compare is a woodland. However, when you're working on creating a seasonal flow of color and interest, the natural ecosystems you may want to study are meadows and prairies. In prairies and meadows around the world, the first flowers appear while tufted grasses are still sound asleep and the crowns of summery perennials are barely showing signs of life. The same can be true in gardens where perennials mingle with ornamental grasses. Dormant grasses can be heavily underplanted with early perennials like lungworts (*Pulmonaria* spp.), which need some shade in summer. Speckle- and stripe-leaved lungwort cultivars are as popular as spotted forms, all of which are at their best in spring. Snugged beside midborder grasses, these sprawlers can be admired during their spring peak and then hidden by taller neighboring foliage as their own foliage declines in quality and mass.

In many parts of the country, native evergreen grasses provide visual continuity between the seasons. You can evoke these natural patterns in the garden by using tough grasses such as blue oat grass (*Helictotrichon sempervirens*) to anchor cluster plantings of early perennials and minor bulbs such as crocus and snowdrops. For long-season punch, pair steel blue oat grass with glossy 'Morning Red' bergenia, a sturdy evergreen perennial whose red-veined, plum-purple flowers appear in early spring above rounded, leathery leaves that remain stained with ruddy winter color until early summer comes to pass.

Late-rising perennials like peonies and Russian sage can be similarly partnered with early flowers. Creeping phlox (*Phlox subulata*) spreads in fragrant pools in spring, encircling silvery sage stems with blue, pink, or white blossoms. Similarly, primroses in deep colors will emphasize the dark wine stems and coppery new leaves of emerging peonies. Early perennials like leopard's bane (*Doronicum* spp.) partner well with tulips and narcissus, joining them in flower, then hiding neighboring browning bulb foliage with their own expanding leaves. Lenten roses (*Helleborus orientalis*) are meadow dwellers that flower in splendor when their companions are dormant, then are swallowed up by maturing foliage that provides needed summer shade. In gardens, hellebores do best in partnerships that provide spring sun and summer shade, and their lustrous foliage remains attractive year-round in mild climates.

In prairies and meadows around the world, the first flowers appear while tufted grasses are still sound asleep and the crowns of summery perennials are barely showing signs of life.

Plant culver's root (*Veronicastrum virginicum*) wherever you need a strong vertical accent, such as at the back of a flower border. Trim fading flower spikes to keep the plant blooming longer.

Early-Summer Splendors

In early summer, prairie plants edge past knee height and lush grasses hide the drying leaves of the earliest flowers. In your garden, the same sort of sequencing can occur. Fading first flowers are masked by summer bloomers already fluffing out wide skirts spangled with buds. When you create layered or sandwich plantings of perennials, a look at a prairie or meadow model will suggest that combinations of clump-formers and moderate runners work well.

For instance, heucheras like wine-leaved 'Plum Pudding' shrink to small crowns in autumn, then expand rapidly and burst on the scene in early summer. They pair effectively with early-flowering carpeters such as *Veronica peduncularis* 'Georgia Blue', a fine-textured sprawler that reblooms in fall, taking on hot foliage tints, as well. By May or June, foliage perennials such as bold rodgersias, rounded hostas, and lady's mantle come into their own, ably assisted by ligularias and ornamental rhubarbs whose huge, bold leaves are as impressive as their fluffy flower plumes.

All have relatively small resting crowns that enlarge dramatically by midsummer. Their early-performing partners must prefer summer shade and drought or retreat into dormancy early. Shady woodlands provide plenty of possibilities, from bluebells and anemones to violets. Larger plants can also overlap if their cycles are compatible. Summer-blooming

baby's-breath sets off jagged-leaved oriental poppies to perfection when the huge blooms open in late spring, then the foamy clouds of baby's-breath blossoms hide the wreckage of the poppy foliage once their fabulous flowers are gone. (I used to be convinced my cats were doing this damage, but I've come to discover that spectacular decay is simply part of the poppy life cycle.) Cut back crashing poppy foliage and the plants will re-leaf neatly, looking tidy well into fall.

High-Summer Showboats

High summer is peak bloom time on the tall prairie, where both grasses and perennials are now head high. Hot pinky-purple wands of brilliant Kansas gayfeather (*Liatris pycnostachya*) sizzle in the sun. Rattlesnake master (*Eryngium yuccifolium*) tips its sheaves of stiff, yuccalike leaves with dramatic candelabra stems that end in explosions of spiky, silver-green globes. Stately culver's root (*Veronicastrum virginicum*) sends its slim white spires skyward with architectural dignity.

Summer is also a delightful time in the garden, where a host of happy plants are flowering generously. Showy sunflowers vie with gold tickseeds, vivid blanketflowers, and daisies of every description. Be careful: It's easy to overfill the garden with summer bloomers, leaving few spots for early and late bloomers. To make room for plants for other seasons, remove any slackers (plants that don't produce well enough or long enough) and discard sulky plants that simply don't enjoy living in your garden. Trade your rejects for something you don't already have, or give them to friends whose conditions might coax a better performance from the underachievers. You can also divide overly enthusiastic plants, reducing them by half, which gives you more room for new plants. If English border beauties don't enjoy your climate, replace the unsatisfying performers with some of those reliable prairie dazzlers and let them carry on into fall.

Autumn Lingerers

As autumn chases late summer away, the still-warm days and cooling nights bring out fabulous fall flames in many kinds of foliage. Certain perennials are quick to join the blaze, such as blue star and balloon flowers, both of which turn to shimmering gold. Fall also brings the burnish of brass and bronze to meadow and prairie, where the ripe grasses are streaked with hot sunset colors and heavy with seedheads. Showy goldenrod burns sun yellow against the blue autumn sky. The silphiums—compass plant, prairie dock, and cup plant—soar 8 to 10 feet tall, their spangled seedheads thronged with goldfinches. Native asters haze the prairie with smoky blue and slumberous purple. Though rough and weedy in the wild, many of these perennials make magnificent garden plants.

You can achieve similarly stunning effects by incorporating plenty of ornamental grasses into borders bright with fall flowers. Native little bluestem's gilded sheaves ripen to a smoldering copper red, while selections of switch grass such as 'Heavy Metal' and 'Cloud Nine' shimmer like spun gold. Combine them with broader-bladed maiden grasses such as 'Morning Light' or zebra-striped 'Strictus', as well as daintier dwarf clumpers like feather grass (*Stipa tenuissima*) and Japanese blood grass (*Imperata cylindrica* 'Red Baron').

Shady gardens can be as full of flowers in fall as in spring when you choose the right plants. Autumn snakeroot spills honeyed scent from slim white bottlebrush flowers. (Our native ones smell a lot less enchanting, but they still look lovely.) Cheerful pink bells of bell-flowered knotweed (*Persicaria campanulata*) still ring out gaily, even in deep shade. Rosy or creamy, Japanese anemones bloom long and hard in dappled light. Arching wands of Asian toad lilies gleam with

Swaying in the lightest wind, the lush greenery of feather grass (*Stipa tenuissima*) changes to a flowing mane of blonde when autumn arrives in the garden. Many garden grasses can be planted solo or in large drifts and can provide excellent erosion control for slopes.

dainty little flowers that stud the stems like so many orchids. Stippled and speckled, freckled and spotted, the little flowers reward the gardener who takes time for closer inspection. Obedient plant (*Physostegia virginiana* 'Variegata') thrives in light shade, where ivory-striped leaves turn the same raspberry as the second flush of flower spikes that often appears in fall.

Winter Wonders

In mild winter areas, a well-chosen array of perennials will keep the color coming right through the winter. The glossy, rounded foliage of bergenias such as 'Redstart' heart-leaf bergenia (*Bergenia cordifolia* 'Redstart') and 'Winter Glow' bergenia (*B.* 'Winter Glow') turn sumptuous shades of ruby and garnet in winter, setting off their own stubby spikes of pink or red flowers. Myrtle spurge (*Euphorbia myrsinites*) tips its lax, blue-scaled arms with lime-color flowerheads in sunny spots, while taller evergreen spurges pop open balloonlike flowers in lemon and chartreuse. Set amid a flurry of evergreen candytuft and rock cress, the effect is charmingly gay all winter long.

Evergreen perennials, including grasses, usually need a light autumn grooming to remain lovely all winter. Don't trim them too hard—most grasses survive winter best when they get their main haircuts in early spring, rather than in fall or winter. Not only are they less likely to be harmed by winter wet or frost, but uncut grasses provide lovely movement, sound, and gentle color even in the depths of winter. With a bit of help, shimmering half-globes of steel blue oat grass, tall maiden and fountain grasses, and tufted blue Lyme grasses can stay on duty indefinitely. Interplant these stalwarts loosely with silvery artemisias, woolly verbascums, and carpeting fleeceflowers, leaving space for early bulbs and summer perennials whose remains can be tidied away as they go dormant.

Where winters are warm, strong winter shapes come from strapping, swordlike New Zealand flax, which has both upright and weeping or cascading forms in a wide range of colors. In colder climes, similarly spiky yuccas can rise dramatically above carpets of evergreen herbs and winter flowers. For visual continuity, encircle these winter performers with easygoing evergreen carpeters, such as speedwells, that can gently fill in gaps where summer plants are slumbering but won't mind being overshadowed later. Masses of minor bulbs such as snow crocus can also be laced through perennial borders without harm to either partner.

Parting Thoughts

You may not be able to take advantage of all the plants and combinations I've described in this book, but by experimenting with various combinations of those that are hardy in your zone, you will discover pleasing partnerships that can fit in with what you already have, expanding the depth and richness of the garden all year-round. Remember that the way to begin is by seeking out adaptable plants that perform early and late in your region. Some of the best advice I can give you is to go plant shopping every month that gardening is practical. Off-season shopping encourages nurseries to stock less-common plants, which in turn encourages us to try them out. Soon, this pleasant circle of reinforcement will result in colorful plantings that will delight your senses throughout much or all of the gardening year.

Care and Feeding of Your Garden

Choosing the plants that will grow best for you depends in good part on where you live, because each region of the country has a distinct climate, and soil and water types vary greatly. If you've done your homework, you will be designing your garden around plants that are well adapted to the **climate and conditions** you can offer them.

By now, you've spent time exploring and learning about your own garden, and you've spent time looking at the bigger regional picture. You've noticed that every garden has its own micro-climates—**pockets of warmth or cold**, sites that are usually wet or very dry, and areas that are windy or protected. You've figured out that **taking time to discover these spots** will help you place your plants well, each according to its particular requirements.

All of these discoveries add up to what I call **guilt-free gardening**. The idea behind guilt-free gardening is that happy plants make happy gardeners. If you give plants what they need and put them where they want to be, they will respond by growing well independently. The goal is to make **healthy gardens** that thrive with the exact amount of time and attention that you have to give. At its heart, this is about sitting happily on the garden bench instead of leaping up to deal with some neglected chore that calls you accusingly whenever you try to **relax in the garden.**

However, no matter how well you've done your homework and how precise your plant and site pairings are, this does not mean that you can simply plunk your plants in place and walk away. Though many gardeners spend a lot of time worrying about how to feed plants, you are better off feeding the soil and letting the plants feed themselves. **Make great garden soil** and you will have happy, healthy plants (as long as you have made appropriate choices as to what to plant). So much confusing advice comes from all sides, especially in the aisles of garden stores. It helps to notice that a great deal of that advice is about things you should buy in order to have a great garden. Luckily, **the truth is a lot less expensive** than product marketers would have you believe.

What Plants Need

FEEDING PLANTS IS GREATLY SIMPLIFIED WHEN YOU understand what plants actually need. The secret to having a lush, abundant garden in short order is to concentrate on getting great root growth from your plants. No matter what you are growing, your plants will be most vigorous when they have the benefit of the best possible root system. Well-rooted plants can take all kinds of environmental stresses in stride, from drought and stormy weather to pests and diseases.

By contrast, overfed plants with lush topgrowth and shallow roots tend to succumb to everything that comes along. They collapse in rain storms (even light ones!), fall prey to powdery mildew, or get picked on by aphids and leafhoppers. Plants without strong roots are always vulnerable. In fact, when you notice that one plant in a group is suffering, chances are excellent that if you investigate, you'll find it has some kind of root damage.

One of the best ways to tell if your soil is healthy is to look at the roots of your plants and weeds. If roots seem vigorous and well-branched and have many tiny root hairs, your soil is friable enough to give the roots room to grow. Roots that are stunted, twisted, sideways, or that have few root hairs are good indicators of unhealthy or compacted soil.

You can promote balanced growth and terrific roots by offering your perennials proper nutrition. Though plant nutrition is fairly complex, the most basic building blocks are nitrogen (represented by N on fertilizer labels), phosphorus (P), and potassium (K). One Master Gardener I know uses the famous poster image of John Travolta dancing in *Saturday Night Fever* to help people understand the role of these key nutrients: The finger pointing up to the sky stands for nitrogen, the force that helps plants grow up. The finger pointing down to the earth stands for potassium, which encourages sturdy root growth. The bent knee that moves round and round stands for phosphorus, the energy exchanger that circulates nutrients throughout the plant.

In somewhat more scientific terms, these essential soil elements can be thought of as the equivalent of proteins, fats, and carbohydrates for plants. Trace elements act like vitamin and mineral supplements, assisting in the construction of healthy plant tissue. Nitrogen promotes leafy growth and combines with trace elements to build the proteins in green plants. Phosphorus controls the transfer energy (plant sugars) and other nutrients between cells, and encourages flower production. Potassium strengthens roots and assists in flower production. Calcium and several other important minerals aid in root growth as well. A balanced blend of all these elements will meet the nutritional needs of a large majority of plants.

Amendments

Organic fertilizers such as lime, alfalfa meal, and soy meal release their nutrients slowly, providing a steady supply of healthy "food" for your garden plants.

IN GENERAL, IT'S WISE TO GROW PLANTS THAT ENJOY THE conditions your garden offers. Most perennials tolerate a wide range of soil types but do best in soils that are close to neutral in pH. Adding plenty of humus (compost) will neutralize pH somewhat and boost root growth as well. Though it's impossible to change the nature of the whole garden, you can alter pH in a small area for special plants.

Before you try to make any corrections, however, it's important to have a soil test taken. Adding more of something that you don't really need can be as bad as not having it there in the first place. Your local extension office can help you obtain a soil test, but they may not necessarily recommend organic fertilizers. Here are a few ways to modify soils organically: To sweeten acid soils, add agricultural lime (not the slaked lime used in outhouses) according to the recommendations on your soil test. Alkaline soils can be brought closer to neutral by mulching with pine needles (which are very acidic). Lean soils can be enriched with soy meal or alfalfa meal for a slowly released source of nitrogen. Horticultural grit or coarse builder's sand will improve drainage slightly, but can create sinkholes. (Making raised beds is still your best bet for improving drainage.)

Commercial fertilizers attempt to correct soil imbalances by increasing nitrogen, phosphorus, and potassium in varying amounts. However, no matter what kind of soil you start out with, the single most important soil amendment you can add is nearly always humus. In simple terms, humus is organic material that has begun to decompose—in other words, it's dead plants. Its role in soil building is a big one, because humus is what makes all kinds of minerals and nutrients available to plant roots, in part by buffering high or low soil pH.

Acid or alkaline soils can lock up important nutrients that bind chemically with several common minerals and become inaccessible to feeder roots even though they remain present in the soil. Humus and compost are generally pH neutral. Both unbind trapped nutrients and facilitate their transfer to plant roots far more effectively than chemical fertilizers do. Humus-builders like compost alter soil texture, opening tight soils and making sandy ones more retentive. Soils are said to be tight when they are compacted, low in oxygen, and offer only a reduced exchange of air and gasses. Retentive soils are those that hold water and soil nutrients for a long time, as opposed to sandy soils, which allow water and nutrients to flush away quickly. The best way to improve heavy or sandy soils on a regular basis is to apply feeding mulches twice a year.

Feeding mulches are light layers of soil amendments that may be scattered evenly over beds and borders or used to spot-feed specific plants. The simplest feeding mulch is a blanket of compost. More complex feeding mulches might include compost, aged manures, and soy meals or alfalfa pellets for a quick nutritional boost, followed by a slower release of longer-lasting nutrients. Mulches of many kinds (including several useful feeding mulch recipes) are described in "The Art of Mulching" on page 202.

When you think about feeding plants, you need to start by improving soil. The frequent addition of compost increases soil tilth and improves its texture dramatically. When farmers talk about the tilth of their soil, they are referring to its texture and structure, or what soil scientists call its "state of aggregation." Healthy soil has a crumbly texture that neither clumps solidly nor sifts away between your fingers. Healthier soil means better soil texture or tilth, and it means better root growth, resulting in sturdier, healthier plants. For all these reasons, organic ornamental gardens are largely fed with soil amendments such as compost, rather than with concentrated dollops of chemical fertilizers.

Caring for Garden Plants

ONCE YOU GET YOUR GARDENS TOGETHER, YOU NEED TO figure out how to keep them growing well. By basing our plantings on models like layered beds and mixed borders, you can greatly reduce the amount of time and energy that you devote to garden maintenance. As plants grow to maturity, they need only a few minutes of care each year and eventually may not ask for anything but admiration from you. Remember that the installation of the garden is by far the most difficult and time-consuming part.

As your plantings mature and the layers knit together, the living tapestry becomes a balanced, self-mulching community. If you have done your homework well, the garden will grow up to be a source of more pleasure than guilt. Congratulations! If you have gotten this far into the process, you are well on your way to delight.

Caring for Trees and Shrubs

Here's the good news: Well-chosen, well-placed, and well-planted trees and shrubs need very little ongoing maintenance. To keep trees and shrubs happy, apply a light (2- to 3-inch) feeding mulch in late winter and again in fall, spreading compost from the main trunk to the dripline. All trees and shrubs will also need to be watered regularly for at least the first full year after planting.

In hot weather, trees and shrubs may need supplemental water once or twice a week. If dry autumns are the norm, continue watering until the first hard frost. Plants that go into winter with dry roots are more prone to frost damage than those with properly watered roots. During their second season, it's wise to keep watering young plants during any prolonged dry or warm spells. After that, established woody plants that are well suited to your climate ought to be as self-sufficient (in terms of water) as your natives are.

As trees and shrubs grow and expand over the years, it may become necessary to edit their size and shape a bit to help them continue to fit well in your gardenscape. As a rule of thumb, no pruning session should remove more than 25 percent of a tree or shrub. Dead wood does not count, of course, but even damaged wood that is clearly past recovery counts to the tree, which may have only recently lost this nutritional resource. Healthy wood should be taken off

respectfully and only after spending some time considering alternative approaches. It's also a good idea to consider what the tree is actually supposed to look like in its natural state. It's definitely best to spread extensive pruning jobs over several years.

When it becomes clear that your woody plants are thriving, you may need to do some editing to give them more room. Often, removing a few lower branches to elevate the canopy of a tree will leave plenty of room for enlarging shrubby neighbors. If branch removal isn't practical, you may want to consider reducing the size of the shrubs. One way to decrease the overall size of a shrub is shovel pruning. Use a shovel to cut away part of the plant at the roots.

Feeding and Watering Natives

Like trees and shrubs, native plants tend to be quite self-sufficient once their basic needs are met. Woody natives should be treated exactly like any tree or shrub for the first season or two. Once established, they will probably need only occasional light pruning to remove damaged limbs or to edit exuberant growth. Where native soils are as good as garden soils, you will not need to amend soil or fertilize natives at all. Where native soils are very lean, it is often helpful to amend the initial planting hole with compost, even for native plants.

It's important to water newly planted natives exactly as you would exotics. Even drought-tolerant plants will need help to get established. If you live in an area where autumn is rainy, you may be able to establish plants in early fall and reduce the need to supplement their water supply. Otherwise, keep them adequately watered until they have a full year of new growth behind them; then you can safely leave them on their own. Again, if you get very hot or dry spells during the second year after planting, it's wiser to water than to wait and see if the youngsters are going to make it alone.

It's also a good idea to mulch every plant, native or not, during its period of establishment. Keeping a young plant mulched for a few years can make a big difference in its growth rate and habit. For a small investment of time and energy, you end up with a larger, healthier, and better-looking plant. Once natives are well established, there is no need to provide mulch, but if you are mingling natives and exotics, mulching the whole planting once a year is certainly not going to harm your plants at all.

Caring for Compact Border Shrubs

Many compact border shrubs will thrive on benign neglect, needing only a few minutes of attention each year to keep them tidy and healthy. Border shrubs in this category include broad-leaved evergreens such as Japanese pieris (*Pieris japonica*), sheep laurel (*Kalmia angustifolia*), and border rhododendrons. It also

At the Sequoia Center, we protect our lovely sequoia trees by using gravel paths as French drains to keep excess water away from the trees' sensitive roots. Do your research before you water in hot weather—summer watering can weaken plants that hail from dry summer regions.

Evergreen shrubs provide safe winter shelter for many birds that don't migrate south for the season. Viewed from a window, the bright dash of a cardinal's color against the warmth of a golden shrub offers a fleeting respite from a bitterly cold, snowy day.

includes deciduous shrubs like fothergilla, star magnolia, and the smaller Japanese maples. These are what I call "character shrubs," plants with a definite shape of their own. All have a strong internal branching pattern with one or more main trunks. These plants should never be sheared or shaped, except with thoughtful attention to the plant's true nature. In terms of nutrition, most shrubs grow best in decent, well-drained soil without commercial fertilizers. An annual feeding mulch (see page 209) in spring and a comforting layer of compost in fall will amply provide for their nutritional needs.

Shrubs' needs for water vary, and as always, you need to consider which plants prefer damp shade or full sun and dry soil before placing them in the garden. Even when you offer shrubs conditions they like, you will need to water them well for their first full year and water them as needed for another year or so before they become independent. Some shrubs, such as hydrangeas, will flag sadly in dry years, even in good soil and well-mulched beds. It's worth clustering thirsty shrubs in the garden and winding a soaker hose around their feet.

Some root-hardy border shrubs may die back to the ground in cold winters, but will reappear in spring. The fluffy pink *Ceanothus* 'Marie Simon' is typical of this group. Shrubs like potentillas and spireas that have a natural bun or blob shape fall into this category as well, since they can be restoratively whacked or sheared as needed and will recover quickly and nicely. For instance, when you want to tidy up the masses of old blossoms on small spireas, you can simply grab handfuls of twigs and clip the ends, or you can shear the shrub back by a third all over.

It's best to do this remedial trimming in late winter or early spring, rather than in fall. The extra topgrowth provides protection from frost damage, and the seedheads will attract goldfinches, chickadees, and other small seed-eating birds. A few broad-leaved evergreens benefit from pruning, and certain daphnes, various leucothoes, and salal (*Gaultheria shallon*) are all amenable to regular clipping, though they may become unnaturally congested if overly controlled.

Larger cane-throwing shrubs include arctic willow, forsythia, quince, and lilac. All of these can be whacked to the ground, if need be, to restore their natural shape. When the roots resprout, selectively choose as many as you think right (you may want 3 or 5 trunks on a lilac, and as many as 20 or so on a large old forsythia). Thin all other shoots, allowing only the chosen to mature.

This practice can be stressful for the plant, however. Even easygoing shrubs like willows and twiggy dogwoods will weaken over time when they are cut back too hard and too often. As a rule of thumb, you can remove up to a third of the oldest, brown stems each year. This will keep a steady supply of juvenile stems coming without harming the plant's health.

Pleasing Perennials

Perennials can be a big problem for the gardener who wants to enjoy flowers, not be in servitude to them. It's quite easy to please plants that are carefully chosen, well placed, and properly planted. When their essential needs are met, a great majority of garden plants grow lustily in return for very little care. Like trees and shrubs, recently planted perennials must be watered regularly during their entire first season. Most natives and many adaptive perennials are quite drought tolerant, once they get their roots deep into the ground. Again, a generous layer of mulch will help to conserve water and repress weeds.

In the long run, all plants grow best with a steady but slowly released supply of nutrients. Newly acquired plants that were nursery-raised on liquid fertilizers may falter when put into the ground, even when the soil is prepared properly. To keep these spoiled beauties growing well, give them a boost of compost tea (see page 226) each month during their first season, spraying both their root zone and the plant itself (as a foliar, or leaf, feed). Most will gain back their lost looks in a few days. Once established, most plants will be satisfied with a biannual feeding mulch.

Border Bulb Care

Garden bulbs fall into two categories—showboats and specialty bulbs. The showboats include buxom border tulips, which can prove to be expensive annuals. These bold beauties are usually force-fed in the fields so they unfailingly produce gorgeous bloom the first year. After that, however, they usually dwindle or vanish altogether. Big bulbs are prima donnas. To please them, you need to provide dedicated space that is only shared by non-needy, shallow-rooted plants such as forget-me-nots and sweet alyssum. Most of these big bulbs are intolerant of poor drainage, which encourages root rots and fungal disorders. To avoid such problems, plant them in well-drained soil in full sun, except in warmer zones like 7 or 8, where the bulbs should be planted in partial shade to keep them from getting scorched. Keep them as dry as possible during dormancy.

One of the best ways to encourage bloom in big bulbs is to offer a feeding mulch of compost and alfalfa pellets in the fall or very early spring. And if you want good bloom on big bulbs, by all means do not remove, braid, twist, or otherwise disfigure the fading foliage. To make it less noticeable, screen the browning bulb foliage with taller, early-rising perennials. You can also tuck yellowing leaves under mulch, where it can wither away in peace.

Specialty (or minor) bulbs are much easier to please. This clan includes crocus, scilla, reticulated iris, snowdrops, and most alliums, among others. Smaller bulbs are apt to naturalize instead of vanish, and many persist in old gardens for generations. Most specialty bulbs are quite independent, needing only decent soil and drainage to grow happily. Their nutritional needs are modest, so a topdressing of compost in fall is sufficient for their needs. Unlike big bulbs, most minor bulbs aren't fussy about dormancy conditions. They do best when allowed to dry out fully in summer, but most will reappear faithfully even in less-than-ideal circumstances.

Garden Grooming

Remove flowers as they fade to keep the garden tidy. For most blooms, just pinch back spent flower stems to the next set of leaves. Late-blooming leggy perennials can also benefit from being pinched back. In late spring, pinch off the plant's growing tips, and you'll be rewarded with a fuller mound of flower stems.

GROOMING CAN SEEM LIKE A CONSTANT CHORE (AND indeed it is), but it's also a delightful way to stay in close connection with your plants. The very dailiness of it is what makes it a refreshment to the spirit, as well as to the plants. As you pass through beds and borders looking for limp leaves and browning flowers, notice the fresh buds and peak blooms that might otherwise flower unseen. What's more, the more often you do this simple chore, the less there is to do. A little goes a long way, and a little is just fine. In the garden, prissy perfectionism may be the only deadly sin. As long as the garden looks tidy, there's no need to overdo things.

I once visited a charming city garden in April, when pale pink cherry blossoms spilled like fragrant snow over a handsome flagged courtyard. When I admired the effect, the gardener laughed, saying, "Yes, I love it too. All last week, I kept trying to show my partner, and every time I came back outside, the petals were gone. Finally I realized that he was cleaning them up with the Dustbuster. To him, they just looked messy."

Garden grooming is not about making the outdoors immaculate. It's about removing flowers and foliage that are past their prime in order to keep plants healthy and the garden looking pleasantly kempt. Grooming also has a productive side. From early summer onward, frequent deadheading (removal of spent blossoms) stimulates prolonged and repeated bloom in many perennials. Deadheading does not mean that you remove only the actual flower, leaving a long, bare stem sticking up. Unless plant form dictates otherwise, spent flower stems are cut back to the next set of leaves, where fresh side shoots and new buds are often lurking.

As autumn draws near, the need for grooming increases. Sloppy floppers (such as daylilies) must be trimmed back before they do damage or begin to rot. Remember, though, to leave in place any plants that promise to hold their own all winter. Some will remain upright and sculptural well into winter, and unfortunately, some won't. It's also important to remember that brown can be beautiful. If you remove every leaf the moment it fades, the garden will soon look threadbare and scrawny instead of mature and full.

When you allow plants to relax into dormancy, and when you choose plants that retreat into dormancy with grace and dignity, the retreating scene in autumn can be almost as lovely as the fullness of summer. When you go to all the trouble of arranging masses of fall color in leaf and flower, it's silly to overgroom their surroundings and make the late bloomers look lonely. Only remove plants that look dreadful and harm others, and leave the rest to melt slowly into the earth or stand tall in the snow.

Grooming the Garden

While you groom, keep your eyes open for problems as well as pretty flowers. Be observant when you work your way through the beds. When problems are spotted early on, it's usually quite easy to resolve them. Watch for telltale symptoms of ill health, such as yellowing or browning foliage, stunted growth, and buds that rot before they can open. Any or all of these conditions may

> When you allow plants to relax into dormancy, and when you choose plants that retreat into dormancy with grace and dignity, the retreating scene in autumn can be almost as lovely as the fullness of summer.

signal root growth problems, poor drainage, compacted soil, overcrowding, or poor planting techniques. If so, the problem will be corrected by altering the improper condition. If not, seriously diseased plants should be discarded or burned (never put them on the compost heap, where they may spread trouble).

If you find puckering foliage, the problem may be sucking insects such as leafhoppers. Sticky leaves often indicate the presence of aphids, while tiny webs are made by spider mites. If caught early on, most insect damage can be controlled with a quick rinse from the hose or a dose of insecticidal soap.

If serious or ongoing problems develop, you may want to dig up the suffering plant and check the roots. Because of the history of root rots in the Northwest, I'm accustomed to checking roots any time I find an unhealthy plant. If one plant is suffering while others are thriving, the culprit is often root damage, such as poor drainage or mechanical damage (for instance, perennial roots that may have been cut or injured during a bulb-planting session). You may be fooled at first, though, by a problem that looks like insect damage. What you should remember is that problems underground may

send invisible distress signals to potential attackers like aphids, who then go in for the kill.

Editing is also a constant job. Even when you make informed and selective choices, the specifics of each site will dictate how plants behave. Be prepared for some surprises—both positive and negative. No matter how well you do your homework, even well-known plants can behave differently in a new setting. Keep an eye on your careful plant combinations, as well. In time, crowding can cause a loss of balance as your plants alter with age.

When eager plants outgrow their allotted spaces before their companions can catch up, shovel pruning will restore the original relationship. Another part of editing is watchful intervention. Plants staked early won't flop and grow deformed. If pinched back in early summer, leggy perennials like asters and 'Autumn Joy' sedum will make bushier, more floriferous plants that don't need staking.

Many common problems can be avoided by thoughtful selectivity at the nursery. When you lose your heart to pretty plants that don't behave well, you need to override sentiment and start assessing plants with clear eyes. Remove slackers that fail to perform and don't respond to feeding or extra care. Also, get rid of plants that do all too well, lest they overrun choicer companions. And be judicious when replacing poor choices—it's silly to replace one problem with another.

With all that said, please don't hesitate to take a few risks and try new things that intrigue you, even if you suspect they won't really work out. Nothing says we *must* succeed equally at everything, that all plants must perform at 100 percent, and that there is no room for imperfection of any kind. Such a garden would hardly be welcoming to humans—who among us could measure up? Gardening is an art rather than a hard science. There are many ways to be right, and the best way to learn is by making mistakes. The best gardeners I know are playful, inventive, and flexible, allowing their plants to drive the design of the garden. Make a point of growing something new each year, and your garden will stretch and grow along with you. As you gain confidence and skills, your garden will gain the depth and polish that turns natural beauty into true art.

Staking Perennials

When selecting perennials, it's a good idea to give preference to sturdy, self-supporting plants. If you're a sucker for big beauties, it's also smart to learn how and when to stake perennials. (Hint: Do it in early spring, long before the need is obvious). Even in the best of circumstances, certain plants will need some unobtrusive assistance to remain upright all season. Where summer rains are heavy or violent, staking will prevent or minimize the collapse of your prized delphiniums. In exposed, windswept gardens, quite a few of the taller perennials will look better for a longer period if they are staked early and well.

Fortunately, inventive gardeners have come up with dozens of methods for keeping plants standing. Many gardeners cheerfully make do with cat's-cradle webs of sticks and string, but it is now possible to buy a wide range of attractive and sturdy supports that look—let's be frank—more elegant. If the bulk of your plants are naturally upright and strong stemmed, you don't really need to invest in expensive hoops and linking systems. In my own garden, I have eliminated most of the weak-spined plants that can't make it on

their own, yet there are always a few youngsters or unfortunates that need some help. I keep bundles of slim bamboo on hand, along with soft, natural-fiber twine in dull shades of brown and green. These materials merge almost seamlessly into the vegetation, and by midsummer, it's very hard to find them even when you know where they are.

Staking with Sticks

Many of the plants you enjoy may need staking, so it's important to learn how to keep them vertical. No matter which method you prefer, the goal is always the same—to design effective, but nearly invisible support systems. Long-stemmed plants such as oriental lilies and delphiniums will need a single stake for every bloom-bearing stem. These stakes need to be fairly hefty if they are to perform in wind and rain. They also need to be a lot longer than you may think. Unless the aboveground portion of the stakes is almost as tall as the main stems will be, wind can snap off the tops of your precious plants in a heartbeat.

When you set your stakes, place them at least 6 inches away from plant crowns, to avoid damaging roots. To make sure tall stakes remain sturdy, push them at least a foot into the ground (use a rubber mallet to pound them in well). For stakes that are holding up plants that are 5 to 6 feet tall, a depth of 18 inches is even better. Secure the lengthening stems to the stakes as they grow, tying in every 12 to 18 inches of new growth. Soft ties of cloth or stretchy tape are better than sharp-edged plastic, which can cut stems in windy weather. My favorite bamboo wands are sturdy and inconspicuous, but last only a few seasons. If you have loose, deep soil, try using slender lengths of steel rebar, which comes in several weights and widths. The original silvery color soon discolors to a dappled, rusty brown that fades almost invisibly into the garden foliage. (Always remember to be careful when bending over to garden around stakes.)

Rebar makes splendid plant supports, especially when swirled into elegant shapes with a pipe bender. These supports can be used as decorative garden objects when not serving the needs of a particular plant. Rebar wands look especially interesting in winter, when the warm, rusty red shines against the snowy ground and the swirling shapes suggest limbs of corkscrew willow or contorted hazel.

Supportive Systems

Mounding plants such as 'Crater Lake' veronica, big double peonies, and oriental poppies often flop open at the heart by midsummer, especially during a wet, rainy year. Peony cages, short-legged border hoops, or half-domes of chicken wire (placed when the first shoots emerge in early spring) will all keep floppy plants from tumbling over their neighbors. Taller tomato cages (those with four tiers) will lend terrific support to tall asters, swaying verbascums, and similar plants that will look awkward and stiff if strapped to straight stakes. You can weave leafy, stems of vines or weeping willow along the glinting metal of cages and other metal hoop systems to disguise the metal in your garden. The green foliage of vines or willow quickly turn a soft brown that melts imperceptibly into the background.

A swirl of bent rebar or a short row of linked stakes will keep tall, arching plants like 'Fireworks' goldenrod and 'Lucifer' crocosmia in line. Shorter plants, such as 'Whirling Butterflies' gaura, can be given a supportive girdle of what English gardeners call pea sticks. Pea sticks are stout, twiggy branches (fruit trees, maples, hazel, or alder wood all make particularly sturdy supports) that are set firmly into the ground near the crown of floppy perennials.

If all else fails, don't forget good old string. When unstaked plants start to slump over their neighbors, weave a strong web with sticks and string, securing the string to slim bamboo wands (some jobs take quite a few). To turn an oversight into a valuable lesson, make a note in your garden journal so you'll remember to stake that plant properly and on-time next spring.

Water-Saving Gardens

DESPITE THE FACT THAT I LIVE WHERE SUMMER RAINS are rare, my gardens seldom need supplemental water. Why don't they need it? Because I plan them that way. As you have seen in previous chapters, you can plan and plant your gardens to make them less needy and more resilient. In many communities these days, water is becoming expensive, and it may be in short supply during hot summer months when use is high. But the good news is that these days, we have better ways to manage watering.

For instance, drip irrigation, once strictly the province of nerdy engineer types, has been simplified to the point where low-tech types like me can master it. Drip irrigation systems feature a main hose with emitters at set intervals that let water drip out at a steady pace. These systems are perfect for watering closely spaced plants. Cover the hoses with mulch to slow evaporation for an even more efficient watering setup.

Soaker hoses are less expensive than drip irrigation systems and can work for gardeners with any size garden. They are a good choice if you're planning to water beds and borders. Soaker hoses are perforated rubber tubes that leak water gently into the soil; they work by capillary action, spreading water through the gaps in the soil. They are most efficient when covered with 4 to 6 inches of soil or mulch, and they're least efficient when draped casually over the surface of the soil. Made from recycled tires, these inexpensive hoses are extremely easy to repair and sturdy enough to last for years. In my garden, these hoses are mainly used

for permanent plantings of shrubs and trees; they also provide the necessary water to help new plantings get through their first summer. After that, most of the plants will get by nicely on their own, and the hidden hose will be capped off until needed (such as when a really hot spell arrives).

For my ornamental gardens, I use a combination of soaker lines that underlie the mulch and overhead sprinklers. True, overhead sprinklers are inefficient, losing water to evaporation, but I water in the morning, rather than during the heat of the day, to reduce evaporation losses. Watering in the evening will also help conserve moisture, but health problems sometimes arise when plants face cooler night temperatures with wet leaves. Because I may only water three or four times in a summer (or not at all), this makes sense for me.

Your climate may make your garden's needs very different. If you find that despite great soil preparation, thoughtful plant selection, and deep mulch, you still need to water regularly, you may want to read some books on xeriscapes (landscapes that do not require supplemental water). Pioneered in Denver, an epicenter of innovative gardening, xeriscaping involves using only those plants that are completely drought-tolerant in your region.

Efficiency counts when you water your garden. A soaker hose is an effortless way to keep large beds and borders evenly watered throughout the season (especially if the hose is on a timer), while a hose and hand-held watering wand will help the less time-crunched gardener direct water right to the roots of thirsty plants.

Wise Watering Reduces Usage

Your garden will tell you in no uncertain terms if you need to develop an efficient watering routine. It's far better to water a little when plants still look good than to put off watering until plants are stressed. If plants flag (wilt a little) during the heat of the day but perk up in the cooler evening and look great in the morning, they are getting enough water. If they always look droopy and flaccid, they aren't. Once the ground is deeply dried out, it can be tricky to rewet the garden properly. If you dig a trowel into the ground and find it dry all the way to the root zone, it's time to water.

Before you can water effectively, however, it's important to soften the crust of dry soil at the surface. Bone-dry earth sheds water—this phenomenon is known in horticultural circles as "crusting." This means that the top inch or so of mulch or soil has dried into an almost-impenetrable crust. Instead of soaking in nicely, water just sheets off the crust. The solution would seem obvious—add moisture-retaining soil amendments.

Unfortunately, though, many common soil amendments actually contribute to the crusting problem. Indeed, peat moss, the most popular amendment, is the worst offender. Dry peat moss sheds water like oily duck feathers. Often it takes a dose of hot water to soften the crust and let water penetrate the hardened soil. But this really isn't a practical solution, since few plants appreciate hot water on their tender parts.

The best solution to crusting is really prevention of the problem in the first place. As usual, mulch plays a key role. Add mulch when the soil is still wet deep down (usually before the middle of May, if you've had adequate winter precipitation). Next, keep the soil evenly wet. Depending on where you live, this may mean frequent and efficient watering. Soaker lines are ideal, especially the flexible, half-inch hoses that drip evenly along their entire length.

When the soil is too dry, it not only slows root growth, but it also hampers plants from feeding properly. Damp soil, on the other hand, releases nutrients, promotes healthy soil flora, and allows for active, strong root growth. Soggy, mucky soil is not the goal. Plants can drown if their roots can't get air. Properly moist soil allows both water and air to reach those struggling roots.

If your garden beds are crusted, try this: Get a soaker hose, thread it through your plants, then cover it with mulch. (Remember, this helps the water to spread underground by capillary action) Now turn it on for a few minutes. The moment you see puddling or runoff, stop. Let the water soak in slowly. Wait half an hour, then turn the water on again, keeping the pressure fairly low. If no puddling occurs, leave it on. After about an hour, dig down and see what's happening. Depending on your soil type, the water will have penetrated to a depth of between 1 and 2 feet.

The worst mistake you can make with soakers is to get carried away and leave them on for too long. Once your soil is properly wet, you may find that it takes as little as 15 minutes of soaker-hose watering once a week to keep it that way. You'll have to do the dig test to find out (just once or twice—not every day). Let the top few inches of soil dry out between waterings, but be sure the soil doesn't get bone dry.

Once you figure out how much you need to water, you simply add turning hoses on and off to your grooming routine. To keep things on track, carry a small kitchen timer in your garden basket. Each time you turn on a soaker line, set the timer for whatever time period your garden requires (mine run for between 15 and 20 minutes). When the timer dings, turn off the first hose and turn on the next. Wise watering is totally worth the effort. The result is less wasted water and markedly better growth.

My Take on Hoses

When shopping for hoses, there are a number of features that I think are worth searching for. Look for hoses that are hard to kink, stay supple in cold weather, and keep on flowing even when a UPS truck is parked on them. I'd also advise you to check the underside of the product label to see if there's a disclaimer about using the hose for drinking water. (You may need to untie the twist-fasteners on the label to read it). Some hoses carry statements that the hose is not intended for drinking water use, or that the hose contains a chemical known to the State of California to cause cancer, birth defects, or other reproductive harm.

In my opinion, it's not a good idea to drink—or to let your kids drink—from a hose that carries a warning like this. And you might not even want to use it on the vegetable patch. Hoses that are labeled as being drinking-water quality are available in garden centers and catalogs and are guaranteed to remain safe for a lifetime. These high-quality hoses last a long, long time; they cost a little more than bargain hoses (usually about $4 more), but for me, the peace of mind is worth a few extra dollars.

Lawn Care for a New Century

If you've filled your yard with beautiful naturalistic gardens, you may only have a small patch of turfgrass to cut. Time to give a reel mower a whirl! They're quiet and lightweight, and perfect for small spaces; best of all, they don't pollute because they run on muscle power.

LAWNS ARE ALMOST SACRED TO NORTH AMERICANS, who seem to think a yard looks nude without one. Across the whole country, nearly every lot—urban, suburban, or rural—is lined from edge to edge with rolling green turf. Lawns are a great place to play catch, watch a baby learn to toddle, or have a picnic. However, all that lush green stuff comes with a steep price tag. The problem is that lawns are not really based on nature. We must impose vigorous controls (often chemical and toxic) to keep lawns looking lush and to prevent weeds from infiltrating the sacred lawn space.

Most lawns require a long cycle of watering and weekly care. In the short term, these considerable efforts seem to produce great results. Sadly, there is a dark side to that lovely lawn. In Seattle, a recent study by King County Hazardous Waste Management revealed that 90 percent of King County neighborhood streams are polluted with Diazinon. This potent poison has recently been banned from use on golf courses and lawn turf farms because it is known to kill birds. You may have read about ducks dying of convulsions after eating Diazinon pellets on lawns. Other birds and many fish are also susceptible. Even so, Diazinon is still available to homeowners. It is a common ingredient in most anti-crane-fly treatments, and it is also found in some weed-and-feed lawn-care products.

Because of runoff, Diazinon is found in many of our streams. We can do a lot to help our endangered wildlife simply by *not* overloading our waterways with excess toxins. Think about it—stuff that kills birds, bees, and fish as well as pesky bugs can't actually be very good for humans, either.

Are there less toxic alternatives to Diazinon? Luckily, there are quite a few. In fact, nontoxic lawn care can be even cheaper and easier than poison-based care. Ask any lawn-care expert about crane fly problems, and you'll learn that a healthy lawn is highly resistant to attack. The best cure is prevention, not poison. Anywhere in the country, proper lawn care begins with a clear understanding of what grass really needs. To grow well, lawn turf needs at least 4 to 6 inches of decent topsoil over a well-drained base.

The turfgrass that makes up your lawn needs at least an inch of water each week to stay green in summer; many ornamental grasses, on the other hand, naturally go dormant if water is not available. Most people water too much and too often during the summer, and the resulting runoff carries excess fertilizers, pesticides, and herbicides into storm drains and streams. Seattle's King County Surface Water Management has a new motto: Everyone lives downstream. That means your toxic runoff may go away, but you'll still be exposed to someone else's. I think we all need to clean up our acts.

Here's how to simply and painlessly break free from using chemicals to keep your lawn looking nice:

Always start with a soil test. It's important to find out all you can about your lawn *before* you take action. A basic soil test should be able to tell you your soil texture, soil pH, and phosphorus and potassium levels. Tests vary by state, so if you live in a state where extensive testing is done you may end up finding out the levels of many micronutrients, as well. In any case, be sure to ask for organic recommendations with your test results.

Feed the soil as well as the lawn. Spread and rake in ½ inch of compost over the lawn twice a year, in spring and fall. If you don't have homemade compost, you can often obtain some for free, or perhaps for a nominal fee, at your local municipal composting site. These days, organic products are widely available, often through city or county recycling programs, or through organic farms.

Feed the lawn a balanced meal. Follow the guidelines given with your soil test results to determine which nutrients need to be added, then treat your lawn to the right stuff when spring rolls around. There are quite a lot of nationally available organic lawn feeds out there; check your local garden centers, Internet sites, and magazines for sources of nutritionally balanced products.

Don't overnourish the lawn. Again, soil testing is important so you know what your lawn is lacking. As a general rule, though, never use more than one pound of nitrogen for each 1,000 square feet of lawn. More than that is not only wasteful, it also puts excess nitrogen into water sources.

Mow high. Adjust your lawn mover to the highest setting and leave it there. Ideally, most lawn grasses should be between 3½ and 4 inches tall. Tall turf photosynthesizes more efficiently than short cut grass. Longer grass shades its own roots, conserves moisture, and outcompetes many annual weeds. Best of all, mowing high is more effective than herbicide for eliminating crabgrass.

Mow lightly but often. As with pruning, grass cutting removes valuable resources. Aim to reduce the total height of grass by no more than one-third each time you mow. This may mean mowing twice a week in high season.

Let the clippings lie. Short clippings make for a self-mulching lawn. As they break down, they release their stored nutrients back into the soil, enriching the lawn just like compost. Contrary to popular belief, letting grass clippings lie will *not* lead to thatch problems. By providing earthworms with steady fodder, this self-mulching technique can eliminate thatch buildup in a single season.

Water wisely. Most lawns are overwatered, leading to anaerobic conditions. In other words, there is so much water in the soil that there's little room for oxygen (and many bad-guy bugs thrive without oxygen). Heavy, clay-based soils may need an inch of water once a week. Sandy soils need briefer but more frequent watering. Since longer turf needs less water than short grass, you'll probably need to reduce your usual schedule.

Do all this, and you'll have a healthier lawn that fights off pests and diseases on its own. If this sounds like too much trouble, consider hiring an organic lawn-care company that can do it for you. Some of these companies provide mowing services as well as lawn and landscaping care. The best will offer organic lawn fertilization programs; nontoxic insect and weed control; and plant, tree, and shrub care. They may also do new and remedial landscaping, as well as pruning for health and beauty.

TOP: Where the gardener wants flowers and the lawn guy (usually) wants grass, a mown area near the house can give way to a low-growing flower and groundcover bed that builds back to naturalistically layered woodlands.

BOTTOM: In woodland gardens, keeping turf tidy can be a challenge. Where lawns grow spotty, trade grass for bulbs and groundcovers. Interplant bulbs with varying bloom seasons for a color-filled floral tapestry.

Making Beautiful Dirt

One of my favorite odors in the world is the scent of the earth. I love the way the wet soil smells in late winter, when snow is in retreat and green shoots are barely pricking through the still-chilly ground. Even better is the intoxicating **smell of spring,** when warming soil wakens a host of happy plants from winter slumber. In summer, flower and foliage perfumes win out, and the subtle earth scents are only noticeable when we pot up a division, pull a fresh carrot, or replace tired annuals. I especially love the sweet, musty fragrance of damp earth and composting leaves in autumn—it's so pleasing to me to see the **cycle of life** in action.

I think most gardeners enjoy the smell of freshly turned soil, and many of us are not afraid to admit that we really like dirt. **There is nothing dirty about dirt,** or about any of the earthy, humble ingredients we use to nourish our plants and ourselves. During my garden school classes, I always tell my students to make beautiful dirt. Often somebody cringes and says, "But dirt is icky! Don't you mean soil?" Nope. Dirt, soil, **good clean earth**—it's really all the same no matter how you dress it up with designer labels.

You may start with great dirt or lousy dirt, but the gardener's job is to protect and improve it, no matter what the initial quality. Great soil makes for a great garden. If there is a secret to making **lush, abundant gardens** in a hurry, it is this: Make lovely dirt, and the garden will support itself.

Clearly, everything we've discussed in terms of plant selection and arrangement is also important. However, making great soil is definitely where healthy, happy gardens begin. Traditional organic farmers and gardeners always teach us to **feed the soil rather than the plants,** because they know that healthy soil makes for thriving plants.

The ideal soil (which does occur naturally in some blessed parts of the country) offers a good **balance of drainage and retention.** Good soil lets air and water pass through freely, yet retains enough nutrients to support active growth. That's a lovely concept, but since many of us don't have ideal soil, we need to learn how to **make the most of what we do have.**

Sweet and Sour Soils

MOST GARDENERS ARE AWARE THAT THEIR SOIL MAY BE classified as either sweet or sour, but they aren't exactly clear about what that means. Simply put, neutral soils are called sweet, while acid soils are considered sour. If sweet sounds good, most folks get nervous that sour sounds bad. However a quick look at natural areas where soils are acidic will reveal that many so-called sour soils can support an abundance of native flora, not to mention thousands of gorgeous plants.

In chemical terms, soil pH describes the acid-alkaline balance, or the relative balance of hydrogen and hydroxide, in your soil. Soils (or water, or anything

else) with more hydrogen ions are acid, while those with more hydroxide are alkaline. Measured on a scale from 0 to 14, a low score (below 7 in pH) means your soil is acid. A high score (above 7) means your soil is alkaline. In a few favored places, the soil is neutral. Technically this means your soil measures 7, but in real terms the range is more flexible.

The progression of pH is not as simple as it looks on a chart. When the pH level is in balance, the soil is considered neutral. When it isn't in balance, each successive pH level is 10 times greater than the last one. This means a soil with a pH of 5 is 10 times more acid than one of 6 and 100 times more acid than one of 7. That's why changing pH even half a step (from 5 to 5.5, say) is quite an undertaking.

This concept is of tremendous importance in the vegetable garden, because most vegetables will grow well in soils that approach neutral. If you have often been disappointed with the performance of your vegetables or flowers despite having given them the best care you can, pH might be the problem. Anything that inhibits the growth of annuals will have a big impact on performance, since they must pack a productive lifetime into just a few months.

Things are a bit different in an ornamental garden where you are mostly growing longer-lived plants with more flexible feeding strategies. In naturalistically layered gardens, pH incompatibilities can largely be avoided by selecting plants that prefer the kinds of soils you can offer them.

What This Soil Needs

TO FIND OUT WHAT YOUR SOIL NEEDS, YOU NEED TO DO a soil test. Your local Cooperative Extension can advise you on how to do the test and where to get results. If your soil results display very high or very low pH, you may want to try to neutralize it by bringing it closer to the 7 range on your pH chart. This generally requires giving the soil a buffering blanket of compost to bring it closer to neutral, and adding other amendments to make the soil more acidic or alkaline as needed. While plants are pretty adaptable, most grow optimally in a fairly narrow pH range (between 6.5 and 7). As always, it makes sense to select a high percentage of plants that are naturally comfortable with the kind of soil you have. Even so, if you are a passionate plant lover, it also makes emotional sense to improve an area or two where you can rejoice in growing plants of all kinds.

While quite a lot of plants will thrive in moderately alkaline soil, fewer are adaptable to very acid situations. When you want to modify the acidity of native soils, the most effective technique is to add agricultural limestone (available in garden centers). Be sure to get your soil tested first, though, to see whether you need to add dolomitic or calcitic agricultural limestone.

(Never use industrial quicklime or slaked lime; these are usually sold at hardware stores.)

In most cases, slightly alkaline soils won't need much modification. Most plants, including vegetables, herbs, and many flowers, will be perfectly content in a soil that's slightly alkaline. If the soil is otherwise lean, adding plenty of humus will help plants make the most of the soil's nutritional value. In extreme cases, alkaline soils can be buffered with pine needles and other acidic amendments. Both acid and alkaline soils are also buffered by compost, which is nearly always close to neutral. Over time, mulching with compost will bring any soil closer to neutral.

Before piling fertilizers and amendments on your garden, purchase a soil test kit from your local extension office. Mix soil samples from several different places in your garden and send it off for testing. The lab will analyze the soil for pH and nutrients, and will offer recommendations on improving the quality of your soil.

If sweet sounds good, most folks get nervous that sour sounds bad.

Getting the Lead Out

THOSE WHO GARDEN IN URBAN SETTINGS, ALONG BUSY roadways, or beside older houses need to consider the possibility that their soil may be contaminated with lead. Most commonly, lead enters soil near an older house, where the walls may have shed many layers of lead-based paint over the years. Lead may also be found in soil where painted sheds, outhouses, and fences once stood. Because wooden structures can easily vanish without leaving visible traces, checking soil for lead is important anywhere there is even the possibility that it may have once been present. Also, even though lead-free gasoline is now the standard, urban, suburban, and even some rural roadside gardens may reveal persistent traces of lead from car exhaust. Lead does not go away, even after many years, so soil should be checked where roads once ran, as well as where they exist now.

If children or pets will use the garden, be sure to have the soil checked in the children's play yard or pet areas as well, since youngsters and small animals are especially vulnerable to lead poisoning. If testing shows that lead is present, you may elect to have the contaminated soil removed altogether. You can also cover the soil with barrier cloth; because lead can't drift up through the cloth, you can then bring in uncontaminated, nutrient-rich soil for making raised beds in the polluted areas.

Soil exhaustion is even more common than lead contamination in urban gardens, where the same plot may have been worked for many years without amendment. Here, the addition of humus (usually in the form of compost) will be of great value. Improving beds and borders with feeding mulches (see page 209) in spring and fall will help, as well. In just a few seasons, exhausted soil will be renewed and the tired plants growing in it will look rejuvenated.

Peeling paint is one of the major sources of lead in soil. Lead contamination is a serious health risk, especially if children play in the garden or if you grow vegetables. If you discover that you have lead in a small area on your site, you can sometimes remove 1 to 3 inches of soil to get rid of the problem. Contact your local health department for more information, including advice on the safe removal and disposal of contaminated soil.

Improving Soil in an Existing Garden

IF YOU'RE ONE OF THE LUCKY FOLKS WHO GARDEN IN deep loam, you have a great deal going for you. When native soil is naturally sweet and good, all you really need to do is respect it and do your best to keep it healthy. Annual feeding mulches of compost will generally provide your plants with all of their nutritional needs, especially if you're growing a combination of natives and well-chosen allies. Once plants are established in the naturalistically layered garden, they will become largely independent. Mulching gives them what they need by providing a slow, steady source of nutrients. It also conserves moisture, reduces competition from weeds, and provides insulation from both winter cold and summer heat.

Where native soils are lean, rocky, sandy, heavy, or badly drained, you need to work a bit harder to make productive, nutritious dirt. Your best bet is nearly always to begin by making new beds. The initial effort of making new beds is by far the most time-consuming part of garden making. Happily, it's a great investment—once made, well-built beds will generally remain fertile and functional for many years. Adding feeding mulches and composts will keep the soil in new beds in good tilth and the plants in good health with little intervention from you.

Starting with Loamy Soil

Where native soils are rich, deep, well drained, loamy, and otherwise desirable in quality, you can begin to make new beds by removing weeds and turf. Before planting, it's always a good idea to improve the exposed native soils at least somewhat with a ½- to 1-inch layer of compost. You can let the worms do the mixing for you with excellent results. If the native soil lacks worms (which it won't if it's really great in the first place), you can add worms and worm castings (which contain worm eggs) to the compost layer.

A manure fork helps you lift, turn, and mix garden wastes, shredded leaves, and kitchen scraps. Occasionally turning a compost pile helps speed up the process of decomposition.

Starting with Sandy Soil

How you build new beds will depend on what kind of soil you are starting out with. With sandy soils, drainage is not an issue, but nutritional deficits are. Because sandy soils drain so easily, many nutrients are quickly carried away by water as it drains. To compensate, sandy soils require frequent and generous humus-building in order to boost nutrient retention. By annually adding compost, you can create a bio-sponge that holds water and nutrients in place long enough for plants to take advantage of them. However, that bio-sponge effect is only temporary, and you will need to continue making regular soil improvements to sandy, quick-draining soils indefinitely.

One excellent way to deal with sandy soils is to make mounded raised beds of heavier, clay-based soil and compost. Because the underlying sandy soil already drains well, the heavier soil will never become waterlogged. To do this, simply bring in as much organic topsoil as you need to create attractive, interestingly shaped beds. The mounds should be sloped gently, to avoid a hard-edged look. Because the soil is heavier than the sandy underbase, it will stay put without any need for edging.

Make beds as deep as you like. Mine are generally between 12 and 18 inches deep at the center, tapering to the level of the path. Since topsoil will settle over time, make them a bit deeper than you really want them to be at the outset (often an extra 4 inches will suffice). No bed should be less than 4 or 5 feet wide, since small islands of dirt will dry out quickly on a sandy base. Once each bed is raked out and shaped, give it a topdressing of compost. Then, presto—you're ready to plant.

Naturally, if you live where sandy or lean soils are the norm, you'd be wise to adapt the garden palette significantly, giving preference to natives and other plants that thrive in such conditions. You will still need to improve the soil, especially in new beds. Once established, those well-adapted plants will usually do just fine with minimal encouragement, such as annual feeding mulches and supplemental water during unusually dry weather.

Lean native soils support native plants best. In dry areas, seek out adaptable plants that prefer soils with relatively low tilth, rather than trying to improve soils to make them rich. This California gardener rose to the occasion and found plants that didn't require supplemental water once they were established.

Starting with Heavy Soil

If sandy soils drain better than you like, clay soils often present the opposite problem—they retain nutrients and water all too well. Clay soils may also be strongly acidic or alkaline. They are terrific reservoirs of nutrients, but those nutrients may be locked up by pH imbalance and a lack of humus, both of which make nutrients less available to plants. What's more, heavy soils are often anaerobic, and the resulting poor oxygen exchange makes it challenging for many plants to grow well. Root rots are a constant problem in heavy soils, particularly where winters are wet. Naturally there are thousands of plants you can grow that are well adapted to clay soils, but even these can be stressed or killed when placed in unimproved soils as youngsters.

When you garden in heavy and badly drained soils, the easiest and most lastingly effective way to make new beds is to bring in new soil of several kinds in order to create mounded raised beds with a well-drained bottom layer. You don't need to remove any turf that's already in place—the new bed will be deep enough so that any existing grasses and weeds will be smothered in short order.

Gardeners often worry that there will somehow be an incompatibility or an impermeable layer where the raw clay meets the new soil. This is not a problem, because the worms will do the mixing for you. Although these raised beds are made in unmixed layers, after a season or two, you can no longer tell where the old soil ends and the new soil begins. Even rough meadow can be converted to garden beds in a few hours without removing the grasses and weeds. (Exceptions are areas filled with tap-rooted pests like Canadian thistles, which must be removed repeatedly no matter what you dump on them.) If the grass is long and rank, you may want to mow it before building the new beds. On the other hand, longer grass tends to mat up and smother itself quickly, so that decision is really up to you. Either way works fine.

To build a layered raised bed on clay soil, begin with a base of sandy loam. Sandy loam is a naturally occurring kind of soil and is pretty much what it sounds like—a fairly sandy soil with enough loam

When all amending efforts fail, use gravel. If site construction left your soil compacted and unworkable, gravel areas will assist drainage. Combining natural local materials like gravel, stone, and wood can create intriguing patterns that prepare the eye for the garden beyond.

Sandy Loam Stand-Ins

If you're building a layered raised bed and have struck out trying to find sandy loam, ask about grit. Road crews often use a coarse grit for minor road repairs; it's also a common treatment for slippery or icy roads in wintertime. This stuff is ideal for mixing with a little topsoil to make a fast-draining underbase for layered raised beds.

You can also use finely crushed gravel that has had the smallest particles removed through a #10 screen. Those tiny little particle bits are the troublemakers in clay soils, so be sure that there are no smalls in your fine gravel mix. Screened ½–¼ crushed gravel works very well. This is a rather coarse crushed rock blend with the largest pieces no more than ½ inch across and the smallest no less than ¼ inch. A crushed gravel underbase will allow the free passage of both water and air through the soil.

Under no circumstances should you use river gravel or pea gravel, both of which are rounded rather than sharp edged. Rounded gravels are very slippery underfoot (which makes them dangerous path surfaces) and they are also extremely migratory, meaning that they move around a lot, even under the weight of a thick layer of topsoil. Rounded gravels don't provide good drainage because they compact together and increase runoff; crushed gravel, on the other hand, has sharp edges that help cut water surface tension and allow water to flow through to the soil below.

Gravel provides excellent drainage when used as a base for raised beds. There are many crushed-rock gravels available, including marble or red stone, but be sure the blend you choose has pieces that measure between ½ and ¼ inch across to maximize drainage.

content to hold its shape. You do not want to substitute sandbox sand or river sand, which are both fine-grained soils that will turn clay into adobe. If you can't find a local source for sandy loam, look for topsoil that has a good amount of sand.

The base layer of sandy loam or grit can be raked out evenly to a depth of about 8 inches. If the underlying native soil puddles or drains slowly during the rainy season, consider making this base layer as much as a foot deep. If you are creating a privacy or screening berm, you can make the initial drainage layer as thick as you want—several feet is not too much, if it is appropriate to your design. Sandy loam is generally the least expensive ingredient in the raised-bed recipe, and it is also very easy to shape and sculpt. Give the beds the general shape you want, then taper the edges down to the original soil level. Where sandbox sand would spill away, sandy loam will remain firmly in place.

Next, add a generous layer of good-quality topsoil, raking it smoothly over your gritty base and tapering the edges. (However, if you are planning to use gravel paths and are building them according to the suggestions on page 33, you don't need to carry this topsoil layer all the way to the ground. The 6- to 8-inch-deep gravel paths will cover up the lower part of the bed, so topsoil spread below this level would just be wasted.) This layer of topsoil can be anywhere from 4 to 8 inches deep or more, depending on what you want to grow and what your budget allows. I often use a depth of 1 foot for this layer, because I want to be able to place larger plants without digging down into the native soil. Thus, my goal is to create beds deep enough to support my largest plants, which may be in 5- or 10-gallon containers.

If your budget doesn't stretch that far, you can supplement or even entirely replace this topsoil layer with homemade compost. I also mulch new beds with pit-washed or composted organic dairy manure, which I pile on in a layer that might be 4 to 6 inches deep. This looks lovely and keeps weeds away until I'm ready to plant.

Even a thin, 1- to 2-inch layer of composted dairy manure is a great idea because this topdressing gives your beds a finished look, suppresses weeds, and keeps the soil nice and moist. Peat moss is not a good topdressing because it contributes no nutritional value to the soil. As a topdressing, peat sheds water rather than absorbing it. Finished compost is a far better choice than peat moss (almost anything is, really).

Getting the Plants In

After all the hard work of making layered raised beds, you're probably wondering when the payoffs start. Well, the first reward is that your beds are ready to plant—there's no need to till or hand-mix layered beds. When you are ready to plant, you simply prepare each planting hole individually, mixing the topsoil and compost by hand in the planting hole before placing the new plant. Set a plant into each planting hole so its neck is no deeper or shallower than it was in its pot. Snug a bit of your topdressing around the whole plant by pressing down on the soil around the neck of the plant. Between plants, you can use a thicker blanket of compost if you have it.

To prevent weed seeds from sprouting and to give your new plants a gentle boost at the same time, sprinkle corn gluten meal around each plant. This natural weed-and-feed product is high in nitrogen and prevents weed (or any other) seeds from sprouting.

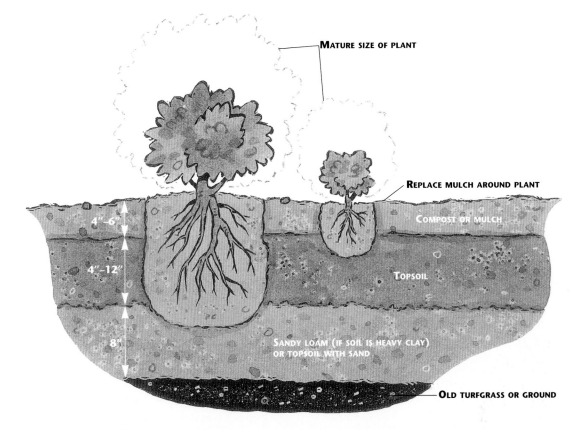

When you're getting ready to plant, consider the mature size of each plant, then space plants to avoid overcrowding. On planting day, use a trowel or shovel to dig a planting hole, mix all the soil layers by hand, then place the plant in the hole so it sits at the same soil level as it was in its pot. Fill the hole with soil, then use your fingers to gently tamp the soil around the plant. Water the plant deeply, then replace the mulch around the plant.

Recycling Manure

DAIRY MANURE MAY BE THE SINGLE MOST USEFUL soil-builder around. My favorite version is called pit-washed dairy manure. I buy mine from a local organic dairy that stores the manure in a large holding pit. They remove the effluent (the "wash" water that passes through the manure-filled pit) and use it to fertilize the dairy's grazing fields. After just a few washings, the manure in the holding pit is fluffy and loose; it looks much like peat moss, but it's far easier to use. Washed dairy manure from healthy cows is just about perfect for garden use; it can be used as a topdressing and for soil improvement.

If organic dairy manure is not an option in your area, almost any kind of animal manure can be used. However, all animal manure should be hot-composted before applying it to the garden. This helps to reduce the probability of passing dangerous pathogens on to people who handle the manure or eat food grown with manure composts. Hot composting (making an actively tended compost that heats up and breaks down quickly) also helps to reduce weeds by killing off seeds.

Understanding Soil Vocabulary

When you add compost to the soil, a community of tiny creatures flourishes. These soil organisms, or biota, bring life to the humus (rotting plants) and minerals that make up the nonliving portion of soil. Dr. Elaine Ingham, a soil ecologist at Oregon State University in Corvallis, coined the phrase "soil foodweb" to describe the interaction of soil fauna—an interaction that is constantly recycling. Here's a brief introduction to the cast of critters that create the soil foodweb and make soil come alive.

Bacteria—Native soils are full of bacteria, and an ordinary sample may contain over 100 million of them. Nitrogen-fixing bacteria dine on particles of humus, and they release nutrients back into the soil in a form that the plants can utilize easily. Bacteria are eaten in turn by scores of fellow soil dwellers. Bacteria help the soil retain nutrients and organic matter. Good garden soils also have a large percentage of fungal creatures, but they're dominated by bacteria (both bacteria and fungi are needed for soil health).

Beneficials and Pathogens—All soil biota, from bacteria to nematodes to fungus, come in many forms. Some help build healthy soil and support healthy plants—these are called beneficials. Others can cause many problems for gardeners, from root rots and blights to molds and mildews—these are called pathogens. Basically, when we improve soil tilth, texture, and nutritional content, we improve the balance between helpful and harmful soil biota.

Earthworms—These hardworking creatures are the soil builder's best friend. Worms do the mixing for us when we layer amendments onto garden soil. Worm tunnels open heavy soil to let air, water, and nutrients get down to plant roots. Worm castings promote sturdy root growth and feed many soil dwellers.

Fungal Hyphae—Like bacteria, fungal hyphae break down organic matter and recycle nutrients through the soil food chain. Healthy woodland soils are fungally dominated, meaning that there are more fungal creatures than bacteria. Most woody plants grow best in a fungally dominated soil.

Microarthropods—These tiny creatures eat bacteria and fungi, as well as plant particles. They are terrific recyclers, making nitrogen and other nutrients more available to plants and soil biota.

Nematodes—Good soil contains an ample supply of beneficial nematodes, which feed on everybody else. Nematodes transform nutrients in the soil into a form that can be readily taken up by plant roots. Pathogenic nematodes, on the other hand, feed on living plant tissue, causing root destruction. Healthy soil contains a high percentage of beneficial nematodes, which keeps the pathogens under control.

Protozoa—You may recall these single-celled critters from high school biology class. Soil protozoa feed on bacteria, then release nitrogen to plant roots. Protozoa are also eaten in turn by nematodes and other soil fauna, releasing nitrogen and other nutrients back into the soil foodweb.

Solarizing Weedy Soil

Covering a bed with black plastic to suppress weeds takes longer than solarizing with clear plastic. But if you live in an area that doesn't have lots of hot summer sun, a season-long black cover may help to smother a tough weed problem.

WHERE PERSISTENT WEEDS TURN GARDENING INTO AN unpleasant chore, you may want to try sterilizing the top few inches of soil before creating a new bed on the site of the unsatisfactory old one. By elevating the soil temperature for 6 weeks (or a full season, if you aren't in a huge hurry to get your garden plans underway), you can clear the new garden of roots and weeds. It's also a good way to rid your beds of soilborne fungal diseases and root-knot nematodes. Soil solarization means giving the earth a good baking by covering the bed with plastic.

You can try using coverings that you have on hand (including old shower curtains, plastic tarps, or drop cloths), but clear, heavy-gauge plastic is what's most widely recommended. Soil solarization is most effective in parts of the country that reliably get plenty of hot, sunny summer weather. Begin by removing any plants you want to keep, as well as any large weeds. Next, scratch up the surface of the bed with a heavy rake or open it with a shovel. Saturate the soil by placing a sprinkler or lines of drip irrigation over the bed and watering until the soil is evenly moist to a depth of 3 feet. Then cover the soil with plastic, pinning down the edges and corners with weed-cloth stakes (the kind that look like giant staples). Heap extra soil or rocks along the edges of the plastic sheet to seal it completely.

This plastic tent will heat up like an oven when the sun hits it. On a bright sunny day, soil temperatures inside the tent will get high enough to kill off most soil pathogens, fungal and otherwise. Lots of weed seeds and roots will also bake to death during the solarization process, which takes a minimum of 6 to 14 weeks. After the allotted time has passed, remove the plastic, but do not cultivate the soil immediately. Wait at least a month, then spread compost over the plot to replace the helpful bacteria that were killed during the solarization process. If you don't have enough time left in the season to plant anything, wait until the following spring to spread the compost.

Soil solarization means giving the earth a good baking by covering the bed with plastic.

The Art of Mulching

Most of us start out gardening with high hopes. We envision ourselves surrounded by healthy, vigorous plants that perform unstintingly. Surely if we just follow the directions and our intentions are good, everything we plant will flower and fruit with **astonishing abundance.** Sadly, many gardeners end up spending more time trying to keep the garden under control than enjoying it.

Most traditional garden design is based on the concept of control over plants. When you make the shift toward **organic gardening** and naturalistic design by improving the soil with compost, layering plants naturally, and tapping into the strengths of your plants, the whole picture changes.

The layered garden's sturdy backbone of woody plants makes it largely independent. When a large proportion of the garden doesn't need you very much, you can **focus your attention** on the few plants that do. If you grow a wide range of plants and make compost from your garden scraps, you help **build the soil** by offering a varied "diet" that satisfies the needs of your native soil flora.

Weeds are the primary enemy of the naturalistic gardener. When the beds and borders are filled with appropriate plants, **there is little room left for weeds.** In most cases, ardent mulching will eliminate the bulk of the weed crop. As your soil improves, mulching helps keep the soil open and loose, so when weeds do appear, they are easy to uproot.

Mulch can reduce the evaporation of soil moisture, help suppress or reduce weeds, modify or stabilize soil temperature, and **improve soil tilth and nutritional quality.** Almost any mulching material, from sawdust to plastic sheeting, can perform the first three functions. But obviously only biodegradable mulch materials can contribute to soil fertility, since nondegradable substances can't improve the nutritional quality of the soil.

As a rule of thumb, mulches are most useful when applied in **late winter or early spring,** and then again in autumn. If you aren't sure how much to use, begin by spreading a fairly thin layer, between 2 and 3 inches deep. As you observe the specific results of mulching on your site and situation, your garden will guide you in refining the timing, amount, and materials you use.

Common Mulches

I'VE FOUND THAT MULCH IS ONE OF THE BIGGEST all-around problem solvers—it conserves moisture, suppresses weeds, and promotes rapid root growth so plants can get established quickly. Here are some of the more common mulch ingredients, along with notable pros and cons that may help you decide which materials are right for your garden. Consider a mulch's ease of use, availability, and appearance (which is a personal reaction), and experiment with several mulches to see what works or looks best in your garden.

Compost

Compost is an ideal mulching material and an important ingredient in most feeding mulches (see page 209). Materials for composting are found inside and outside of your home—leaves, grass clippings, kitchen scraps, shredded newspapers, garden waste, wood ashes, coffee grounds, pet hair, and many other things. (Do not add pet or human waste, grease, oil, or dairy or meat products into your compost system.) See page 211 for more on making compost.

Finished compost can be pressed through a fine screen to make an even-textured mulch for topdressing in ornamental beds. Coarser, less-finished compost can be used at the back of deep beds, around shrubs and trees, and anywhere that plantings won't be seen from close-up. Compost improves soil tilth, texture, and nutritional value.

Leaves

If you live in a wooded neighborhood, you can employ nature's own bounty to your advantage. Small, fine-textured leaves from birch or willow trees can be used as mulch, but larger leaves like those from chestnut and large maple trees tend to mat and clump up; large leaves are best for mulch when they're dried and shredded. Shredded leaves make a wonderful mulch that's light, easy to handle, and very attractive. In mixed borders, use a leafy mulch around woody plants, spreading it 3 to 4 inches deep. Shredded leaves can be mixed half-and-half with compost and used on ornamental beds of all kinds.

Grass Clippings

Anybody with a lawn (or neighbors who practice organic lawn care) probably has a great supply of grass clippings for at least half the year. Add a thin, 1-inch layer of grass clippings to beds and borders as the clippings accumulate; don't pile them much thicker than

1 inch, though, or they may clump together so tightly that air can't penetrate. Grass clippings are a great source of nitrogen, so compost them half-and-half by volume with dry leaves, straw, or another dry material, and then use the resulting compost as mulch.

Hay and Straw

Hay and straw may be the original mulching materials; they've been used for centuries in gardens and fields. Traditional farming methods included recycling rotted or spoiled hay into the midden (manure heap), as well as using it on growing plots. Technically, hay that's sold today contains the grain or seeds of the plant; straw does not. I say "technically" because you'll find that most straw does contain a fair amount of seed, most of which will sprout.

Field straw works well, and a little goes a long way. A bale of straw consists of many tightly packed flakes that can be fluffed into a loose, easily handled mulch. Coarse in nature and light in color, straw is best used at the backs of large borders or in new beds to keep them weed-free during the winter. For a finer texture, you can run over it with a lawn mower.

Pine Needles

In woodland settings, a deep mulch of pine needles looks rustic and natural. When alkaline soils need buffering, a mulch of pine needles can add a valuable and balancing acidity. However, a pine-needle mulch can look inappropriate in a more open setting and may be too coarse to make a suitable mulch for small plants that are easily smothered. Be aware, too, that thick layers of pine needles (more than 2 to 3 inches) can mat down and shed water instead of allowing it to filter down to the plant roots. It's usually best to add pine needles to your compost pile rather than using them on their own as a mulch.

Buckwheat Hulls

Lightweight and deep brown in color, buckwheat hulls are easy to spread and look quite nice in mixed beds and borders. They do tend to sprout a fair amount, giving you an extra cover crop of buckwheat that can be a bit of a pest. But since young buckwheat is a splendid thing to add to the compost pile (chickens also love it), consider the tiny buckwheat volunteers to be gifts to your compost heap.

Bark, Sawdust, and Wood Shavings

Wood by-products include several extremely common mulching materials that are inexpensive, readily available, and easy to use. However, some have a drawback that needs to be considered. To a greater or lesser degree, most tie up soil nitrogen temporarily as they decompose (fresh sawdust uses the most nitrogen, while coarsely ground wood chips use the least).

Wood chips come in several grades of coarseness. They can be a useful material for pathways, especially in wooded settings. A 6- to 8-inch layer of coarse chips will last for several years without replenishment. Because the rotting wood starves the soil, weeds are rarely a problem in wood chip paths.

Although I never use shredded bark as a mulch on planting beds of any kind, many gardeners do. The

> In woodland settings, a deep mulch of pine needles looks rustic and natural.

bark is removed from the trees before they are made into paper. It makes for an attractive, deep brown mulch, but unlike the chips, it does not tend to rob nitrogen from the soil as it breaks down.

Sawdust is almost as common as wood chips, and it has some of the same problems. Even more than chips, fresh sawdust quickly depletes soil nitrogen as it rots. You will often see plants yellowing where sawdust has been used as a mulch. This is a sign of stress and nitrogen depletion. Remedy the situation by removing the sawdust and substituting several inches of compost; sprinkle with alfalfa pellets to help replace the lost nitrogen.

Sawdust also clumps easily, creating dry, airless pockets where roots can't survive. Thick layers of sawdust (more than an inch) tend to crust over, shedding water rather than absorbing it. Sawdust breaks down slowly, which makes it a fair choice for pathways where drainage isn't a problem.

Wood shavings are an awkward mulching material because they are too lightweight to stay put, too light in color to be a backdrop for plants (they compete visually), and practically waterproof, repelling water instead of absorbing it. However, they do make delightful paths. Springy and cushy underfoot, an 8- to 12-inch-thick pathway of wood shavings makes you feel like you're walking on clouds.

Dairy Manure

Composted cow manure is endlessly useful in the garden. If you live near an organic dairy, consider mulching all your beds with a generous layer of composted cow manure each fall. I'm able to get pit-washed dairy manure that's been washed to a fluffy, light consistency, and I use it for all my beds and borders.

If you're not fortunate enough to live near an organic dairy, there are likely to be other materials available in your area that will work just as well. Composted mushroom soil, a mixture of composted manure and straw left over from growing mushrooms, is widely available in many regions and makes a great mulch.

Peat Moss

Once widely popular, peat moss is becoming more expensive and less in demand. This is good because peat has no place in most gardens. Peat ranks among the very worst things you can use as a mulch, since it sheds water and is difficult to rewet once dry. Peat adds virtually nothing in terms of nutrition to the soil.

Weed-Barrier Cloth

Artificial mulch cloth is everywhere. Woven or punctured, the cloth allows the free passage of air and water, but blocks weeds from growing up through the it. Weed cloth comes in several weights and is rated for various uses, from lining pathways to suppressing Johnson grass and other pests. Most barrier cloths are not biodegradable, though they may begin to disintegrate over time, especially if they're exposed to sunlight. They do not contribute to soil tilth or add nutritional value, even when they do fall apart.

Mulch in Many Ways

FORTUNATELY, MULCHING IS NOT PARTICULARLY HARD work. You don't have to till these slow-working amendments in, you just scatter them evenly over each bed. Take care not to cover the crowns of your plants, of course, but don't worry about mixing the compost into the soil, because the worms will do that for you. Here's a guide to the various kinds of mulches.

Annual Mulches

Annual mulches are generally applied in early spring or in fall. They are used mainly to suppress weeds and maintain healthy soil. Established trees and shrubs will respond well to an annual mulch of compost and shredded leaves. In most cases, adding 2 to 4 inches of this mixture each year will keep a well-rooted plant content. When mulching trees and shrubs, begin at the trunk of the plant, using a lesser amount of mulch (1 to 2 inches) to avoid smothering the crown. Work out to the dripline of the tree or shrub, mulching more deeply as you go. This helps keep the root zone moist, well fed, and free of weeds.

Topdressing

Topdressing refers to any kind of fertilizer or amendment that is added to the surface of the soil; it's called a topdressing because it is not tilled or worked into the soil. Topdressing provides nutrients to individual plants that have already been established. Before you mulch plants, you may add a topdressing of a specific amendment, such as lime (to buffer pH), or a fertilizer, such as soy meal (for extra nitrogen). This may be lightly scratched or mixed into the surface of the soil around the plant before adding the mulch. With ornamental plantings, a thin, 1- to 2-inch layer of an attractive mulch such as compost or shredded leaves may be added to give the beds and borders a uniform and tidy appearance.

Smother Mulches

Smother mulching is an easy and practical way to rid the garden of challenging weed patches. Basically, you just create a barrier to prevent light and air from getting to the weeds until they die off. Anywhere you have an infestation of weeds, you simply heap a mixture of green grass clippings and shredded dry leaves or straw on top of the area. Be generous here; a 2-foot-thick layer is not too much. This makes a small static compost pile that slowly decomposes. Almost anything already growing in

The task of spreading mulch and aged compost in well-planted borders like this one can be performed most readily in early spring and late fall, when plants are at their smallest. On sloping sites, I've found that compost clings beautifully to the soil, even after drenching rains.

Many of the garden school borders are almost self-composting. Shrub foliage is allowed to rot in place, as is waste from many perennials that recycle themselves without smothering companions or groundcovers.

your weed patch will be smothered by that heavy a blanket, and no new weeds will grow through it.

Tough weeds like English ivy, nettles, and blackberries need coarser cover. For these, I use a thick layer of very coarse bark chips. My supply comes from the road crews who trim trees around power lines. This material is not suitable for garden use in the ordinary sense, but it does make a superior smother mulch. As it breaks down,

the coarse bark draws a lot of nitrogen from the soil, leaving it depleted and very lean. This, coupled with the weight of the bark and the lack of light and air that it lets through, is enough to discourage almost any weed. Before dumping the bark, cut back any topgrowth (be sure to wear heavy gloves and long-sleeved, protective clothing), then heap the chips over the problem spot.

If the weeds are thuggish and well-established, consider removing as much root as possible before applying the smother mulch. The more you take away, the less you need to starve out. Short-handled mattocks and heavy picks are great tools for root removal. It also helps to put down a layer of newspaper or plain cardboard to create a secondary barrier between the weeds and the mulch. Keep a watchful eye on the area, and be vigilant about removing any and all shoots and stems that make it through the layers.

For smaller problem areas that also have poor soil, an effective way to use a smother mulch is in combination with a hot-composting mulch. Begin by mowing or cutting back all weeds, then add a generous blanket (2 to 3 feet high, if you have enough material) of a hot-composting mulch, such as a mixture of one-third grass clippings and two-thirds dry shredded leaves. The heat created from this hot composting discourages weeds from making a comeback. When this layer has broken down, the soil beneath it will be loose, making it much easier to dig out any persistent weed roots. Add a secondary smother mulch of coarse wood chips. Any weeds that do emerge will be easy to pull out, and the mulch will break down peacefully for as long as you like. When you want to garden in that spot, pull the chips away (they make a fine path material) and replace them with compost and a booster of alfalfa meal. This will restore the nitrogen level of the underlying soil in a hurry.

Feeding Mulches

Feeding mulches do everything ordinary mulches do—suppress weeds and maintain soil moisture and temperature—but they also add significant nutritional ingredients to the soil. As they break down, feeding mulches release a steady supply of nutrients, such as nitrogen and other soil builders.

Feeding mulches can be tailored to meet specific needs and altered to suit the climatic requirements of various parts of the country. A good feeding mulch adds both soil amendments and some readily available nutrients to the soil. Which you use will depend in part on where you live. For example, in the Pacific Northwest, the moist climate drains nutrients out of the soil quickly, so I use generous amounts of compost and manure on my garden beds, along with some bonemeal and rock phosphate to supplement the phosphorous that tends to be lacking in our soils. Soils in drier regions of the country will burn through organic matter much more slowly, so gardeners there won't need to use as much mulch, but may need to add other nutrients that are not found in their soils. A simple soil test will help you identify which nutrients are lacking in your soil. It's always a good idea to have an analysis done before adding any amendments or fertilizers.

My own favorite feeding mulch is one I learned from an old rosarian; he swore it made his roses twice as big as anybody else's. This simple feeding mulch consists of a 2- to 4-inch layer of composted dairy manure and alfalfa meal (available at feed stores), both of which promote good soil tilth and add a boost of nitrogen to the soil. (The ingredients for all of the recipes in this chapter can be found at nurseries that carry organic supplies or through organic mail-order suppliers, such as Peaceful Valley Farm Supply; see page 270.)

Where native soils are acidic, you can buffer the pH by adding dolomite or agricultural limestone to your feeding mulches. Where soils are seriously alkaline, near-neutral compost will bring the pH closer to neutral. Alkaline hardpan or clay soils can be improved by applying gypsum, which helps to develop a finer soil texture and increase the naturally low levels of calcium and sulfur often found in these difficult soils. No matter where you live or what kind of soil you have, your feeding mulches will be improved by the addition of kelp meal, which supplies a broad range of trace elements and minerals.

It's easy to spread compost in new gardens because there's plenty of room between the plants. In the newly planted courtyard at the garden school, a midsummer mulch of aged compost adds nutrients to the garden.

Basic Feeding Mulch

4 parts compost
4 parts shredded leaves
4 parts composted dairy manure

Basic Spring Feeding Mulch

4 parts compost
4 parts shredded leaves
4 parts composted dairy manure (do not use bagged steer manure)
2 parts alfalfa meal (sold as rabbit food at feed stores)

General Purpose Booster Feed

4 parts pesticide-free cottonseed or soy meal
1 part dolomite or agricultural lime
1 part rock phosphate
½ part kelp meal

All of the recipes here are measured by volume rather than weight. To make them, simply choose a specific container or bucket to represent one "part." It's easiest to combine the ingredients in a large tub or a wheelbarrow, where you can see that the mixtures get evenly blended (a lightweight soil scoop works best for mixing the ingredients). Store any unused feeding mulches in a tightly closed container (small, heavy-gauge plastic garbage cans are excellent). You'll find you'll come back to these soil boosters again and again.

The Basic Feeding Mulch can be spread generously almost anywhere and is equally valuable in spring or fall. The Basic Spring Feeding Mulch adds a lot more nitrogen and is best used in late winter or early spring, when plants begin active growth. Spread these basic feeding mulches evenly over established beds and borders, taking care not to cover the crowns of any resting perennials. Start with a 2- to 4-inch layer and take notes about how your plants respond.

Booster Feeds

More concentrated than the feeding mulches above, booster feeds should be applied to the root zones of your plants as a topdressing. My favorite booster feed recipe, General Purpose Booster Feed, is adapted from a recipe published many years ago by the Territorial Seed Company, a mail-order seed company specializing in regionally appropriate vegetables for gardeners west of the Cascades (though they also have a national catalog of vegetable, herb, and flower seeds). Territorial founder Steve Solomon created many organic feeding mulches and booster feeds like the one here. This multipurpose booster feed works for ornamental

pH-Neutral Spring Border Booster

5 parts compost
4 parts pesticide-free cottonseed or soy meal
⅓ part raw bonemeal
⅓ part steamed bonemeal
½ part kelp meal

borders or vegetable gardens and is especially valuable where native soils are poor or exhausted.

To make the most of a booster feed, scatter a small amount around each new plant and gently scratch it into the top inch or two of soil. Give small plants about a tablespoon of booster, medium ones a scant quarter of a cup, and larger ones half a cup. A mature shrub or tree with a broad dripline could use a cup or more.

Many native soils are either acid or alkaline, and though thousands of plants will adapt happily to either condition, many popular ornamentals prefer soils that are closer to neutral. I find this ornamental border booster pleases natives and exotics alike, and it can be used in mixed borders containing native plants. Both raw and steamed bonemeal are used, because steamed bonemeal is available to plants right away, while raw bonemeal breaks down more slowly. Spread this booster feed thinly around each plant as a topdressing, extending outward to the dripline of shrubs. Allow about a quarter cup per plant, adding more (½ to 1 cup) for larger shrubs. Lightly scratch the booster into the top inch or two of soil, and cover it with a thin topdressing.

Composting Basics

Cement block compost bins are useful in a garden that's still being designed. You can stack the blocks without mortaring them and then dismantle and move the bin when you expand or change your garden.

THOUGH COMPOSTING HAS A MYSTIQUE ABOUT IT, IT IS really a very simple process that anyone can follow. Basically, compost is about making plant materials rot in a beneficial manner. If you have never made compost before, don't worry, it's easy to get started. There are many books that describe composting techniques in detail, but if you want some hands-on instruction, contact your local Master Gardener program (through your local extension office) and see whether your area has a Master Composter program.

Everything that comes out of the garden goes back in, one way or another. The most important way to do this is through composting. Sadly, most commercial compost products are not nearly as well balanced as homemade compost. Happily, homemade ones are generally excellent (partly because they are not stored for long periods in plastic bags).

Homemade compost is a highly effective soil amendment because it is full of microbial life. A teaspoon of compost may contain up to 6 billion microbes that feed plants by feeding the soil. You can encourage microbial diversity by growing a wide range of plants and by making compost from more than just two or three ingredients (such as grass clippings and shredded leaves). When you mulch with homemade compost, your airy compost "blanket" turns the top few inches of soil into a beneficial environment for healthy soil organisms.

How Big Should the Bin Be?

The best place for a compost system is within easy reach of the garden. If you plan to add kitchen scraps, place your bin close to the kitchen. Since few composting areas are extremely elegant, use a simple screen or fence to mask the work area from the house and outdoor seating areas. The size of your composting system matters, too, since very small piles are not efficient. The minimum size is about 3 feet high by 3 feet wide by 3 feet deep. An average suburban garden may provide twice that volume in garden waste, and that much waste will be composted most efficiently in an enclosed space (such as in a bin with deep sides rather than a free-form heap or mound). Twin bins are easier to use than a single pile—the first bin can contain the finished, usable compost, while the second can contain wastes that are still actively composting. If your garden is larger than ¼ acre, you will probably need a set of three connected bins. The bins can be as big as you like, but remember that large bins are harder to fill, reach into, and mix.

What Should Be Composted?

The simple rule of thumb for composting piles is to use one-third green and two-thirds brown materials. Green materials are nitrogen-rich materials such as fresh foliage and grass clippings, and brown materials are high in carbon, like dry leaves or straw. In summer, when the bulk of the garden grooming leftovers are fresh and green, you can keep a bale of straw next to the compost. When you add a layer of fresh green materials, add twice as much dry straw to keep the pile in balance. The goal is to have the nitrogen in the green stuff in balance with the carbon-based brown stuff.

If you use kitchen scraps, do not include anything with animal fat, such as fish, meat scraps, or cheese. These will attract dogs, rats, raccoons, and mice—any of which can wreak havoc with your pile. If you have problems with rodents in your compost pile, one way to use kitchen scraps is to put each day's accumulation of vegetable matter in the blender or food processor with some water and whirl it into a slush. This slurry can be added to the pile all year-round without attracting anybody's attention.

Garden weeds are welcome, so long as they aren't heavy with seed. (Seeds can persist and cause much worse weed problems when they're reapplied to the garden as compost.) Some obvious exceptions are the more aggressive weeds that spread by root, shoot, or seed. Thugs like field bindweed, stinging nettles, and brambles are all dreadful pests in the compost *and* in the garden. Bag these and discard them in the trash.

Is Smaller Better?

Reducing the size of compostable materials will speed up the rotting process considerably. Fine-textured materials like grass clippings or small leaves can be added directly to the compost pile. Big leaves, large stalks, and coarse stems will need to be reduced in size before they go on the heap. The smaller the bits, the larger the surface area for the bacteria to munch on, making decomposition faster. In other words, if you chop up your materials, you'll get finished compost much quicker.

To do this quickly, you can use a leaf shredder, which may be a hand-crank or an electric model. If you own a lawn mower, use it to run over heaps of leaves and other soft garden waste. Try to have a mixture of ingredients that are relatively uniform in size so they all decompose at roughly the same rate.

How Does It Work?

Compost heaps are made by creating layers of nitrogen-rich (green and wet) and carbon-rich (brown and dry) materials in quantities sufficient to build up heat. A well-constructed compost heap gets hot enough to kill most weed seeds, as well as many pathogens (such as fungal diseases and bacterial blights). The goal is to get your new pile off to a quick start, then maintain a slow, sustained heat. If you use

Fall leaves are abundant in most neighborhoods, so put your rake to the ready. Lawn debris is a major ingredient in a successful compost pile, which should be one-third green materials and two-thirds brown materials.

bottomless bins, start by raking the soil surface. This rough, open surface allows the free exchange of water, air, and beneficial soil microbes between the native soil and your pile.

Begin your new pile with a brown layer. Fill your bin with a thick layer of shredded dry leaves, dry grasses, and any garden scraps, heaping them about 6 to 8 inches high. Top this layer with a smaller layer of fresh green materials, which might be foliage, grass, and chopped stems. Toss in a shovelful of soil or old compost between each layer to inoculate the pile with decomposing microbes. Repeat the layers until you fill the bin, ending with a carbon-rich brown layer.

How Wet Should It Be?

Green materials are usually moist enough to keep the pile going, but the brown, carbon-rich materials may be quite dry. If so, sprinkle each brown layer with just enough water to make it damp (but not dripping). This moist but airy condition encourages and speeds decomposition. In really hot, dry regions, you may need to cover the pile with burlap, heavy plastic, or a tarp to maintain an ideal moisture level.

Within a few days, your new compost heap will feel noticeably warm to the touch; you may also notice steam rising from it. Once started, an active compost pile can poke along on its own with no more help from you; the process can take months, however, especially in cooler weather. To rev up the composting process, you'll need to add more oxygen when the pile begins to cool down after that initial heating. If you turn the compost heap (use a manure or composting fork) you'll aerate the heap and reactivate the heat by redistributing the cooler outsides and the hotter middle. This is very

The Tea Cure for Failing Drain Fields and Soggy Lawns

A fascinating new technology offers hope for those whose backyard ecology has been abruptly changed by recent building or landclearing. Research done in part at Oregon State University at Corvallis has created mechanical tea brewers that make a compost tea product with wide-reaching applications. On soggy soils, regular applications of this tea changed percolation times (water seepage rates) dramatically after just a few months of use. Where standing water puddled for months in winter, there is now quick drainage. Researchers have also seen rapid changes in soil texture, worm count, and plant growth. Although all the initial research has been directed toward farm crops, researchers are running the first trials at my garden school to examine using this compost tea in ordinary backyards.

To create concentrated compost tea, we fill a mesh basket with a combination of worm castings and complex garden compost. To feed beneficial bacteria and fungi (the critters that make soil come alive), we also add blackstrap molasses, rock dust, soluble kelp, and a mix of other ingredients. In the brewer, a vortex air nozzle extracts organisms from the compost and maintains consistent oxygen levels in the tea.

Over an 18-hour brew cycle, beneficial bacteria and other organisms multiply. Thanks to the constant presence of oxygen and the competition between different bacterial species, the solution has a high concentration of beneficial biota and a very low percentage of pathogens.

The resulting blend can be used as a soil drench or it can be sprayed on plant foliage. To be effective, the tea must be kept well aerated and must be used within 15 to 24 hours of the time it finished brewing. If the tea is not kept well aerated, the shelf life is only a few hours.

On plants, the tea fills the sites where beneficial biota battle with pathogens for primacy, tipping the balance toward plant health. In soils, the food resources added to the tea encourage the bloom of beneficial biota and create an excellent environment for root growth.

easy to do if you use the side-by-side bin method. When the first bin needs turning, you mix it into the empty second bin. Now you can start another batch in the first bin. A few weeks later, you can turn the second bin into the third, move the first batch into the second bin, and start yet another batch. If the compost seems dry, sprinkle on a little more water during the turning, and cover the pile with fresh soil or finished compost.

After three or four turns, the homogenized mixture looks less like ingredients and more like compost. When you want to use compost, you sieve it to reduce its lumpiness. If you don't have a soil sieve, wrap a piece of stiff screen around your wheel barrow and rub the compost through it with the back of a flat-bladed shovel. Any large, coarse pieces can be tossed back for another trip through the cycle.

The Brush Pile as Habitat

Large brush piles that are passively composting are ideal if you have a large property; you can create many heaps, one for every area that's being gardened. My garden has several wooded sections, so I make small heaps wherever I'm planning to create a bed in the future. I try to use mostly small, finely textured materials that will rot fairly quickly for these small piles. For larger pieces of garden waste, I start my pile with a base of fallen tree branches. As these rough piles age, they become havens for many small beneficial creatures, from birds to bees to garden snakes. Over time, these brush piles may be moved or mined for usable compost, but they can also become part of your landscape.

When left mainly undisturbed (except for new additions after cleanups), brush heaps can support a delightfully diverse range of birds and small animals, as well as beneficial insects such as orchard mason bees and bumblebees. If you have a large property and are considering making a permanent brush pile of this sort, placement is of paramount importance. Otherwise, you inevitably discover that the spot that seemed so convenient a few years ago is now precisely where you want to make a path or place a pond. Moving a large brush pile is not an easy job and it defeats most of the point of creating a sustainable habitat, since shy woodland animals dislike having their home dismantled and moved, even if it's only moved a few feet away.

A wooded spot near the perimeter of your land is generally a good place for a static brush pile, since presumably you will want to protect and build up the property-line plantings to protect your visual privacy. It's also a good idea to consider what such a pile may look like from neighboring properties, if it is visible at all. If the neighbors can see your pile, consider providing some courtesy screening by planting a small thicket of red twig dogwoods or low evergreen conifers at the back of your pile. Soon the heap will be lost to view, and the dense backdrop will make an even safer cover for your favorite small animals.

Passive, Static, or Cool Composting

At its simplest, composting is a very slow process that can take several years. Static or passive piles are simply heaps of garden leftovers, combining everything from branches and corn stalks to leaves and grass clippings. You don't need to turn or mix static piles; you just need to add raw materials continuously, layer by layer, as they present themselves. After a year or so, you can remove the top layer to find that much of the inner heap has decomposed on its own. Remove the more finished compost, screen it by pressing it through a coarse screen for a more uniform texture, and use the result as a mulch anywhere in the garden. Toss back any large pieces to cycle through the pile again.

In yards that have been gardened for a long time, most of the compostable pieces will be fairly small, a factor that accelerates the process. Where gardens abut woodlands or greenbelts, and in neglected gardens with many older, overgrown plantings, the materials you're tossing into your pile may be coarser and larger. This makes the process slower, but it can be an advantage if you are trying to tame a wild garden. In this case, consider creating two different piles, one for faster-rotting materials such as leaves, grass clippings, and fine-textured garden debris and a second for larger, coarser materials. The second pile can be heaped in an out-of-the-way corner, where it can become a habitat for all kinds of wildlife.

Active or Hot Composting

Passive composting heaps may be almost work free, but you do wait quite a while for the compost payoff. Faster composting methods (called active or hot composting) create a regular supply of usable compost in a relatively short time. Active composting systems work best when one-third of the waste is green or high in nitrogen and two-thirds is brown or high in carbon. It's important to alternate the layers of green and brown for quick, beneficial rotting. Smaller-size materials decompose more quickly than larger pieces, so chop or shred materials before adding them to the pile. A healthy compost pile needs air and moderate moisture to keep the process hot and working.

Sheet Composting

Sheet composting can be a great way to start a new ornamental bed. In simple terms, sheet composting means piling compostable materials in thick layers on the site of a new bed. Alternate thick layers of wet, green materials such as fresh leaves and grass clippings with dry, brown ones such as dried leaves and chopped straw. Add some large twigs and branches to maintain good air flow to the center of your pile, which should resemble a large mattress.

In an ornamental bed, sheet composting is a slow, passive method. Because you won't be turning the

materials, the layers will take quite a while to break down. You can continue to add to the top layer every time you work in the area. Simply toss weeds, twigs, and other biodegradable materials on the pile. By the time you get ready to plant the area, most of the materials will be rotted into compost. You still don't need to do any mixing; simply add some compost to each planting hole and top off the new bed with more mulch as needed. This is an excellent way to establish perimeter plantings of trees and shrubs on a large property.

Although you can compost almost any organic material, certain weeds can cause trouble in your compost if the pile doesn't heat up enough to kill the weed seeds. Avoid throwing bishop's weed, Canada thistle, quack grass, comfrey, and Johnsongrass on the pile because they can be extremely invasive if added to a garden while the seed, root, or rhizome is still viable.

Troubleshooting in the Healthy Garden

Here's the good news—you should be able to quickly skim through this chapter. That's because when you make layered, naturalistic gardens with care, you experience few problems that require intervention. Any garden will need periodic editing, of course, and as long as the world is full of weeds (many of them imported Europeans), you will be dealing with them. Weeding is work when it gets out of hand, but in a **well-filled, happily growing garden,** it becomes a different experience. Some gardeners consider weeding to be part of their regular meditation practice and genuinely enjoy the opportunity to be among plants in such a calm and purposeful way.

Editing involves paying attention to a number of things, including the health of individual plants and the **overall health of the garden.** When one plant suffers where others thrive, the problem is very often traceable to root damage. **If the root system is healthy** and the problem was caused by mechanical damage (an errant shovel, a cat fight, a straying ball), the plant will usually recover just fine.

Other problems arise when the balance between your plants is disturbed. Perhaps one group of plants grows all too well at the expense of their companions. In this case, editing consists of watchful attentiveness and the periodic thinning or removal of the aggressors. A very slow grower may need a secure position in a smaller bed or even a container, where it will get **daily attention** instead of getting lost in a bed full of stronger partners. This kind of editing is an ongoing process—part of the dailiness of garden making and keeping. Like weeding, these minor interventions are a way to **keep in touch and interact with the garden.** When you work in and with the garden each day, you gain an immeasurable advantage of closeness.

Beauty Is Just the Beginning

IT'S IMPORTANT TO LOOK BEYOND THE EVERYDAY CHORES and enjoy your garden for its overall beauty. This way, you won't miss seeing beautiful buds and blossoms in your quest to tackle weeds and work. It took me years to realize that the beauty of gardening wasn't just what I saw when I was "finished," but what I did along the way, as well. One day, after spending several hours clearing a large garden bed, I realized that I had crawled through a great swath of creeping wood iris in delicate bloom, as well as a small host of minor bulbs in full bloom. Since none of them were squashed flat, I knew that I had "noticed" these blossoming treasures; however, I was so busy working and weeding that I hadn't even taken a moment to acknowledge their presence in the bed.

That moment of recognition turned my gardening life around. Ever since that day, I have made admiration part of my working schedule. As I garden, alone or with others, I take time to notice blooming flowers, swelling buds, and emerging shoots. When you tidy or replenish a bed, take time to admire your handiwork, to notice the contribution each plant makes, and to appreciate the way the garden looks as a whole. Whenever I hold gardening workshops, we always end each session with an extended admiration period. As we walk around, nearly everybody discovers beauty that was overlooked while we were in "working mode."

This point is a simple one, of course, yet one that can make a world of difference to the way you experience the garden. Your garden can be a source of refreshment and renewal or an unending series of musts and shoulds. When you allow the chore list to override the ability to see what's right and wonderful despite a few imperfections, you deprive yourself of so much joy that's readily available and free for the taking.

Learn to see your garden with the same charitable eye you use when visiting other gardens. You can admire someone else's garden for hours without finding imperfections. When visitors tour your garden, refrain from telling them how much better your garden looked last week or how much better it will look next month. Don't point out what needs doing instead of what looks great. Enjoy your garden as happily and wholeheartedly as you enjoy other gardens.

> Take time to smell the roses! I learned years ago that garden chores aren't chores at all when you weave your way through breathtakingly beautiful plants as you go about tidying and deadheading. Even the task of weeding can be softened by the scent of a rosebud, the sparkling silver foliage of an artemisia, or the abundant flowers in a mound of coreopsis.

Think Big, Start Small

TO INCREASE YOUR ENJOYMENT IN THE GARDEN, IT HELPS to adopt a principle I call "working toward." What this means is that each time you need to deal with a problem or perform a chore, you should consider the overall goal—not just the next step. Anybody who has moved a pile of rocks three or four times in order to get it out of the way of an encroaching project will see the beauty of this simple idea. Repeated chores often arise because you aren't perfectly clear about the many stages of a project (or more often, a whole related series of projects). When planning becomes a habit, you save yourself a significant amount of time and a tremendous amount of energy.

Working toward is also about making daunting tasks seem less overwhelming. The idea is to break a big job into a number of smaller ones that can be worked on over time. And it's important to plan your tasks in such a way that you don't lose ground; you want your small pieces to remain done, so that they can be built upon. For example, if an area is weeded once then left untended, when you come back to it, it will simply need weeding all over again. But if the area is weeded and well mulched, it will be ready to work on when you come back to it.

The secret to success with any project is to start small and work on it often. When my kids were little, I learned the power of the 15-minute work increment. Before that time, I didn't believe that anything worthwhile could be accomplished in under an hour or two. Now I know that putting in as little as 5 minutes a day, every day, can make a great deal of work melt away.

A large task can seem like an impossible one, but well-planned persistence can make it manageable. If a large and visually important border looks ratty, "working toward" cleaning it up might mean pulling weeds for 15 minutes each day and using the weeds to smother the next chunk. Instead of carting the rank weeds off to the compost pile, create static piles in the direction you're working, so they help to smother more weeds that cover the area where you want to work next. When clearing wild woods, making new beds, breaking ground, or weeding trouble spots, use mulch as an ally. Use plenty of chips or straw on the newly exposed ground, whether it's a path or bed. Mulch your way ahead, step by step, inch by inch.

Keeping all project pieces at a size you can manage also helps. Instead of tilling up a great big bed and watching it fill up with weeds while you struggle to plant one part of it, take the bed on a bit at a time. Only uncover as much new earth as you can care for and keep under control. This might mean building up borders one tiller session at a time until you reach the desired size. Despite the temptation to see how it will look, don't take on more than you can deal with. When projects are designed in small units, everything you do flows into the next step. Instead of feeling constantly frustrated, you'll feel efficient and practical. What once felt like daunting work will now feel almost effortless.

In a new bed or border, a once-a-week foray will keep weeds to a minimum. Besides, weeds are easiest to pull when they're still small— firmly grasp the weed at the base of the stem and give a steady but firm yank. To remove more tenacious weeds, you may need to use a cultivator or pronged weeding fork.

Working with Weeds

Not all would-be weeds are unworthy, at least from an ornamental standpoint. Star chickweed (*Stellaria pubera*) is a pretty spring wildflower, blooming from March to May.

ASK A GROUP OF GARDENERS ABOUT THEIR TROUBLES AND you'll get varied responses. Some will complain about deer or slugs, but sooner or later, all will mention weeds. Before you spend a lot of time and energy on removing weeds, it's worth asking yourself what, if anything, the weeds might be doing for you. For instance, chickweed is a very common spreader that has several beneficial qualities. Fine-textured and lacy, it seldom harms the plants it surrounds, and it can act as a living mulch, conserving moisture and shading out worse weeds with its webby doily of foliage. Its fine roots penetrate deep into the soil, pulling up trace elements and minerals that add valuable phytonutrients to the compost pile. Chickweed is easy to uproot, making it a good candidate for temporary groundcover.

Some of the annual clovers can also be considered temporary groundcovers, particularly those that are easily uprooted (these don't include the creepers). Clovers are nitrogen fixers, improving nitrogen levels in the soil. Some of the oxalis tribe (sorrels and false clovers) are also worthy temps, including the ubiquitous types that come in lovely shades of copper, bronze, red, and purple. These make a dense and handsome groundcover and can be sheared back if they get leggy late in the season.

Weeds to avoid at all costs are rampant spreaders like bindweed (also known as wild morning glory or creeping Jenny), taprooted terrors like Canadian thistle, and relentless creepers like creeping buttercup. Where aggressive weeds proliferate, it's a good idea to clear the ground before trying to garden. Generally, though, methods that involve soil disturbance only make matters worse. Seeds of many weeds are opportunistic, lying dormant until some disturbance triggers sprouting. Repeated tilling can fill the ground with scraps of weed root, each of which will grow with determined vigor. Instead, consider soil solarization with clear plastic or a deep smother mulch (see pages 201 and 207).

Frequent mowing inhibits flowering, which makes it easier to control many kinds of weeds. Mow a rough meadow regularly for a few seasons, and soon you will have something resembling a lawn. Mowing eliminates many coarse grasses, reeds, and taller weeds quite quickly. However, it won't control taprooted weeds that make flat basal rosettes, such as dandelions, hawkweeds, and many thistles. Control of taprooted weeds like dock and dandelions requires time and patience. If we simply cut the tops off, the roots resprout quickly. To avoid this, use a Japanese farmer's knife (a hori-hori), a long or thin-bladed weeder, to cut away at least 4 or 5 inches of the root. The rest will generally rot without returning.

Flame Power

In my gardens, the gravel paths, sidewalks, driveways, and other paved areas are kept weed free with a flamethrower. Flame has been used by organic growers for years to keep orchards, vineyards, and vegetable beds weed free. Many organic farm and garden supply

Boiling water kills weeds by literally burning the leaf tissue. Simply pour a kettle of boiling water over the weeds in sidewalks, patios, and driveways. But use boiling water cautiously in and around borders and beds because it can harm worms and other beneficials and healthy plants nearby.

catalogs carry flamethrowers with cart or backpack fittings to make the flamethrowers easier to use. There are also several kinds of flame valves that allow you to fine-tune and direct the open flame.

Flamethrowers work by heating the water in the cells of weed foliage. It's not necessary to burn the weed to the ground; a brief, 3- to 5-second blast is enough to evaporate the water within a young weed and kill it. Larger ones (especially taprooted weeds) may require several sessions before they succumb. Many grasses are genetically programmed to face fire, and established clumps will return from a burning undismayed. Young grass seedlings are far less resilient, however, and flaming grass seedlings in gravel will kill them quite quickly.

Where large patches of ground are infested, weed flamers are very satisfying to use and can be extremely effective on persistent weeds. However, it's hard to use this tool selectively in the garden, where the heat from the flamethrower can scorch shrubs and damage perennials that are too close to the target area. To avoid unintended plant damage, restrict use of flamethrowers to nonflammable surfaced paths and patios—flamethrowers should not be used near bark paths or pine needle mulches, or near anything that could easily catch fire. What's more, flamethrowers can be dangerous during droughts, when wildfires easily escape control. To keep flame weeding safe, make sure you have a reliable water source on hand, and always enlist a partner to help you watch for runaway sparks.

Boiling Water

Where an open flame is unsafe to use (in bark paths, for instance), boiling water serves the same purpose without the danger of fire. It is awkward to try and use large amounts of boiling water this way, but a daily visit with a teapot can keep a given area clean year-round. Spot watering persistent weeds in cracks with boiling water will kill even the worst pests in time.

Cover Crops

When a large space is overrun with weeds, planting it with a cover crop can reduce the weed return rate. Fast growers such as crimson clover, oats, and buckwheat can outpace the weeds. Instead of harvesting a crop, till under these green cover crops to replenish the soil with stored nitrogen and other nutrients. If you don't want to till, you can simply mow your cover crops and let them compost on site. When it's time to resow the next cover crop, you can scratch the soil with a heavy rake or simply broadcast seed a bit more heavily than usual.

Cover cropping has one major disadvantage—it takes time. You often need several cycles of cover cropping to get tired, weedy soil into better condition. However, when you have a large property to contend with and are not ready to take on the whole place at once, this system is an excellent way of getting and keeping wild areas under control while building tilth and soil nutrition levels.

Dealing with Pests

YOUR ORGANIC GARDEN MAY NOT BE PROBLEM-FREE, BUT by taking care of the soil and selecting native plants, you may find you have few pests to deal with at all. However even happy, healthy, and well-suited plants can occasionally start to lose a battle with a mightier foe.

You may be relieved to know that there are a few low-impact environmental approaches you can use when insect pests attack. Hand-picking visible pests and dropping them into soapy water may be the best place to start; this method is particularly effective against Japanese beetles and slugs. Sprays of cold water (make sure you hit the undersides of leaves, too) or insecticidal soap are usually effective against pests like aphids and spider mites; you may have to repeat the treatment every few days when infestations are heavy. You can also remove severely infested leaves to get rid of pests; be sure to throw the foliage into the trash or burn it; do not add it to your compost pile.

Deer, rabbits, and rodents (like moles, voles, and groundhogs) are also potential troublemakers, and there may be little you can do for long-term effectiveness. Sometimes you can deter animal pests from mowing down prize plantings by offering them other menu options—plants that aren't as special or as expensive. At other times, nothing but a fully developed plan of attack will do; that's when I get out the recipes for concoctions and repellents to chase away these nuisances. Below, I've highlighted a few of the most common pests and my solutions for controlling them.

Aphids

You'll know when you have aphids in the garden because they usually appear by the hundreds. It's disheartening to see a seemingly healthy plant turn so quickly into a yellow, distorted, sick-looking plant. Aphids attack by sucking sap from a plant; the leaves and flowers soon fall, and molds and viral diseases take over the weakened plant. The quickest way I've found to get rid of these pests is with a strong shot of water. Even a heavy, driving rain can kill them because their soft bodies are easily damaged. You can attract native predators and parasites by planting pollen- and nectar-producing plants near plants that are attacked frequently by aphids.

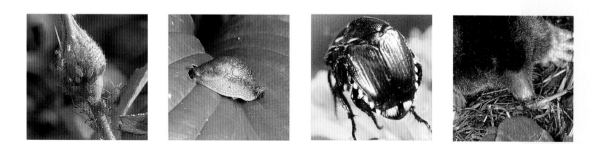

Four-footed animal pests can be more damaging to a garden than insects are. If deer fencing is an impractical option, you may need to live with the damage the deer cause. Contact your local extension office for a list of plants that deer tend to avoid in your area.

Deer

The very best deer deterrent is a dog, without question. Barring that, gardeners resort to a whole host of strategies, all of which work for a while. My garden abuts a large public forest and is on a deer superhighway. We see deer daily and I've found that there are no deer-proof plants. What they gorge on one year may be ignored the next, while plants they have disdained for years suddenly become irresistible. Young deer are often more adventurous and curious than their elders, happily taste-testing almost everything in their path.

Deer fencing must be at least 8 feet high to be effective—and 10 feet is better. I've decided not to fence, but instead provide a large assortment of plants, including many kinds of local favorites. When there is enough variety, something will always survive to look great. For instance, deer adore our native redtwig dogwood, which normally grows to 8 feet high and wide. The local deer keep it trimmed at about 3 feet. The presence of the redtwig dogwood protects several other, more ornamental dogwoods I grow, which are barely touched when so many luscious red twigs are available. This is what I call "win-win" planting.

There are other good solutions, as well. In one garden I know, a young boy planted a hedge of "dog" roses (free roses that nobody really liked) around his mother's garden. He figured that the deer would nibble these and leave the choicer ones inside the garden alone. (He was correct, I might add.) Another neighbor protects her woodland garden by an irregular "hedge" of recycled plants that distract the deer from the garden's more valuable flowers.

In my own garden, I find it useful to plant several varieties of plants that deer tend to feed on, such as the twiggy dogwoods and smaller willows. By offering a small smorgasbord, I generally escape the wholesale damage that occurs when deer find a concentration of one special plant that they really love. When you incorporate roses, lilies, and other delicious plants into naturalistically layered gardens where they're planted alongside many other kinds of plants, deer are less likely to find them than when their favorites are massed together. It's silly to set plants out like a salad bar and then get angry when something takes you up on your offer. Mixing tasty plants into mixed borders makes them harder for deer and other pests to find.

Young deer are often more adventurous and curious than their elders, happily taste-testing almost everything in their path.

A Concentrate to Repel Moles

When you make this recipe, you can double or triple the ingredients for a larger batch, depending on the severity of the problem and how much of the repellent you need to make. If you have lots of moles, make a big batch and use it daily (or share it with friends).

A few drops dishwashing liquid
⅛ cup castor oil

Mix together until foamy. To use, add two tablespoons of the mixture to 1 gallon of water. Use a tank or backpack sprayer to apply the mixture over the lawn and around mole holes. This usually works within a day.

Japanese Beetles

You've heard it a million times—"the best defense is a good offense." With Japanese beetles, it's advice worth following. You can start by avoiding plants that Japanese beetles love, such as astilbes, four-o'clocks (*Mirabilis jalapa*), hollyhocks, peonies, and roses. Japanese beetles aren't the easiest pests to control. When beetle numbers are high in midsummer, handpick or vacuum them (with a handheld vacuum) from the plants in the early morning, or shake them from the plants onto plastic sheets. You can kill them by drowning them in soapy water or crushing them underfoot. By all means, don't use Japanese beetle traps. They attract far more beetles to your yard than you'll ever kill in the trap.

You can keep Japanese beetles away by dealing with their larvae (the fat, white grubs you find just under the grass layer). To kill the grubs, apply milky disease spores to the lawn. This bacteria survives for many years in the soil and will eliminate Japanese beetle grubs over the course of a few seasons. Apply the material in late spring or fall when the soil temperature is at least 70°F, but while grubs are still present in the soil.

Moles

Moles come to the garden for worms. When you make great soil, you're inviting moles to partake of a tasty feast. My favorite way to deal with moles is to create small static compost piles in an unobtrusive area near the point of attack. I stock the compost pile with some almost-finished compost and blended kitchen scraps, then add a supply of red wigglers from the worm bin. This rich concentration of worms convinces the moles to dine here, instead of digging through the garden. This is a bit like putting a pot of jam out for wasps when they appear at a picnic.

Another highly effective way to deal with moles is to use a homemade version of a commercial mole repellent. I have found it to be very effective in my own gardens. This recipe, at left, has also been tested by many home gardeners, who report excellent results.

Rabbits

Rabbits can be real pests. They'll always go for the tender new growth on a plant, and they often leave the plant devastated and struggling for life. Unfortunately, there are few organic controls that keep rabbits away altogether. They do tend to avoid plants that are tough to chew or aromatic, though, so planting artmesias, catmint, lamb's-ears, and yarrow could discourage them. If your plants live past infancy, you can continue to keep rabbits away by sprinkling bloodmeal or hot-pepper spray around your garden early in the season.

Slugs

Unless you live where slugs are rampant, you may not even be aware of these little pests. In the maritime Northwest, however, our native wood slug is nicknamed "the banana slug," both for its color and its size. In truth, these local slugs are composters that feed on dying foliage. They are important recyclers in woods and damp meadows and should be welcome in gardens as well. In contrast, the European field slugs and snails are unwanted imports that feast on live foliage and do a great deal of damage.

Traditional slug controls include beer traps (containers that hold enough beer to drown an unsuspecting mollusk), as well as diatomaceous earth (tiny, ground-up particles sharp-edged enough to slice slugs into sushi).

Dealing with Diseases

I HARDLY EVER HAVE TO COPE WITH SERIOUS PLANT diseases, so I am not really an expert on plant pathology. In naturalistic layered gardens, it's quite easy to find the right ecological niche for almost any plant. When you take time to make great soil before planting, your plants get off to a healthy start. When you keep the soil healthy with regular feeding mulches, you avoid a multitude of common diseases and growth problems. When certain plants persist in having problems, whether it be black spot on roses or mildew on phlox, I exchange the sufferers for roses and phlox that are resistant to these problems.

On the other hand, every garden has its share of difficulties. Where I live, for instance, soilborne diseases such as root rots are as common and as prevalent as athlete's foot in a locker room. In most of my gardens, there have been whole sections where root rots killed off numerous plants despite the most careful soil preparation. Rather than try to use deadly soil drenches to combat the pathogens responsible for the damage, I chose to find plants that had natural resistance to the root rots that are found in my area.

I began by looking at the survivors—plants that grew just fine while their neighbors perished. Then I introduced relatives of the healthy plants, building a base of resistant families that could be grown successfully in the trouble spots. Interestingly enough, these varied from place to place, probably because the exact pathogen also varied. I had my soil tested to find out what the overall problem was (I didn't bother to find out precisely which pathogen was the culprit in each case, since the tests can be expensive and not always precise). Instead, I looked at what was working well and worked from there.

Even with the best culture, some plants will have problems. How you choose to deal with those problems depends on how much time and energy you are willing to devote to those particular plants. For example, when peonies get botrytis, as they do in these parts, I have several options. The easiest solution would be to toss out the ones that have it—coddling the sick usually leads to plants with lifelong problems. Look on the bright side: Getting rid of troublesome plants allows you to make healthier choices when you replace them.

If you've lost a few plants in your ornamental garden and have some holes to fill, try planting plants that do double-duty, producing edible food and making a splash with color and form. The blazing colors of 'Bright Lights' Swiss chard prove that many food-producing plants have ornamental qualities, as well.

Clump-forming *Phlox paniculata* 'David' is one of the most mildew-resistant garden phloxes available. Planting resistant varieties is one way to prevent the problem of mildew. If it gains a foothold in your garden, keep it under control by spraying the leaves of affected plants with a strong spray of water.

My other option would be to watch my peonies with care and pick off buds and leaves that show signs of the disease. But I choose to deal with botrytis in another way. I spray peonies with weekly applications of home-brewed compost tea. I make compost tea by filling a cheesecloth sack with aged compost and soaking the sack in water overnight. I dilute the liquid with water until it's the color of weak tea. I spray the compost tea on all surfaces of the plant (including the undersides of the leaves) and it controls the problem nicely.

Baking Soda Spray for Fungal Disease

1 tablespoon baking soda
1 tablespoon horticultural oil
1 gallon water

Mix the baking soda, oil, and water in a 1-gallon pump or backpack sprayer. Spray each plant completely, including tough-to-reach spots. Spray about once a week, but try to limit your spraying to the cool times of day because the oil may react with sunlight and burn plant leaves. It's always a good idea to test the spray on a few leaves before spraying the entire plant.

In general, you have a couple of options when it comes to battling diseases in your garden. Weekly applications of compost tea are a good start; it contains beneficial bacteria that give plants the upper hand when fighting off fungal diseases. You can also prune diseased, dead, or dying plants to remove disease-scarred areas.

You can fight fungal diseases like black spot and powdery mildew with a baking soda spray you mix yourself (see recipe above). Developed by researchers at Cornell University, this disease-fighting formula can be applied with a pump or backpack sprayer.

For serious disease problems, contact your local extension agent and ask about applying organic controls. If the controls don't seem to be working, you may have to remove the infected plant and choose a more disease-resistant plant or cultivar.

Pollination Nation

IT'S CURIOUS TO THINK THAT WE HUMANS MAY OWE OUR culture, if not our very existence, to bees. Nearly two-thirds of the world's flowers are pollinated by bees and other insects like moths, mosquitoes, and wasps. The majority of fruits, vegetables, grains, and herbs are also dependent on pollinators. While some plants can be pollinated by wind, gravity, or a passing animal, others depend on birds or bats. Most, however, are propagated by the humble bee.

Over thousand of years, humans have developed a respectful, even affectionate working relationship with bees. Beekeeping has been commemorated by poets as long as humans have kept records. Unfortunately, that relationship has become increasingly strained. Even as exploding populations demand ever-greater yields from our crops, encroaching development, chemical farming, and pollution are destroying the natural habitat of bees and other pollinators.

What can ordinary gardeners do about it? It's easy to feel that such huge problems can only be solved by huge repairs, and in many respects, that is sadly so. Even if we devote our whole backyard to creating a habitat for bees, birds, and other native pollinators, one small patch can't support enough wildlife to really matter. But there is great strength in numbers. If many of us devote even part of the land in our trust to supporting bees and other pollinators, we can weave a living green web that stretches from coast to coast.

Nearly one-third of all North Americans have some kind of garden. If we each set aside a portion of our yards for plants that provide habitat and food for our native pollinators, that adds up to hundreds of thousands of acres. If each of us makes the choice not to use pesticides and herbicides, we can enormously reduce the toxic runoff that pollutes our waterways and soils. Then, if each of us makes a point of taking the idea a bit beyond our own backyards, we can stretch our influence further still.

One Idea, Many Believers

The term "each one teach one" has been used as a slogan for many charitable causes. In gardening circles, wouldn't it be wonderful to expand that idea to "each one teach many" to help spread the word about the benefits of organic, naturalistic, and sustainable gardening? For instance, in my town, a family began

If many of us devote even part of the land in our trust to supporting bees and other pollinators, we can weave a living green web that stretches from coast to coast.

planting daffodils in public places, offering them free to any neighborhood that would help plant. Now about 8,000 new bulbs go in each year and the roads are bright with blossoms in spring.

Another family decided to plant lilacs in public areas, adding 100 each year. A local conservationist joined in, offering native red currant bushes (*Ribes sanguineum*) to anybody who would plant them in appropriate sites. In just a few years, the idea of creating public plantings has taken firm hold. Volunteer groups make bee, bird, and butterfly gardens at local schools and teach kids to observe the creatures who come to feed and live. A larger pollinator garden has been installed at the local library, and others will be made at the city hall, the performing arts center, and even along the town's roads.

Gardeners anywhere can plan programs like this for their own towns. The best way to begin is with small projects that are inexpensive and simple to maintain. Schools are good places to start because teachers are always excited about projects that will actively involve kids in learning about science and help them to connect with the natural world. A pollinator garden can be used as an outdoor classroom for science and ecology classes. It's usually easy to get help and seed money from parent-teacher groups, and it's important to involve them in the planning and planting of bee, bird, and butterfly gardens so they can be involved with the ongoing maintenance. Such outreach has a long arm—once folks begin paying attention to the small creatures around them, they are often willing to stop using pesticides.

If these public pollinator gardens teach people only one thing, it should be this: Think before you spray. For so many years, advertisers (and experts who ought to

have known better) urged us to rush out and buy poison spray the moment some poor bug annoyed us. If we were inconvenienced by wasps—well, zap them all dead. If ants got in your peonies, just wipe them out before they attack another plant. Hopefully, we can turn the tide and teach people how important pollinators (and all insects) are to healthy and sustainable gardens.

Even though few people actually try to get rid of honeybees, all-purpose bug sprays don't discriminate. Bees and many other small pollinators are just as susceptible to these pesticides as their less-desirable relatives are. What's more, many commonly used pesticides will kill bees a long way from your yard. Drift from sprays can carry toxins clear around the block. Downstream, those powerful toxins can kill fish that certainly never did anything to anybody's lawn.

Helping the Bees

It won't be as easy to undo the harm as it was to cause it. Luckily, there are steps you can take to help bees and other pollinators. First, stop using toxic pesticides and herbicides. Next, seek out organic or ecologically sound solutions to disease and insect problems. If you aren't sure what organic steps to take, ask your local nursery or buy a book or magazine on organic gardening. In the meantime, call your local Master Gardener hotline (you can find these folks through your local extension office). In other words, do your homework and ask for advice *before* you reach for the spray can.

Honeybees in particular are suffering in great numbers. Besides the lethal effects of pesticides and herbicides intended for other targets, millions have

Outdoor garden classrooms provide kids with an instant science lesson. Working closely with plants, insects, and animals, they begin to understand how delicate and interconnected the natural world is and how organic gardening can create abundant and beautiful landscapes.

died because of tracheal mites, tiny pests that lodge in their windpipes. Despite their widespread range, honeybees don't really belong in the New World. Originally, a few hives were brought to New England by settlers from Europe. Soon the bees adapted to the new land and were so naturalized that many people forgot their non-native status. These imported European honeybees are hive-building bees that made their way west with the wagon trains and can now be found in every state.

All native American bees, on the other hand, are solitary bees that nest alone rather than in hives. Solitary bees (like the orchard mason bee) do a fine job of pollinating, but need our active encouragement and a clean environment in order to thrive in great numbers. Some ecological watch groups estimate that the native bee population is only about 5 percent of what it was 2 decades ago. Nobody knows how many native bees lost out to the more efficient honeybees. Over the past decade, disease has evened the score, but at a terrible price for both team players and loner bees.

With the increased interest in the plight of the bee, many gardeners are intrigued by the idea of creating a garden that will attract and nourish bees, birds, and butterflies. Such a garden can make a genuine contribution to the well-being of wild creatures. If you have noticed poor fruit set or low vegetable yields in recent summers, lack of pollination may well be the underlying cause.

The best way to avoid such problems is to encourage native bees and other pollinators to make their homes in your garden. Not using poisons is a huge step in the right direction. Providing housing is another. In return for your hospitality, bees will make quick work of pollinating your garden. Many nurseries now sell native bee and wasp houses and mason bee kits, which include little apartment houses for solitary bees. These contain blocks of wood with a zillion holes drilled into them. Some models come with paper straw sleeves so you can change the "sheets" after each season's guests leave.

You can also use plants to create a welcoming environment for bees. In my garden, I usually spy the first bees on snow crocus, especially early-blooming species like golden bunch (*Crocus ancyrensis*), which appear in February and March. The whole mahonia clan (*Mahonia* spp.) are excellent bee plants, especially forms of early-flowering Oregon grapeholly (*Mahonia*

aquifolium). You can often find mason bees gorging themselves on lily-of-the-valley shrub (*Pieris japonica*). There are many forms of this attractive evergreen, all decked with clustered white, fragrant flowers from late winter through spring. Blueberries, huckleberries, lingonberries, kinnikinnick, and salal are equally popular with early bees, whose gentle hum enlivens the garden as much as any early bird's chirps.

Plant the flowers that bloom first in your garden on the sunny south side of the house, where the bees will find them close at hand when they awaken from winter slumber. Add bee-attracting plants to your garden each year, and each spring when the garden is abuzz with busy pollinators, you'll be glad you made room for our mild-mannered, productive native bees.

If you love the idea of attracting and keeping bees, want to make your own honey, or find your fruit and vegetable production is not what it should be, contact your local beekeepers association. (Check with your local extension office to find the nearest branch.) These kindly and informative folks will give you the buzz on how to get started with honeybees, as well as other kinds of bees.

Bee houses can attract one of the best pollinators around—the orchard mason bee. Hang houses at least 3 feet off the ground on the sunny sides of outbuildings or fence posts, and provide a sheltering overhang to keep the nest holes dry and sheltered from wind.

Saving Lady Beetles

LADY BEETLES (COMMONLY REFERRED TO AS LADYBUGS) are among the gardener's best friends because these little beetles have a voracious appetite for aphids. Lady beetles are often released in greenhouses and fields where aphids plague all sorts of commercial crops, from vegetables and salad greens to annuals and perennials. When growers use natural controls like lady beetles to get rid of pests, they reduce chemical pollution.

An introduced Asian species of lady beetles (*Harmonia axyridis*) is spreading slowly throughout the country. They were deliberately imported by farmers to assist our native lady beetles, and they do a terrific mop-up job in gardens where aphids are a problem. The markings on this species are varied, so in any given group you can find lots of different colors and patterns. Some of the lady beetles are spotless, with a solid body color of red, tomato orange, or glossy black. Others have just a few big spots or many small ones. You might see a black lady beetle with orange spots, a tomato orange lady beetle with black spots, and a "normal" red lady beetle with black spots.

Asian lady beetles get through the winter by hibernating, and they begin their search for a safe shelter in the fall. In their native land, they would head for the side of a cliff, but here they often have to settle for a warm, light-color wall. They often work their way indoors through cracks in walls or around windows. If you discover lady beetles cozying into your home for the winter, don't panic. Consider their presence a blessing—a blessing for your garden, that is.

You don't have to let them roam freely until the garden warms up, though. Just harvest them and store them in the refrigerator in a clean jar with a lid. The most effective collection system for lady beetles is a small hand-held vacuum. Fitted with a clean bag, these totable vacuums will swoosh up the ladybugs as fast as they appear—but if you use this method, accept that you may loose some lady beetles in the process. Seattle Master Gardener Jo Phillips uses a gentler method to clean up lady beetles—a plain old whisk broom. "They're still a little slow when they first wake up," she says, "so just sweep them into a clean dustpan and then into a jar."

Once the lady beetles are in the jar, add a damp paper towel or a few drops of water—they need some moisture to survive—but don't add so much liquid that they drown. In late April or May, when the hungry aphids arrive in force, you'll know it's time to waken your sleepy lady beetles. Turn them loose in the garden (just set the open jar on the soil on a nice day), and they'll eat their way through the aphids before you can say "Thank you."

When growers use natural controls like lady beetles to get rid of pests, they reduce chemical pollution.

Help Is at Hand

You may enjoy the solitude and peacefulness you find in your garden, but you might come across a gardening situation where you need someone with a fresh perspective or expertise that you don't have at your fingertips. Seek out plant societies or Master Gardener organizations to learn about native plants, tackling garden problems, and the latest trends in garden design. You just might meet a host of new friends who are as passionate about organic gardening as you are.

NO MATTER HOW WELL YOU CARE FOR YOUR GARDEN, troubles may arise that common sense and simple organic remedies can't eliminate. When serious, persistent trouble plagues your garden, seek help from your local Master Gardener organization. This excellent program consists of well-trained problem solvers who can offer a wide range of solutions specific to your region, including organic and less-toxic alternatives to the chemical quick-fixes readily available in garden centers.

This program began in Washington and Oregon almost 25 years ago and is now operating in every state in the union. Master Gardeners are volunteers who receive training in all aspects of gardening, from planting and harvesting to controlling pests and diseases. They, in turn, perform many hours of community service helping other gardeners. The program is run through the Cooperative Extension Service. Feel free to contact Master Gardeners if you have problems or questions, or are simply looking for some great ideas (see page 270).

In fact, once your naturalistic layered borders are in place and you've enjoyed your garden for a few seasons, you may find yourself wanting to return some of your joy to your community. If so, please consider joining a Master Gardener program yourself. You will find that it is every bit as rewarding to help others discover the secrets of having a healthy, abundant garden as it was for you to do so in your own backyard.

Organic Garden
Design School
Workbook

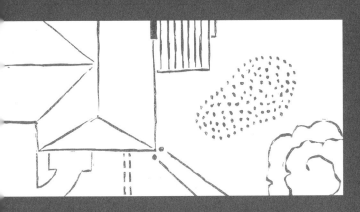

Designing a garden is an exhilarating and rewarding process, but it's important that you do your homework before you start. Even in a small area, there's a lot to discover and learn. The following workbook exercises will help you amass information and keep it accessible. You'll also learn how to assess your property, evaluate its assets and drawbacks, and "edit" the space to suit your design.

Clearly, there's a lot to making a garden design, so it's not wise to rush through the process in a single weekend. Take your time, explore your options, and consider new possibilities as they emerge. By the end of the workbook, you'll be able to create a site map, set clear goals for your garden, and develop an overall plan that suits you and your lifestyle. Once this is done, you can create a workable timeline and set a budget for each project. Congratulations—you're on your way to your dream garden!

Start a Garden Notebook

A garden notebook is the ideal place to keep track of your design ideas, plant lists, site maps, past successes and failures, and most of all, your garden dreams. It doesn't have to be fancy—remember, it's a work in progress, and it's one that's meant to be used. And if you do use it, it can be your best friend, helping you create a garden that works for you.

Your notebook can be a design guide for your specific site. Start with a simple three-ring binder or loose-leaf notebook, or find a large-size journal. Use paper tab dividers to create sections for each part of the garden you plan to work on or want to think about. Keep design ideas and lists of possible plants in each section, as well as the names of books that inspire you. You can also paste cutouts from magazines or photographs of gardens you've visited into your notebook.

Include or designate a few blank pages for simple sketches. In this notebook, you'll learn how to make a site map as your first step in garden making, and you'll want to include this map in your notebook, as well. You may also want to enlarge relevant sections of your site map so you can tackle each part of the garden separately. These sample maps are the ideal places to try out your new design ideas.

Make a Site Map

Map-making may seem intimidating, especially if you don't draw. However, all you need for making a perfectly serviceable site map is a contractor's measuring tape, a buddy, a clipboard, some graph paper, and a pencil. Oh, and an eraser—just in case.

Contractor's measuring tapes come in several lengths, but you should look for a cloth one that's at least 100 feet long (unless your lot is really small, of course).

To measure your site, have your buddy hold one end of the measuring tape at fixed points throughout the site while you take the other end to key boundary lines, structures, plants, paths, and other features. Record the distances you measure, and make notes as necessary. Every site will have a variety of distances and spaces to measure and evaluate. Just to keep you on track, follow this general checklist of things you should measure.

Site Checklist

- ❑ Length of property
- ❑ Width of property
- ❑ Dimensions of house
- ❑ Dimensions of garage
- ❑ Dimensions of outbuildings
- ❑ Length of driveway
- ❑ Width of driveway
- ❑ Sizes and placement of existing hardscape, like decks, paths, patios, retaining walls, or fences
- ❑ Sizes and placement of existing large trees and shrubs, including canopy line for large trees and overhanging trees from neighboring properties
- ❑ Placement of existing overhead wires, telephone poles, or other stationary objects
- ❑ Placement of existing underground pipes, septic field, well, invisible fencing, or power lines

Finding Hidden Features

If you don't have the original blueprints for your home, you may not know exactly where underground pipes, power lines, or the septic field is located. But you'll need to find these things before you dig, plant, or build on your site. Start your search with household papers, like deeds or surveys, or check with local utility companies or local zoning and building officials. If you have an older home, you may have stone markers sunk in the soil that indicate the location of septic fields or wellheads. Or ask older neighbors for information; you may be surprised at how much they know about the neighborhood and your site.

Draw the Map

To make the site map functional, you'll need to combine a sketch of the property with all the measurements you've taken. Graph paper makes this part of the exercise a breeze. When you draw the map, remember that strict accuracy is less important than relative accuracy—as long as you have the house in pretty much the right place and the overall size on the map is about right, your map will be useful. It's also worth remembering that even the best designs on paper will always need some tweaking when it comes time to plant the garden. Gardens designed on paper are always a little different from what you'll actually find on your site.

I like to make an overall site map on the largest sheet of graph paper I can buy. Before you buy graph paper, though, decide what scale you want to use. If you have a tiny urban lot, you can decide a foot of ground equals ½ inch on paper, and make a decent map on an 8½ × 11 sheet of paper. If your site is acres wide, you'll need to tighten things up, making ¼ inch on graph paper equal a foot or even a yard. If your site is really large and you plan to garden in many different areas, you may want to make additional maps in larger scale, each map showing a particular area in detail. Whatever scale you decide on, your local paper or art supply shop may carry (or be able to special-order) oversize sheets of graph paper. These oversize sheets cost a

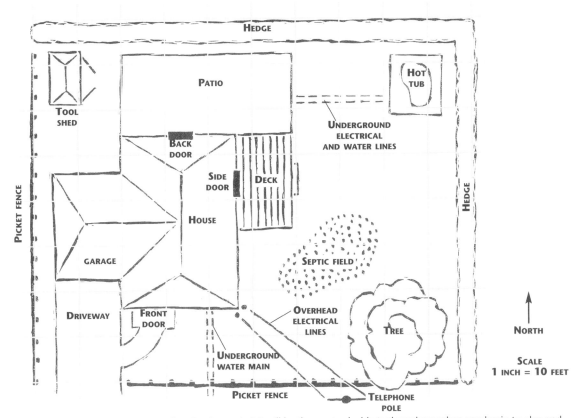

Making an accurate site map may take a few hours, but it will be the most valuable tool you have when you begin to plan and design your garden. Draw the elements to scale, starting with an outline of the yard, house, and other major features (such as sheds, trees, driveways, and patios). Add your yard's dimensions, any low or high points, an arrow indicating north, and underground or overhead features like water lines and electrical wires.

few bucks, but you'll only need one or two, and the time and effort saved by having a fairly accurate map will repay many times over the modest investment you make.

If you want to draft a large, very detailed map, invest in a drafting scale ruler. These three-dimensional rulers only cost a few dollars and are triangular—each side of the triangle has a different scale, such as ⅛ inch, ¼ inch, or ½ inch. The ruler translates graph paper–size measurements into feet, making it easy to see the actual dimensions of your site. Be sure to note on the graph paper what scale you're using. Then follow the steps on page 236 to identify features and draw your site map.

Step-by Step Mapmaking

1. Draw the overall shape of your property and any topographical features, using the gridlines on the graph paper as guides. For instance, if you're using ½-inch graph paper and you've decided that ½ inch equals 1 foot, 40 graph paper spaces represent the width of your 40-foot-wide property. It's best to use a pencil so you can easily erase any misplaced lines.

2. Indicate changes of grade by drawing a series of lines that follow the contour of the slope. Be sure to record whether the slopes are slight, moderate, or steep.

3. Add structures such as houses, garages, and driveways, plus features like sidewalks and paths, and foot traffic patterns.

4. Add an arrow indicating north.

5. Add any large trees and shrubs, noting both trunk size (a rough estimate is fine) and canopy (also called dripline, meaning the spread of a tree's branches).

6. Indicate any underground and overhead objects with a broken line, small dashes, or a new color of pencil. These marks will remind you of landscape features you may not see when you're on-site.

Use Bubbles to Design

Designers use "bubble maps" to indicate areas of the property that have specific characteristics, such as full sun or wet soil. On your site map, you might draw a bubble—a more-or-less circular shape—over the sunniest area and write "sun" in the center. Make another wherever there is consistent shade and write—you guessed it—"shade." In addition, note areas that are damp, dry, well drained, or washed out. Add bubbles where the kids play, the dog naps, and the meter reader tramples, too.

Indicate places where foot traffic needs to be redirected or sections of the garden that need to be improved.

If you want to play around with many ideas, copy your master sketch a few times and move those bubbles to different areas. You can use pens of different colors to indicate bubbles that can't move, such as for a vegetable garden that really needs the sun or a hammock that really should be in shade. Anything else can be placed more flexibly and noted in a different color.

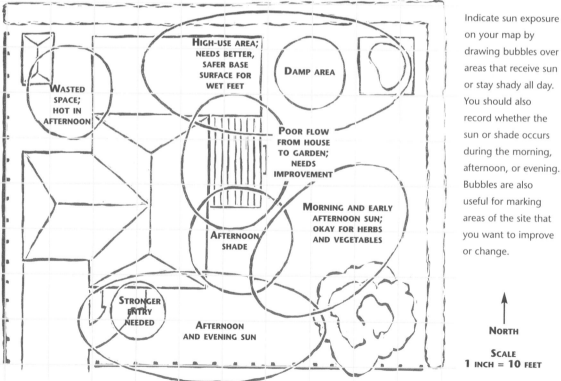

Indicate sun exposure on your map by drawing bubbles over areas that receive sun or stay shady all day. You should also record whether the sun or shade occurs during the morning, afternoon, or evening. Bubbles are also useful for marking areas of the site that you want to improve or change.

Assess Your Garden's Potential

To make a design that fulfills your needs, you must be as clear as possible about what you want. However, it may take some time to understand what you want in a garden design. Entertaining too many choices can be as frustrating as having too few choices. It's less confusing to figure out what you want from the garden if you begin by considering three things: what you want, what you need, and what you have.

This means deciding what you (and by "you" I mean anyone who will use the garden space) will do in the garden and what you want to have in the garden, as well as how much space is actually available. The easiest way to do this is to list all the activities and chores that you will do in your garden space. Use the questions and spaces on page 238 to explore your ideas and record your thoughts. Add to the list any and all services you want the garden to provide, such as room for an herb and vegetable garden, a cutting garden, an ornamental pool, or a naturalistic mixed border that provides privacy and beauty all year long.

To help you evaluate your site's potential, take some time to consider the three questions on page 238: What do you want? What do you need? What do you have?

To answer them well, it's helpful to examine your assumptions. Often, what you think you know about your site can get in the way of seeing what is possible or probable. It's also useful to clarify the difference between dreams and practical needs. Revealing your hidden ideas helps you to create a realistic garden plan that makes optimal use of the available space, light, shade, and other attributes.

When you assess the importance or usefulness of existing plants, keep in mind that these factors may depend on how your garden develops. Both plants and objects may have a temporary value that makes them short-term keepers, even if they eventually will be removed.

I like to develop a 5-year plan for clients. During Year 1, we implement two aspects of the overall plan—the parts that are most important for safety reasons or accessibility and the parts that will give the most immediate pleasure, such as a patio or enclosed garden "room." The remaining years in the overall plan are devoted to growing and filling in garden rooms, spaces, and beds.

Seasons of Change

Your garden will grow and change through the years, and your "needs" for the garden will change, as well. For instance, 10 years ago, my garden's activity list included having Cub Scout races each week. We had to make room for a barbecue and a large picnic table, find space for a water slide, and designate places for children and a goodly assortment of animals to play. I also grew lots of organic vegetables and herbs, had a large compost area, and maintained a small orchard. In those days, the ornamental planting that edged our meadow was called The Soccer Border because nothing in it could be harmed by a straying soccer ball.

These days, my garden needs are very different. My children are grown, most of the animals are gone, and the old farm with its rolling meadow has been sold. At my new home, I still have a large compost area, but most of the features I had in my old garden aren't as necessary now. Space on my new property is given over to teaching gardens that demonstrate how to plant a sloping, shady hillside; a dry, sunny roadside strip; a high-traffic pathway; or the area over a septic field.

Time has changed the way I use the garden, too. It has also changed the way I garden, because I can no longer do the back-breaking work that traditional gardening requires. Instead, I've designed beds and borders that I can maintain in less time each week than it used to take to mow our lawn. In return for modest attention, the plants I've chosen provide me and all who visit with beauty throughout the seasons.

What Do You Want?

? Think about your garden. What do you like best about the way it is now?

_____
_____
_____
_____
_____
_____

? Imagine your dream garden. What would it have that your present garden lacks?

_____
_____
_____
_____
_____
_____

? What do you want to be able to do in your garden? (Grow vegetables, feed the birds and bees, or enjoy year-round ornamental borders?)

_____
_____
_____
_____
_____
_____
_____

What Do You Need?

✓ List all the activities and chores that you intend to do in your yard. Include things like washing the car or the dog, playing ball games, eating dinner, and reading in a shady corner.

_____
_____
_____
_____
_____
_____
_____
_____

? Which of these activities and chores will take place in the garden area?

_____
_____
_____
_____

? Where could the others take place?

_____
_____
_____
_____
_____

What Do You Have?

✓ List the features of your yard and garden, even if they're things you'd like to eliminate. Include features like sidewalk beds, compost piles, large turfgrass areas, wooded property lines, and privet hedges. For now, a simple list will suffice; you'll continue to evaluate what your garden contains as you go along.

_____
_____
_____
_____
_____
_____
_____
_____
_____
_____
_____
_____
_____
_____
_____
_____

Imagine Your Garden

Much of what you have to work with will be detailed on your site map. However, you are probably beginning to see that there are more to gardens than what meets the eye. The process of site mapping is only the beginning. Intangibles (like a wonderful sense of welcome or terrific flow) won't show up on a map. In this section, you'll analyze your garden space in terms of enclosure, clutter, entry, and access. Most of my students find that they have a lot more confidence in their own judgment after doing the first few exercises.

Assessing Enclosure

Enclosing the garden can give it presence and privacy. Enclosure also creates a firm backdrop for your plants, setting them off in the way that a gallery wall sets off the pictures hung upon it. One caveat I feel compelled to mention, however, is that most gardeners over-screen their gardens. This is especially true with hedging plants, most of which are tall trees by nature. Fences don't grow taller with time, but laurels and privet and maples certainly do. When analyzing your own yard in terms of enclosure, try this simple exercise to get a fresh look at your site.

✓ Record the kinds and sizes of enclosure presently in place around your property. Use these questions to guide your observations.

◆ Is there enough enclosure?

◆ Is it functional and attractive?

◆ Is there too much enclosure (overgrown plantings, high fence) already?

◆ Do any enclosed areas require repetitive maintenance (shearing, monthly clipping, clearing of debris)?

◆ What would be gained if you removed or altered the present enclosure (time, valuable garden space, more sun, more inviting outdoor dining area)?

◆ Is there a simpler, inexpensive, more attractive alternative?

◆ Front yard observations at a glance:

_____

_____

◆ Side yard(s) observations at a glance:

_____

_____

◆ Backyard observations at a glance:

_____

_____

_____

✓ Stroll through several neighborhoods in your area, noticing the different ways other gardeners achieve enclosure. Take a notebook and jot down enclosures you'd like to remember and incorporate into your design.

◆ What types of enclosures did you see?

_____

_____

_____

_____

◆ Which look most attractive?

_____

_____

◆ Which seem most practical?

_____

_____

◆ Are any obviously unsuccessful? Why?

_____

_____

✓ Visit the library and browse through picture books of gates, fences, hedges, and so on. Sketch any ideas you find appealing, and add them to your notebook. Or cut out photographs of enclosures you like from magazines and catalogs and place them in your notebook, too.

Many people have a hard time imagining what space would look like if it were enclosed or planted in a different manner. To help you imagine what could be there, work through this list of questions.

? How might you use any open space differently if it were enclosed? For example, if your side yard were enclosed, would you turn that area into a private patio?

_____

_____

? How might you use any enclosed space differently if it were not enclosed? For example: If an overgrown hedge takes up most of the front yard, what would you gain by removing it and substituting a fence?

_____

_____

_____

_____

? Are there any views, like wonderful neighborhood trees, distant mountains, or a beautiful mixed border, to frame?

_____

_____

_____

_____

? Are there any views you'd like to screen to gain privacy, such as a neighbor's deck overlooking your pool, or views you'd like to block because they're unattractive, such as curbside garbage cans or a compost pile?

_____

_____

? How much screening is actually required in each of the following areas of the yard to give a sense of enclosure? Keep in mind that, in many cases, a screen that's just 6 to 10 feet tall is sufficient.

◆ Screening needs for front:

_____

_____

_____

◆ Screening needs for back:

_____

_____

_____

_____

◆ Screening needs for side(s):

_____

_____

_____

_____

Assessing Clutter

Many designers begin a garden renovation by mentally uncluttering the site, a process that's a bit like pruning. You'll need to mentally eliminate anything that is unneeded, unattractive, nonfunctional, or dead. What's left (often very little) will generally look quite different when uncrowded. Plants that have been squeezed for years may initially seem too misshapen to keep, but thoughtful, remedial pruning may reveal unsuspected sculptural qualities.

It's not uncommon for a small urban lot to hold many overgrown plants that are no longer in scale with the site and that require ceaseless hard pruning. When you remove these usually unhealthy plants (nobody likes to be cut in half for years!), a surprising amount of usable space is suddenly available.

If your site is overgrown and you are having a hard time getting around what's there, try this exercise that allows you to thoughtfully evaluate all the features of your site. Record your findings on the Clutter Questionnaire on the opposite page.

✓ 1. List all the major features of your site.

2. Cross out any that can't be removed (for instance, the house and the garage).

3. Ask yourself the questions on the opposite page about each remaining feature.

Is it functional? Does that sagging old hedge in the side yard screen the street well? If so, you may decide that even though the function (screening) is important, it might be better fulfilled by another element. If the hedge does nothing but fill space, you may decide to simply remove it.

Is it necessary? Sometimes an object or plant may not be healthy or attractive, yet it seems necessary (usually to provide privacy). You may decide that its function is vital and, if removed, it will need immediate replacement. In which case, you'll need to analyze its function (screening, muffling road noise, or filtering dust) carefully so you can choose a replacement that meets those same needs.

Is it healthy and in good condition? If the answer is "yes," the object or plant may be a keeper and something you want to preserve. If the answer is "no," you may decide the object's function (screening, privacy, or beauty) is important, but you may find something else that will better fill the space.

Is it attractive? Sometimes a fence or shrub may be sturdy and functional, yet ugly. Ask yourself whether remedial action, such as pruning, painting, or disguising, would help.

Emotions can also affect your choices. However, when a plant with sentimental value harms the garden (through ill health, old age, or overwhelming size), consider whether it's really worth keeping. Perhaps you can immortalize the plant by recycling it into garden art or by capturing it in a photograph.

Clutter Questionnaire

Major feature of your site	Is it functional?	Is it necessary?	Is it healthy and in good condition?	Is it attractive?

Assessing Access and Entryways

Once you have looked with care at the kind and quantity of enclosures your site offers or requires, you can move on to issues of access. If you want your home to be welcoming, you need to create an obvious and attractive main entrance. The entrances to your garden also need to be attractive and well defined. Both of these points may seem obvious, yet it is very easy to get used to awkward situations that have changed slowly or not at all over many years.

To start, work through this exercise with just your home in mind. To get a good look at your home's entryway, walk across the street and examine what your neighbors see. Think about the view as a whole, then look individually at the aspects that make up your entryway. Then, walk up to your entryway and take time to really see what's there. At right are a few of the questions you should ask yourself. (Don't spend time finding a solution at this point; in most cases a simple "yes" or "no" will suffice.)

Before reacting to what you see and making on-the-spot decisions about what you want to cut down, plant, build, or change, take time for some mental editing. Think of things that could be changed slightly rather than drastically, or brainstorm major changes you could make to achieve an entirely new look.

Access and Entryway Assessment

◆ Is an overgrown hedge or shrub eating up your sidewalk and obscuring the door?

◆ Are the foundation plantings reaching for the sky?

◆ Is the front yard lost beneath a broad canopy tree whose lower limbs block house windows?

◆ Is the main entryway to your home easy to use at all times?

◆ Can it be used by a person with a baby stroller and bags of groceries?

◆ If your entry has steps, is there a handrail to assist children or adults?

◆ Is there adequate lighting at night?

◆ Do entryway plants or container plantings block access?

◆ Is the entryway area surfaced with a non-skid paving material such as concrete, brick, or stone?

◆ Is the footing safe in the rain or snow?

◆ Would the entryway change if a few lower limbs came off the tree?

◆ What if the hedge were gone altogether?

◆ Could those overgrown foundation plants be moved and perhaps used to block an unsightly view from the backyard?

◆ Does the access path really need to be arrow straight?

◆ Could a gentle curve create interestingly shaped planting beds, soften the linear front yard, or add a pleasing touch of naturalism to the entryway?

◆ If the main entry path is already winding, do its curves create problems for people trying to reach the front door?

◆ Is the path visually confusing?

◆ Do people get lost trying to find your front door?

After filling out this checklist, you will see the garden with fresh eyes. By now, some solutions will probably be obvious, while others may require more information, more thought, and more study. If you decide you want a second opinion or design help, a professional garden designer can guide you to a solution and can provide garden renovation services for projects of all sizes. Be aware, though, that few professional designers understand natural-istic design principles or consider organic solutions to common garden problems. To find qualified help, contact local organic growers for ideas. Organic growers often work together and share information and resources, and they may be able to connect you with garden designers who value organic principles.

Now that you've worked through the exercise using your home's access and entryways as the sub-ject, turn your thoughts to garden access—it's just as important as home access. To decide whether garden access requires improvement, designers look at how garden visitors enter or reach different garden spaces. If getting in and out of the garden is awkward, complicated, or inconvenient, the garden space will not be used to its maximum potential. To assess the effectiveness of your garden access areas, ask yourself some of the same questions you've answered in the previous list, then home in on the specifics of your situation.

Many access problems can be corrected by improving the garden paths and placing other hardscape elements, such as fences, gates, and arbors, appropriately. Begin your design process by finding the right places for each garden or yard activity, then link these areas with wide, safe, well-drained paths. Certain things must happen in cer-tain places, and it's your job as a garden designer to make logical designs when creating garden space.

Place activity areas according to their relative importance in your life. Herbs and vegetables need great sun to thrive, so they may share the sunniest spot with a picnic table, creating a multi-use area. Service areas (like electrical meters and trash con-tainers) need to be accessible, but can still be hid-den from view. Compost should be kept close to the kitchen, but not readily visible from seating areas. It's important to consider the practical aspect of every activity in your garden or yard as you're evaluating access and entryways.

Garden Access Assessment

◆ How do you reach the garden? Does everyone who uses the garden access it from the same entryway?

◆ How might this entryway be improved?

◆ Is entry to the garden from the house easy and obvious?

◆ Are there or might there be multiple entrances to the garden?

◆ Should the entrance or entrances be formal or informal?

◆ Should entry be from the sidewalk?

◆ Should entry be from a driveway, covered walkway, or garage?

◆ Should the entrance be open (through an arbor), or should it be closed (through a gate)?

Moving Toward More Naturalistic Design

Many of you may have started gardening when beds were always poker-straight. Gardening has evolved over the past few decades, though, and gardeners now look more to Mother Nature to create gardens that emulate the patterns found in her unplanned wooded areas and meadows. Changes happen slowly, though, and you may have a site that harkens back to the era of hard lines and geometric layouts. If you allow yourself to draw outside the lines, you'll be able to bring a fresh, more naturalistic look to your gardens by making changes one at a time.

Consider design alternatives to the rectangle. When faced with the task of making a garden design for a rectangular side yard, most folks initially respond by creating some version of a geometrically based design. Garden visitors may find these geometric designs overly formal and may not enter because they feel the sanctity of the garden shouldn't be disturbed. While these gardens may have appeal for certain areas and regions, they do

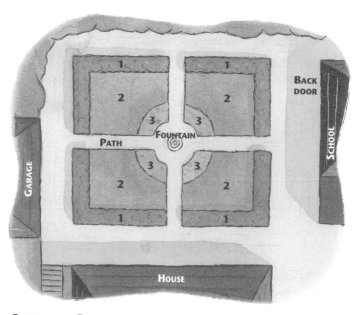

PLANT KEY

1. PRIVET (6' HIGH)
2. ANNUALS AND PERENNIALS
3. HERBS AND BULBS

GEOMETRIC GARDEN: This typical geometry-based design fits neatly into the space between my house and the garden school, but it doesn't help to connect the courtyard garden with the surrounding woodland gardens. The design's straight lines and angles emphasize the separation between the two garden areas, rather than making one garden flow naturally into the other.

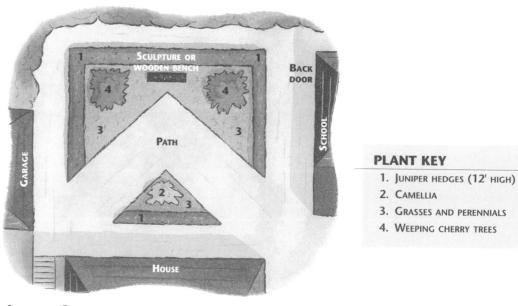

PLANT KEY

1. JUNIPER HEDGES (12' HIGH)
2. CAMELLIA
3. GRASSES AND PERENNIALS
4. WEEPING CHERRY TREES

ANGULAR GARDEN: Clean lines, crisp angles, and generous pathways make for a playful division of space. This kind of design looks great from a window, but is less attractive to strollers, who find little to keep them lingering here. It's hard to imagine a feeling of privacy in this garden, with such wide-open areas dominating the design.

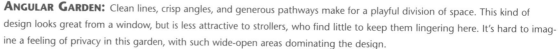

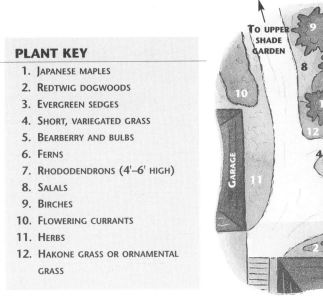

PLANT KEY

1. JAPANESE MAPLES
2. REDTWIG DOGWOODS
3. EVERGREEN SEDGES
4. SHORT, VARIEGATED GRASS
5. BEARBERRY AND BULBS
6. FERNS
7. RHODODENDRONS (4'–6' HIGH)
8. SALALS
9. BIRCHES
10. FLOWERING CURRANTS
11. HERBS
12. HAKONE GRASS OR ORNAMENTAL GRASS

NESTLING GARDEN: Looser lines and eccentrically shaped island beds make this garden seem like an extension of the backdrop woodland. Sculptural rocks and a water feature would look convincing here because you could naturalistically nestle them into the gently sloping hillside.

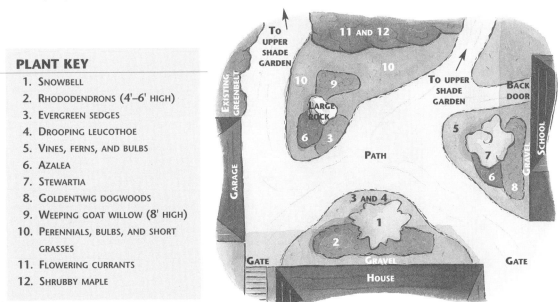

PLANT KEY

1. SNOWBELL
2. RHODODENDRONS (4'–6' HIGH)
3. EVERGREEN SEDGES
4. DROOPING LEUCOTHOE
5. VINES, FERNS, AND BULBS
6. AZALEA
7. STEWARTIA
8. GOLDENTWIG DOGWOODS
9. WEEPING GOAT WILLOW (8' HIGH)
10. PERENNIALS, BULBS, AND SHORT GRASSES
11. FLOWERING CURRANTS
12. SHRUBBY MAPLE

FLOWING GARDEN: These soft, inflated bed shapes gracefully open the courtyard space to foot traffic flow. Tuck a few seats in here and there in the widest gravel area, and they'll look comfortably at home. You can link this courtyard garden to the shade gardens just ahead with naturalistic groupings of small trees and shrubs.

not take into consideration the naturalistic approach to garden design.

If you have a rectangular area on your property, consider developing it in a nonlinear manner, using natural, fluid forms instead of straight lines. Start by drawing bubbles on your site plan to indicate the main areas of use, then add curving lines to indicate the possible flow of movement from one area to another. Add planting beds and plants on the map to help you visualize how the garden is shaping up. Use these two naturalistic alternatives to the stoic rectangle for inspiration.

Now it's your turn to tackle the geometry-based areas on your site. Sketch the approximate dimensions of your garden, then throw caution to the wind and try new ideas for paths and beds. Add a serpentine pathway, cluster plantings along an oval walk, or create a recessed area along a bed for a grand bench. Think about how you want to use the space and how you walk through the area as you explore the possibilities.

Consider ways to create a more powerful sense of entry for an important part of your garden. Choose an area in your garden where you'd like to improve the entryway. This can be an entry to your house, an entry to the backyard, or an entry from one part of the garden to another. Take a photograph of the area, then use a photocopy machine to enlarge it to a size that's easy to work with and that provides a sense of scale (8½ × 11 inches is great). You should make a handful of copies so you can try out a variety of ideas and designs. Next, sketch your ideas directly on the copy, or create a sketch and cut out any interesting shapes and place them on the photocopy.

To improve an entry point, try adding a curve in a straight sidewalk; wide, flowing steps to a slope; or an arch to announce a new part of the garden. Instead of turning a 90-degree angle to get to a front door, flow one path into another to keep the visitor moving forward. Substitute plants with fluid textures and movements for rigid hedges and privet. Or change an insignificant entry of stepping stones into a welcoming path and seating area that beckons the visitor. The Before and After entry designs on this page illustrate how a little creative thinking can create a powerful impact.

Once you've tested a few designs on your photocopies, transfer your ideas to graph paper to begin the plans for your new entry. Use your imagination and don't limit your ideas.

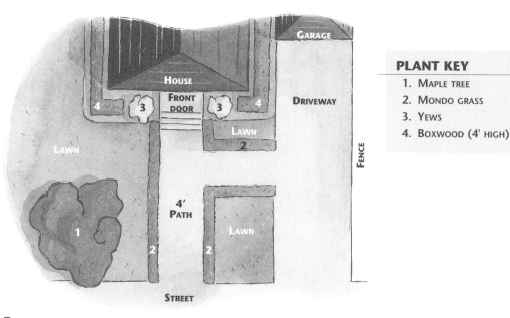

PLANT KEY

1. MAPLE TREE
2. MONDO GRASS
3. YEWS
4. BOXWOOD (4' HIGH)

BEFORE: This typical entryway features linear paths and uninspiring plants. When foundation beds are too narrow, like these are, you'll need to prune constantly to keep the plants at the "right" size. You'll recognize another typical front yard feature—a big lawn interrupted by a single shade tree (in this case, a dreadfully invasive Norway maple).

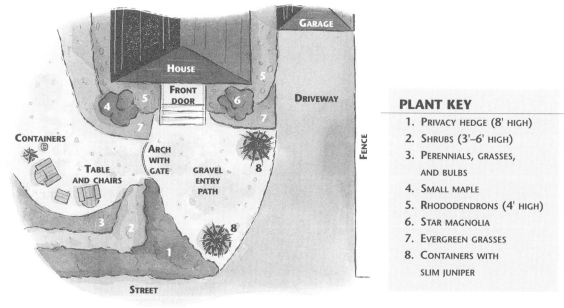

PLANT KEY

1. PRIVACY HEDGE (8' HIGH)
2. SHRUBS (3'–6' HIGH)
3. PERENNIALS, GRASSES, AND BULBS
4. SMALL MAPLE
5. RHODODENDRONS (4' HIGH)
6. STAR MAGNOLIA
7. EVERGREEN GRASSES
8. CONTAINERS WITH SLIM JUNIPER

AFTER: Soften a few lines, and the same entryway has a totally different feeling. Generous curves entice visitors toward the front door, while decorative containers create a sense of entry without the expense of a large arch or gate. A loose, unsheared privacy hedge provides enclosure for the yard, and smaller replacement trees provide shade and screening for the house.

PLANT KEY

1. LARGE CHERRY TREE (VERY OLD)
2. LAWN
3. JAPANESE HOLLY

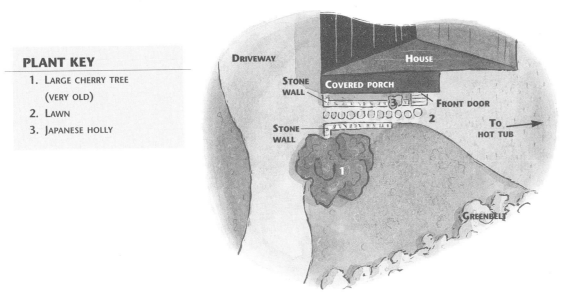

BEFORE: Though this site is large, the entryway feels cramped, narrow, and awkward. Visitors to the house are squeezed through a constricting pathway lined with stone retaining walls. An elderly, oversize cherry tree dominates the scene, while a seldom-used hot tub appears in plain site from the walkway.

PLANT KEY

1. GOLDENTWIG DOGWOOD
2. FLOWERING CURRANTS
3. NEW CHERRY TREE
4. EVERGREEN HERBS, SHRUBS, GRASSES, PERENNIALS, AND BULBS
5. STRAWBERRY TREE (12' HIGH)
6. DWARF CRABAPPLE
7. EVERGREEN HERBS
8. DAPHNE
9. EVERGREEN FERNS
10. RHODODENDRON (8' HIGH)

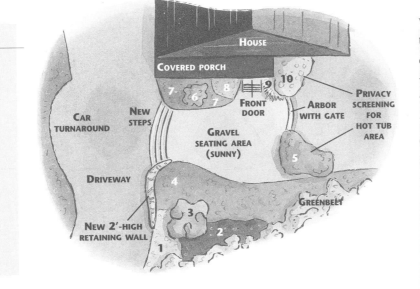

AFTER: Expanding the space and softening the lines makes the entryway accessible and inviting. An arbor, gate, and enclosing shrubs now screen the hot tub, which gets far more use when not overlooked by drop-in visitors. A new wild cherry tree and native shrubs knit the garden back to the greenbelt, continuing the privacy screening.

Consider ways to alter geometrically oriented pathways into nonlinear paths with more naturalistic form and flow. Make a bird's-eye view sketch of each straight-shot pathway, then blow it up to an easy-to-use size like 8½ × 11 inches. Lay tracing paper over the sketch and mark immovable objects (like the house and garage). Leave off the existing straight paths completely. You'll end up with a pathless map that shows the relative positions of main areas of access. You can do the same thing with a map or blueprint of your property. For a head-on view that's more reality-based, take a few snapshots of the area, enlarge them on a copy machine, then sketch different ideas right on the copies.

If you can't immediately see any alternatives to what's already in place, sleep on it for a while. Leave the new drawing in a drawer for a few days so you come back to it with fresh vision. If you're working with a sketch, you can use the method outlined in "Use Bubbles to Design" on page 236 to explore the possibilities. If you're working with a photocopied enlargement, cut out pathway shapes from paper and tape them to the copy to help you visualize your ideas. And prepare to be amazed!

Making Natural and Flowing Paths

Paths and walkways should lead you naturally from place to place. Stroll around your site and evaluate whether your paths entice you and your garden visitors to stop here and there in a relaxed setting, deliver you posthaste to another section of the garden, or need widening or tidying in order to accommodate increased foot traffic.

The Usability Factor

By simply changing the line of a path (either by widening or curving it), you can make an enormous difference in the way you use the garden. If you have to brush by an overgrown hedge to get to the compost heap or squeeze between the garage and the house to reach the herb garden, you won't recycle food scraps or use fresh herbs very often. When you create clear, simple paths that lead to your objectives, your often-unconscious hesitation vanishes, and it becomes a matter of course to use the paths frequently.

Perhaps the most common design flaw you'll come across is paths that are too narrow. You may not need an 8-foot-wide entry path in a tiny urban garden, but anything under 4 feet is going to seem cramped—5 or 6 feet will look more in scale and will function better. Side paths should never be less than 3 feet wide—4 feet wide is better still. That said, let's take a look at how you can evaluate and make changes to your pathways.

What's Underfoot

First of all, consider what kind of surface you want to use. Most folks assume that garden paths must be paved with stone, brick, slate, or some similar hard surface. This is especially true of main entry paths. Hardscape paving can indeed give a path a look of permanence, but only when it's well planned and properly implemented.

I've experimented with many path materials, and I now prefer to make most paths of crushed gravel. When the gravel is tamped with a compactor, it makes a surface hard enough to allow for wheelchair use. Gravel drains so quickly that it eliminates the worry of messy puddles or treacherous ice spots in most climates. And when you use it in combination with rounded or raised beds, the gravel particles stay put in the pathway.

For a more artistic look, you can incorporate flat slabs of granite, slate, or stone into a gravel pathway at any time (though it's easiest to set them in place when you're initially creating the paths). I've heard many complaints from gardeners that gravel driveways and paths become weedy in just a few short months, but I've discovered that this usually happens when the gravel in the path isn't deep enough. For a minor foot path, use gravel at least 4 inches deep to prevent most weeds. For wider areas such as main paths and driveways, use at least 6 inches of gravel to keep the path surface largely weed free. Flame weeders (see page 220) are an excellent way to keep gravel paths clean.

In most situations, though, the material of the paths contributes less to the overall design than the line and width of the paths, so those should be your overriding design considerations. Simple, generous lines lead the eye forward and entice the foot onward. Broad paths invite company along the garden path and greatly facilitate maintenance. And paths that curve in and around plants create an air of excitement and discovery that can't be matched by beds and plants alone.

Before you make any definite decisions about pathways, you may want to get a second, or even a third, opinion. Sometimes you've lived with a situation so long that it becomes natural to want to keep it the same. Don't let fear of time- or labor-intensity stall your creative thoughts. These fears may, in fact, inspire even more creativity. Instead of ripping out a too-small walkway entirely, you may dream up a solution that widens it and makes it more scenic by just adding to the sides of the existing walk!

Path Assessment

	Current size	Current characteristics	What is the path's function?	How can it better meet your needs?	Design ideas
Path 1					
Path 2					
Path 3					
Path 4					
Path 5					

Fine-Tuning Screening Points

You've already identified areas where you need to screen unwanted views or where you want to improve a view with plantings. It's time to delve a little deeper and pinpoint the exact requirements of those areas so you can begin to look for plants that fit the bill. Keeping an open mind about plantings is a good strategy here—even if you have your heart set on a triple planting of barberry to screen a particular spot, you may find that it's not tall enough to block the view entirely. But, as you explore the attributes of other, larger shrubs for that area, you may find one that you like even better than the one you had your heart set on originally.

Views from Inside and Outside

It's important to explore viewpoints from within the house and from any seating areas outside when planning your garden. This exercise will help you identify unwanted views from both inside and outside vantage points and will help you explore the size and shape of screening plants you'll need to eliminate these undesirable views.

You'll need at least one partner, a dozen or so stakes, colorful plastic ribbon, an indelible marking pen, a notebook, and photocopies of the worksheet on the opposite page. One partner stands indoors with the copies and notebook, looking out at the garden. The other person stands in the garden, armed with stakes, ribbon, and the marking pen. The inside partner directs the placement of stakes, each of which represents a key screening plant or group of plants.

"Stake" Your Goal

The goal for each stake's plant or planting should be clearly defined. Stake 1 might represent a plant that is required to block the view of the neighbor's junky cars or an ugly street sign. Goals should be direct and tangible like "screen the neighbor's empty dog cage," not "improve the property line." The clearer the goal, the easier it will be to find a potential candidate for each position. One thing to note: If the house inhabitants are of markedly different heights, it's wise for all interested parties to take a turn viewing the garden from inside.

Using the marking pen, the outside partner numbers each stake, then ties a ribbon around it. (This is especially important in a crowded garden, where a lone stake can easily get lost.) The inside partner writes notes about each stake and the size of the plant that will need to be placed in that area.

For instance, the notation for Stake 1 might read "Need a single plant here, no more than 8 feet high. It could be as much as 8 feet wide, but 5 feet would cover the ugly view just fine." To help the indoor person figure out the needed heights and widths, the outdoor person must pretend to be a plant. Raised or outstretched arms give a good idea of the desired height and girth for each.

Further notations for each stake should include specific facts about each site. Stake 1 might be in sandy soil in full sun, or it might be in shade in heavy clay soil. If the screening spot is a vital one, an evergreen plant may be called for, or you may elect to find twiggy shrubs to fill the bill. If it is an area that is seldom viewed or is only used in summer, a deciduous shrub will work just fine.

The stake-placing and note-taking process should be continued from every important window. What's an important window? If you spend time at the kitchen sink or in a certain room, those views are important. If you pass by a hall window daily without ever looking out of it, that's less so.

Within the garden, important viewpoints are places where you spend a lot of time (or plan to do so). Seating areas, barbecue pits, porches, pools, and patios are places where good screening can make a vital difference in how often an area is used. To give you an idea about how far-reaching your information can be, see the example I've given in the chart.

Views from Outside

Location	Goal	Site conditions	Plant size needed	Plant candidates
Example View from: *Kitchen window*	*Beautiful flower garden with long season of bloom to view while washing dishes*	*Full sun, clay soil*	*Size not critical; long bloom important*	Echinacea, Nepeta, Salvia, Sedum, *a few evergreens for winter color, possibly an evergreen groundcover*
Stake 1 View from:				
Stake 2 View from:				
Stake 3 View from:				
Stake 4 View from:				

Record Weather Events

Understanding the relationships between plants and weather can help you plan and take care of your garden. Four important factors affect plants: temperature, rainfall, sunlight, and wind. Many ornamental plants are native to warm climates, so freezing temperatures are bound to injure, if not kill, them. Cold-weather frosts damage plants when the water in the plants' cells freezes and ruptures the cell wall. Plants that are native to colder climates go dormant for the cold months to protect themselves.

Another factor in plant care is rainfall. Your region's rainfall will determine which plants you can grow without a lot of supplemental watering and which water-thirsty plants might be better if they're admired only in a catalog. You can get average rainfall statistics from your local weather service or Master Gardeners. (Contact your local extension office to locate Master Gardeners in your area.) If you'd like to keep track at home, buy an inexpensive rain gauge, or simply use an empty can and a ruler. Whatever amount of rain falls in the can equals the amount of rain that's fallen in the garden.

Sunlight and shade are equal partners in determining which plants will thrive on your property. Every plant has its own tolerances of the amount and intensity of sun or shade, and knowing when the sun hits certain areas of your site is vital when choosing plants.

Wind is a little less predictable than sun, but it will influence plant health, growth, and stability. Too much wind can dry out soil and plants, stunt growth of new plants, and knock over shallow-rooted plants. Wind can work in your favor, too, because air circulation can help reduce disease problems in some plants.

Keep a Weather Diary

Learning about the weather patterns in your area will help you take better care of your plants. Keeping a weather diary is a great way to track patterns. To start a weather diary, use a regular calendar (make sure it has large boxes for each day), make notes in your garden journal, or photocopy pages from a calendar and add it to your garden notebook each month.

Make notes every day so you can see how varied the weather can be from week to week. Be sure to record temperature highs and lows, rainfall, storm types and intensities, and any extreme conditions, such as hail or flooding. After 2 or 3 years, weather patterns may be readily identifiable.

Track Sun on the Site

Observant gardeners can carefully match plant and site by simply taking note of what's going on in the garden. Once each season, spend a day recording the sun's path and the patterns of sunlight and shade on your site from sunup to sundown. Walk around the site and note how shadows fall around buildings, trees, and other plantings about every 2 to 3 hours. Record the information in the chart on the opposite page. (This information will be vital when you plan beds and borders, site trees, and choose plants.) For example: If it's a spring day at 10 A.M. and you're observing the front of your north-facing house, you may find that the sun reaches all of the front yard except the house foundation bed. Simply write "Almost all" in the "Areas in sun" section and "2-foot-wide foundation bed" in the "Areas in shade" section. Continue observations throughout the day. If your foundation bed never gets sun or gets it for less than 3 hours, you can conclude that the foundation plants you choose should be shade-tolerant.

Sun and Shade Tracking

Season:	Time of day:	Time of day:	Time of day:	Time of day:	Time of day:	Time of day:
Location on property	Areas in sun: _____ _____ Areas in shade: _____ _____	Areas in sun: _____ _____ Areas in shade: _____ _____	Areas in sun: _____ _____ Areas in shade: _____ _____	Areas in sun: _____ _____ Areas in shade: _____ _____	Areas in sun: _____ _____ Areas in shade: _____ _____	Areas in sun: _____ _____ Areas in shade: _____ _____
Location on property	Areas in sun: _____ _____ Areas in shade: _____ _____	Areas in sun: _____ _____ Areas in shade: _____ _____	Areas in sun: _____ _____ Areas in shade: _____ _____	Areas in sun: _____ _____ Areas in shade: _____ _____	Areas in sun: _____ _____ Areas in shade: _____ _____	Areas in sun: _____ _____ Areas in shade: _____ _____
Location on property	Areas in sun: _____ _____ Areas in shade: _____ _____	Areas in sun: _____ _____ Areas in shade: _____ _____	Areas in sun: _____ _____ Areas in shade: _____ _____	Areas in sun: _____ _____ Areas in shade: _____ _____	Areas in sun: _____ _____ Areas in shade: _____ _____	Areas in sun: _____ _____ Areas in shade: _____ _____
Location on property	Areas in sun: _____ _____ Areas in shade: _____ _____	Areas in sun: _____ _____ Areas in shade: _____ _____	Areas in sun: _____ _____ Areas in shade: _____ _____	Areas in sun: _____ _____ Areas in shade: _____ _____	Areas in sun: _____ _____ Areas in shade: _____ _____	Areas in sun: _____ _____ Areas in shade: _____ _____

Track Wind on the Site

It may be hard to know exactly how the wind affects your garden, but you can make informed decisions about new plantings (especially windbreaks) if you look and listen when the wind is blowing. Observe how wind affects your current plantings by spending time outdoors on a windy day when the trees are in leaf and your perennials have reached mature height. Walk around the site, watching how wind gusts blow branches and stems; take notes to remember which plants seem strained under the windy conditions, which may be damaged by heavier winds, and which seem to tolerate the hearty gusts. If you have older trees on your property, you may be able to tell where past windstorms have broken off limbs or split trunks. Record what you see, then keep this information in mind when you're planning new beds.

Wind Patterns

Location on property:

Observations:

Sturdy plants in this location:

Less-sturdy plants in this location:

Location on property:

Observations:

Sturdy plants in this location:

Less-sturdy plants in this location:

Location on property:

Observations:

Sturdy plants in this location:

Less-sturdy plants in this location:

Location on property:

Observations:

Sturdy plants in this location:

Less-sturdy plants in this location:

Location on property:

Observations:

Sturdy plants in this location:

Less-sturdy plants in this location:

Location on property:

Observations:

Sturdy plants in this location:

Less-sturdy plants in this location:

Placing Key Trees and Shrubs

Trees and shrubs add structure to the garden and help create the garden's backbone. They are often the centerpiece of a yard or the focal point of a mixed border. With all eyes focused on these structural beauties, it's important to carefully plan where you'll plant them.

You'll need to do a bit of research before committing to a particular tree or shrub because you'll need to have a clear sense of the ultimate size and shape of any plant you choose for your garden. Because you'll want your plantings to look good for years to come, you need to allow enough room for the plants to mature in the space you have to work with. You may also want to consider how a plant's seasonal changes, including its winter silhouette, will contribute to your overall design.

Elevation Drawings

This exercise will help you evaluate your choices and will help you visualize how the trees and shrubs you're considering will look in your garden. Most garden plans are drawn from a bird's-eye view, which is helpful when planning space

allotments. Garden designers often take plans one step further by drawing elevations—head-on views showing the height and width of proposed plantings to make sure the plants work together. If you have a hard time visualizing how plants will look, this exercise is extremely helpful and enlightening.

MATERIALS YOU'LL NEED

- Snapshots of garden areas where you want to place key trees and shrubs
- Roll or sheets of tracing paper or clear Mylar sheets (often sold as clear copy "paper" used for overhead transparencies)
- Colored pencils for tracing paper or dry-erase colored markers for Mylar
- Illustrated encyclopedia of trees and shrubs (from library)
- Nursery or garden catalogs with photos of trees and shrubs
- Double-sided or removable tape

If you feel comfortable drawing simple shapes and outlines, enlarge the snapshots of each garden area on a color copy machine ($8\frac{1}{2} \times 11$ inches is good; 11×17 inches gives an even better view). Tape one of the copies to your desk or drawing board, then tape tracing paper or Mylar over the

photograph as an overlay. Using the illustrations in the encyclopedia as models, sketch the shapes of your chosen trees and shrubs onto the tracing paper or Mylar in the desired spots. Use pencils for drawing on tracing paper and markers for drawing on Mylar. Don't worry about creating great art here; use a loose, impressionistic style to give the sense of each plant's habit and size.

You may find Mylar easier to use than tracing paper at first because Mylar is clear, not cloudy. But once you get started, you may find that tracing paper and colored pencils are easier to use with finesse. Either way, once you get the hang of making an overlay, you can whip off a number of alternative versions of your proposed plantings very quickly.

If you have trouble sketching or aren't happy with the results you've had with the plant outlines you've drawn, you may want to turn to plant catalogs for help. Given the scale of most catalogs, you may be able to use your landscape layouts at their regular size, or you may need to enlarge them a bit. Cut out photographs of the trees and shrubs you want to test-drive from the catalogs, then tape them lightly (double-sided or removable tape works best) to your tracing paper or Mylar overlays. If the cutouts are too small, use the pencils or markers to build them up a bit, following the contours of the trees and shrubs for shape.

Tree and Shrub Choices

It's helpful to keep track of the trees and shrubs that you're considering so you have an at-a-glance record of plant sizes and shapes. This section can get you started while you're testing different trees and shrubs in your elevation drawings. You should consider, however, adding a permanent section to your garden notebook listing the features of the trees and shrubs you're considering and actual or catalog photos of your possible choices.

Tree and Shrub Possibilities

Tree or shrub name	Height at maturity	Width at maturity	Soil and exposure preferences	Proposed planting location	Best time to plant

Solving Problems

Many gardens have obvious problems. Do you have an uninviting front entrance; an old, rotting fence that you want to replace with something more natural; or an outbuilding that needs to be disguised? The best solutions aren't always apparent, and problem solving takes patience. But it is rewarding when you come up with the right solution.

Or maybe your garden is in okay shape, but you want to make cosmetic changes. My problem-solving method can work in this instance, as well. Instead of concentrating solely on making a change in your garden, identify a problem that needs to be solved and pair your solution with the change. For example, you may want to replace the 40-year-old concrete sidewalk from your back patio to your garage. It's not that the existing sidewalk is un-usable, but you'd prefer it to be brick or stone. A simple change, right?

Possibly. But before you make any decisions, stop and ask yourself if the sidewalk could be improved in any way. Would it be easier to carry groceries if it had night lighting or was wider, or could you eliminate a damp, soggy spot if you created a raised bed along the path's edge when you were "repaving?" Perhaps you could add an inter-esting curve in the path and a nook for a bench so you could enjoy the hummingbird garden you planted nearby last spring.

Whether your garden problem is an obvious one or not, work through this exercise and explore as many options as you can think of before settling on a solution. Identify your problem first, then write down anything that would be affected by a change, both positively and negatively. Record possible solutions, then evaluate each one by walking through the site and visualizing the change. You may have to refine your solution a few times or enlist the help of a friend to find a solution that solves the problem. The best solution to your garden problem may ultimately end up being a combination of ideas.

Solution Possibilities

Problem: How may it be affected by a change (drainage, view, foot traffic, exposure, etc.):	Problem: How may it be affected by a change (drainage, view, foot traffic, exposure, etc.):
Possible solution 1:	Possible solution 1:
Possible solution 2:	Possible solution 2:
Possible solution 3:	Possible solution 3:
Possible solution 4:	Possible solution 4:
Solution to pursue:	Solution to pursue:

Unshearing a Hedge

If you have a big, tightly sheared hedge, getting it back into a more natural shape can seem a daunting task. The restorative process is not difficult, but it does take time and patience. It's not enough to simply let tight-sheared shapes grow out, because this won't address the problems of poor air flow and too little light at the cores of the plants. The goal is to reduce the unnatural density of the plants that make up the hedge by opening them up to more light and air. Gentle thinning creates a looser, softer appearance that improves each year. This technique also works for freestanding shrubs that have been repeatedly pruned into bowling-ball or gumdrop shapes.

MATERIALS YOU'LL NEED

- Sharp bypass or scissors-type pruning shears
- Sharpening stone
- Small pruning saw (pull-stroke pruning saws are easier to use with finesse in tight spots, such as the interior of an overgrown shrub)

HOW TO DO IT

1. Reach into the body of your sheared hedge and grasp a modest handful of twigs.

2. Use sharp bypass pruning shears (not anvil-type pruners, which can damage plants) to snip off your twigs. Cut each stem back to the trunk or a main branch.

3. Observe the result; it should not look like a gaping hole. If it does, ruffle the twigs around your cut until the gap is hidden. Next time, take a smaller handful. Think about taking nibbles, not big bites.

4. Select a spot about 1 foot away from your first cut and repeat the process.

5. As you continue making cuts, be sure to keep moving to different places around the hedge so that it ends up being thinned evenly from all directions. Stop pruning when you have removed about 25 percent of each plant's mass (or before that, if it looks great). Taking off too much foliage causes stress and can actually trigger a density-increasing growth spurt in many shrubs.

6. Mulch and water your newly pruned hedge to reduce shock and stress.

7. Repeat the process each spring (or fall) until the hedge looks natural.

If a hedge has been sheared repeatedly into a geometric shape, a cross-section will reveal very dense, twiggy branching near the surface of the hedge, letting little light and air into the cores of the shrubs.

To unshear the hedge, study the shrub, then prune carefully selected stems back to a main branch. Prune the shrub from all directions. You can remove up to 25 percent of a shrub each year until it regains its natural shape and form.

Creating a Layered Sandwich

Dabbling with simple bulb-and-groundcover sandwiches is rewarding, but the ability to create a layered, easy-care planting of natives and allies that provides a long sequence of color and interest will be the most useful skill to have when designing naturalistic gardens.

To get started, evaluate the conditions where you plan to create your layered sandwich. You'll need to identify the type of soil you have, determine whether you have moist or dry conditions, and analyze whether the proposed bed is in sunlight, in shade, or both.

Using the plant lists in "Sandwich Gardening" (see page 112), make a master list of plants that would be appropriate for your site. Expand and refine the list by seeking advice from your local extension office, local native plant societies, and other gardeners. Visit nurseries and local gardens to see which plants grow best in your area. Instead of choosing a huge list of plants, you could select a few large families (such as anemones, asters, and penstemons) and combine several members from each to simplify the selection process.

Sample Planting List for a Sunny Sandwich

COMMON NAME (BOTANICAL NAME)	BLOOM TIME	DORMANT	HARDINESS ZONES
Beard-tongue (*Penstemon grandiflorus*)	Summer	Winter	3–9
Bird's foot violet (*Viola pedata*)	Spring to summer	Winter	4–8
Common snowdrop (*Galanthus nivalis*)	Winter to spring	Summer	3–9
Fall crocus (*Crocus kotschyanus*)	Fall	Winter to summer	3–8
Golden bunch (*Crocus ancyrensis*)	Winter to spring	Summer	5–8
Grecian windflower (*Anemone blanda*)	Spring	Summer to winter	4–8
Heath aster (*Aster ericoides*)	Summer to fall	Winter	5–8
Japanese anemone (*Anemone hupehensis* var. *japonica*)	Summer to fall	Winter	4–8
Leadwort (*Ceratostigma plumbaginoides*)	Spring to fall	Winter	6–9
Lily leek (*Allium moly*)	Summer	Winter	3–9
Nodding onion (*Allium cernuum*)	Late spring to summer	Fall	4–10
Pasque flower (*Pulsatilla vulgaris*)	Spring	Summer to winter	5–7
'Purple Sensation' onion (*Allium aflatunense* 'Purple Sensation')	Summer	Winter	4–8
Shooting stars (*Dodecatheon meadia*)	Spring	Summer to winter	4–8
Silky aster (*Aster sericeus*)	Summer to fall	Winter	4–8
Slender beard-tongue (*Penstemon gracilis*)	Spring to summer	Winter	3–8
Smooth aster (*Aster laevis*)	Summer to fall	Winter	4–8
Smooth penstemon (*Penstemon digitalis*)	Summer	Winter	2–8
Snow crocus (*Crocus chrysanthus*)	Winter to spring	Summer	3–8
Star of Persia (*Allium christophii*)	Summer	Winter	5–8
Upland white aster (*Aster ptarmicoides*)	Summer to fall	Winter	2–9

When you plan your garden, arrange your plants according to bloom and dormancy periods, as well as height. Place early bloomers where their fading foliage will be disguised by later-rising perennials. An exception to this rule occurs when plants have interesting seedheads (such as heath asters). These will hold their looks into fall.

To plant your sandwich, prepare a nursery bed by covering the soil with 4 to 6 inches of aged compost. With the plants still in the pots, lay them out according to your plan, adjusting the spacing as necessary. Mix compost into each planting hole when you set each plant in place. Water plants well and topdress any low or bare spots with more aged compost.

Composing with Perennials

Your plant combinations will have undeniable impact if you pay attention to plant architecture and tonal value when you select plants. It's important to consider new ideas and combinations and to train your eye to see plants as more than just brilliant bursts of color. You can even practice combinations at the nursery without buying a thing—just select a handful of plants in their pots and nest them together to evaluate their overall structure and foliage colors.

Plant Architecture

Many gardeners are skilled at creating plant combinations based on flower power (combining pleasing flower color with various textures and forms of foliage), so incorporating plant architecture into the selection process is a logical next step.

The architecture of a plant is its shape, and many plants have distinct shapes that add variety to a combination planting. If you pair a dwarf Alberta spruce (a perfect upside-down ice cream cone) with a billow of catmint (*Nepeta* spp.) the two

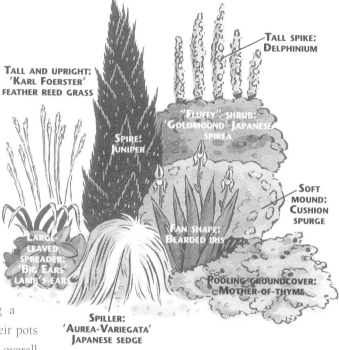

TALL SPIKE: DELPHINIUM

TALL AND UPRIGHT: 'KARL FOERSTER' FEATHER REED GRASS

"FLUFFY" SHRUB: 'GOLDMOUND' JAPANESE SPIREA

SPIRE: JUNIPER

SOFT MOUND: CUSHION SPURGE

LARGE-LEAVED SPREADER: 'BIG EARS' LAMB'S-EARS

FAN SHAPE: BEARDED IRIS

POOLING GROUNDCOVER: MOTHER-OF-THYME

SPILLER: 'AUREA-VARIEGATA' JAPANESE SEDGE

Playing with plant shapes helps you discover what kinds of combinations look best in your garden. Pairing plants that have powerful natural forms with fluffy, indeterminate shapes will keep a combination balanced and tidy.

textures complement each other. Adding a smooth mound of penstemon will change the texture palette and lend more visual appeal. Try mingling three or five shapes—perhaps a cone, a mound, a sprawl, an arch, and a spire—to make an architecture vignette. When you combine plants, use more of the mounded, billowing, or sprawling varieties than you do of the strong vertical plants.

Plants with Strong Architecture

Arches, Fans, and Fountains
Ferns, grasses, irises, and yuccas, and many border shrubs

Balls and Mounds
'Autumn Joy' sedum and other upright sedums, catmint (*Nepeta* spp.), 'Chameleon' spurge (*Euphorbia dulcis* 'Chameleon'), chrysanthemums (*Chrysanthemum* spp.), cushion asters (*Aster novi-belgii* and others), cushion spurge (*Euphorbia polychroma*), and sages (*Salvia officinalis* and others)

Columns and Cones
Culver's root (*Veronicastrum virginicum*), desert candles (*Eremurus* spp.), Dwarf Alberta spruce and other evergreen conifers, and foxgloves (*Digitalis* spp.)

Eccentrics
'Blaukappe' blue sea holly (*Eryngium planum* 'Blaukappe'), globe thistle (*Echinops* spp.), rattlesnake master (*Eryngium yuccifolium*), and verbascums

Spikes and Spires
'Album' white fireweed (*Epilobium angustifolium* 'Album'), astilbes, delphiniums, lupines, and South American verbena (*Verbena bonariensis*)

Spills and Sprawls
Creeping artemisias, creeping bellflowers (*Campanula portenschlagiana* and others), creeping mints, creeping oreganos, creeping sedums, creeping thymes, and creeping veronicas (*Veronica peduncularis* and others)

If the combination will be viewed from various spots in the garden, walk away from your setup and approach it from a different angle. Do the various shapes blend into a single mound, or do they create visually interesting combinations? Does one particular plant seem out of place, or is each plant's architecture adding interest to the group? If the plants you're using change shape dramatically over the course of the year, it may be helpful to revisit your combination in different seasons.

Tonal Value

An architectural plant doesn't just count on its shape for its allure—its color and tonal value (the intensity of its color) contribute to its overall good looks, as well. When you assemble an assortment of plants, choose ones that have flowers and foliage in your usual preferred color range. Then choose an assortment of plants that will provide powerful contrasts of both color and tonal value to your favorite palette. If you lean toward pastels, look for stronger shades of the same colors. Deeper colors will amplify and strengthen your basic palette.

For high tonal value contrast, add paler plants such as creamy variegated iris (*Iris pallida* 'Variegata'), silvery artemisia, steel blue oat grass (*Helictotrichon sempervirens*), and 'Variegata' obedient plant (*Physostegia virginiana* 'Variegata').

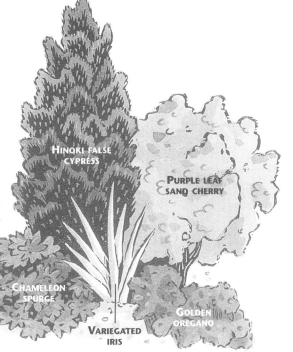

Create visual impact in your garden by using plants with contrasting tonal values. To make contrasts that tickle your fancy, visit a nursery and play around with potted plants, creating combinations that mix light and dark colors.

Sandwich each of the plants from your preferred palette between a light and a dark companion and see what happens. Notice how colors come alive when they share a common tint or tone with a neighboring plant, even if the actual color is quite different. Notice how the difference in tonal value creates "pop," or high contrast. Do you prefer the darker plant to be behind or in front of the preferred plant? Place the plants side-by-side in the combinations you're considering, and assess the

Plants with Strong Tonal Contrast

Dark Foliage Plants

Autumn snakeroot (*Cimicifuga simplex* 'Brunette' or 'Braunlaub'), burgundy or purple coral bells (*Heuchera* spp.), 'Diabolo' black ninebark (*Physocarpus opulifolius* 'Diabolo'), 'Nigrescens' black mondo grass (*Ophiopogon planiscapus* 'Nigrescens'), painted fern (*Athyrium nipponicum* var. *pictum*), purple sand cherry (*Prunus* × *cistena*), and 'Ravenswing' black chervil (*Anthriscus sylvestris* 'Ravenswing')

Golden Foliage Plants

Golden feverfew (*Tanacetum parthenium* 'Aureum'), golden hostas, golden lemon balm (*Melissa officinalis* 'All Gold'), and golden meadowsweet (*Filipendula ulmaria* 'Aurea')

Blue or Gray Foliage Plants

Blue oat grass (*Helictotrichon sempervirens*), blue wheat grass (*Elymus magellanicus*), 'Jackman's Blue' blue rue (*Ruta graveolens* 'Jackman's Blue'), 'Silver King' artemisia (*Artemisia ludoviciana* 'Silver King'), 'Silver Mound' silvermound artemisia (*Artemisia schmidtiana* 'Silver Mound'), and 'The Blues' little bluestem (*Schizachyrium scoparium* 'The Blues'), plus many silver and gray sages

impact. You'll immediately make a judgment about what works and what doesn't. Change the arrangement in the layout or make substitutions if necessary. Take a break and walk away, then see if you're happy with the changes you've made.

Creating a Seasonal Sequence

The best way to master the art of seasonal sequencing is to make some plantings, watch them for a season or two, and then fine-tune the mixture to suit your site. Sounds like fun (and believe me, it is), but planning still needs to be part of the process. And I've found that even experienced gardeners can dread the process of planning when they're itching to plant. This planning exercise will give you the basic groundwork for exploring the excitement and satisfaction of seasonal sequencing.

I've created sample designs for two 8 × 12-foot plantings, one for a shady garden (opposite page) and one for a sunny garden (page 265). Look through the plants I've used in each garden to get inspiration for the gardens you'll create. The goal of this exercise is for you to create variations of these plantings that would be suitable for your region. You'll find possible plant candidates in the charts that accompany each of my garden designs, but of course, feel free to add other favorite plants to your sequence garden, as I've done in my two designs.

Each of the designs I've created includes an assortment of plants with different seasons of

(continued on page 264)

Shady Sequencing Palette Choices

COMMON NAME (BOTANICAL NAME)	SEASONS OF INTEREST	HARDINESS ZONES
SHRUBS		
Azalea (*Rhododendron* spp.)	All seasons	4–9, varies by species
Dwarf fothergilla (*Fothergilla* spp.)	Spring, summer, fall	5–8
Enkianthus (*Enkianthus* spp.)	Spring, summer, fall	6–8, varies by species
Rhododendron (*Rhododendron* spp.)	All seasons	5–8
Witch hazel (*Hamamelis vernalis* and some hybrids)	All seasons	4–8
PERENNIALS		
'Amethystina' purple toad lily (*Tricyrtis formosana* 'Amethystina')	Spring, fall	6–9
Autumn fern (*Dryopteris erythrosora*)	All seasons; evergreen	6–9
Black snakeroot (*Cimicifuga racemosa*)	Summer, fall	3–8
Epimedium (*Epimedium* spp.)	All seasons; evergreen	5–8, varies by species
Japanese anemone (*Anemone hupehensis* var. *japonica*)	Summer, fall	5–9
Labrador violet (*Viola labradorica*)	Spring, summer, fall	2–8
'Rubra' red wood spurge (*Euphorbia amygdaloides* 'Rubra'; also sold as 'Purpurea')	All seasons; evergreen	6–9
Spotted lungwort (*Pulmonaria saccharata*)	Spring, summer, fall	4–8
Stinking iris (*Iris foetidissima*)	All seasons; evergreen	7–9
'Wester Flisk' stinking hellebore (*Helleborus foetidus* 'Wester Flisk')	All seasons; evergreen	6–9
White wood aster (*Aster divaricatus*)	Spring, fall	4–8
Yellow corydalis (*Corydalis lutea*)	Spring, summer, fall	5–8
BULBS		
Algerian iris (*Iris unguicularis*)	Fall, winter	7–9
Autumn crocus (*Colchicum autumnale*)	Fall	4–9
Grecian windflower (*Anemone blanda*)	Winter, spring	4–8
Hardy cyclamen (*Cyclamen hederifolium*)	Fall, winter	5–9
'Pictum' Italian arum (*Arum italicum* 'Pictum')	Summer, fall, winter	6–9
Showy Japanese lily (*Lilium speciosum*)	Fall	4–8
Tomasini's crocus (*Crocus tommasinianus*)	Winter, spring	3–8
Winter aconite (*Eranthis hyemalis*)	Winter, spring	4–9

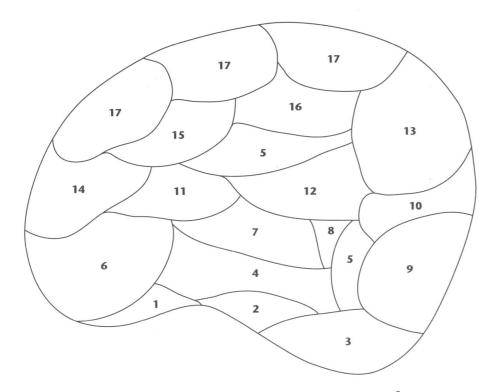

Plant List for the Shady Sequencing Garden

Numbers in parentheses indicate the number of plants in the garden.

1. White wood aster (3)

2. Hakone grass (1)

3. Spotted lungwort (3)

4. Autumn fern (5) and autumn crocus (100)

5. Tomasini's crocus (100), hardy cyclamen (12), and epimedium (3)

6. Japanese anemone (5)

7. Epimedium (3) and Grecian windflower (50)

8. Stinking iris (1)

9. Enkianthus, 5' high (1)

10. Japanese anemone (3)

11. Yellow corydalis (3)

12. White wood aster (5) and Grecian windflower (50)

13. Dwarf fothergilla, 4' high (1)

14. 'Rubra' red wood spurge (3)

15. Stinking iris (3)

16. Autumn fern (5)

17. Rhododendron (*Rhododendron yakushimanum*), 3' high (1)

Made in the Shade Sequencing

Create your own sequenced shade garden! Use a photocopier to enlarge the bed shape below, then add plant division lines as you choose plants for different areas of the bed. Use the list of shrubs, perennials, and bulbs on the opposite page for inspiration when designing a seasonal sequence, and include any other shade-tolerant plants you've admired in gardens, nurseries, or plant catalogs. My plant suggestions are just guidelines, so feel free to add any plants that fulfill your individual needs. For the garden to look its best, try to find a site that already has some screening and backdrop plants in place. (Some of the shrubs I suggested could fill that role nicely if you need to plant a backdrop, as well.)

A successful sequence won't happen overnight, so create a few variations. I hope you'll come up with a garden design that you'll actually want to plant in your yard. It's always rewarding to see the fruits of your labor firsthand.

interest. I've arranged the plants in clusters in the bed, yet the seasonal performers weave in and out of each cluster, so there are as few blank spots as possible during any given season. Depending on where you live, you may not even be able to see the winter performers because they'll be covered with snow. In those regions, I suggest that you substitute combinations of shrubs for the perennials. In areas where snows alternate with thaws, you will glimpse the winter vignettes each time the snow retreats.

While plants may have main seasons of interest, many plants contribute to the overall look of the garden even when out of bloom, whether through their foliage, texture, or structure, so don't be overly ambitious when it comes to fall tidying. Seasonal interest to a gardener can also mean seeing a cardinal swaying on a browned hydrangea head or enjoying the antics of a junco trying to extract seeds from switch grass. Plants left in place for the cold months can be appreciated just as much as plants alive with color during the growing season.

Experimentation is key when designing a garden that rises and falls through the seasons. Sequencing successfully means learning by trial and error and discovering when to make substitutions and additions to the plants in your garden design.

Sunny Sequencing Palette Choices

COMMON NAME (BOTANICAL NAME)	SEASONS OF INTEREST	HARDINESS ZONES
SHRUBS		
Barberry (*Berberis julianae, B. koreana*)	Spring, summer, fall	6–9
Deutzia (*Deutzia* spp.)	Spring, summer, fall	5–8, varies by species
Forsythia (*Forsythia* spp.)	Spring, fall	6–9
Japanese flowering quince (*Chaenomeles japonica*)	Spring, summer, fall	5–9
Summersweet (*Clethra alnifolia*)	Spring, summer, fall	3–9
PERENNIALS		
Basket of gold (*Aurinia saxatilis*)	All seasons	4–8
Black-eyed Susan (*Rudbeckia fulgida*)	Spring, fall	4–9
Blue star flower (*Amsonia tabernaemontana*)	Spring, summer, fall	3–9
Boltonia (*Boltonia asteroides*)	Spring, fall	4–9
Calico aster (*Aster lateriflorus*)	Spring, summer, fall	4–8
Cushion spurge (*Euphorbia polychroma*)	Spring, summer, fall	4–9
Frikart's aster (*Aster frikartii*)	Summer, fall	4–9
Horned violet (*Viola cornuta*)	Spring, summer, fall	7–9
Leadwort (*Ceratostigma plumbaginoides*)	Spring, summer, fall	6–9
Pasque flower (*Pulsatilla vulgaris*)	Spring	5–7
Russian sage (*Perovskia atriplicifolia*)	All seasons	3–9
Sea holly (*Eryngium* spp.)	All seasons	6–9
Sweet violet (*Viola odorata*)	Spring, summer, fall	8–9
Tall sedum (*Sedum telephium* and cultivars)	Spring, summer, fall	4–9
Western white false indigo (*Baptisia lactea*)	All seasons	4–8
BULBS		
Common snowdrop (*Galanthus nivalis*)	Winter, spring	3–9
Golden bunch crocus (*Crocus ancyrensis*)	Winter, spring	5–8
Golden-rayed lily (*Lilium auratum*)	Fall	4–8
Fall-blooming crocus (*Crocus medius, C. pulchellus,* and other species)	Fall	3–8
Fall snowflake (*Leucojum autumnale*)	Fall	5–9
Narcissus (*Narcissus* spp.)	Spring	4–8

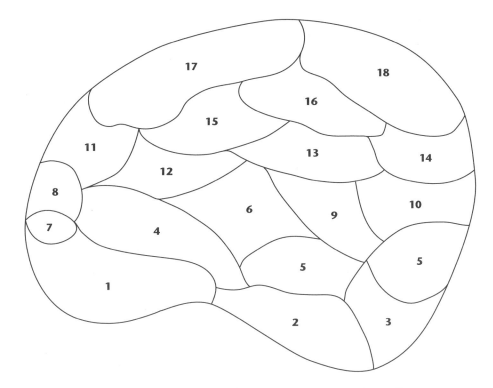

Fun in the Sun Sequencing

Try your hand at designing a sequenced garden for a sunny area. Use a photocopier to enlarge the bed shape below, then add plant division lines as you choose the plants for the bed. On the opposite page, I've provided a list of shrubs, perennials, and bulbs that can be the framework for your garden, but don't limit yourself to only these choices.

Seasonal sequencing isn't an exact science because climate, rainfall, and temperature play significant roles in when and how a plant blooms and performs. During times of drought, plants may wither and die much sooner than in a normal rainfall year, and late-season perennials may never amount to much at all. In wet and stormy years, plants can flourish to the point that they collapse in a heavy rain or suffer wind damage when they're not supported. As you develop and refine your sequenced garden, you can edit out plants that don't stand the test of time, and substitute sure-fire winners.

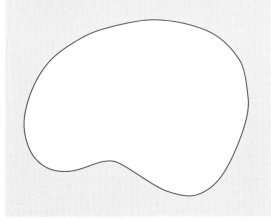

Plant List for the Sunny Sequencing Garden

Number in parentheses indicates number of plants in garden

1. Golden bunch crocus (100), common snowdrop (100), and sweet violet (12)
2. 'Autumn Joy' sedum (5), daffodil (50), and sweet violet (6)
3. Golden bunch crocus (65) and cushion spurge (2)
4. Cushion spurge (5)
5. 'Cameo' Japanese flowering quince (1), golden bunch crocus (65), and common snowdrop (50)
6. 'Nanho Purple' butterfly bush (*Buddleia* 'Nanho Purple') (1)
7. 'Autumn Joy' sedum (1)
8. 'Cabaret' maiden grass (*Miscanthus sinensis* 'Cabaret') (1)
9. Russian sage (3)
10. Frikart's aster (*Aster frikartii*) (3)
11. 'Nikko' slender deutzia (1)
12. South American vervain (*Verbena bonariensis*) (1)
13. Black-eyed Susan (5)
14. Sea holly (3)
15. Russian sage (5) and fall-blooming crocus (135)
16. Western white false indigo (3) and fall-blooming crocus (135)
17. 'Crimson Pygmy' barberry (*Berberis* 'Crimson Pygmy') and golden bunch crocus (135)
18. 'Cabaret' maiden grass (*Miscanthus sinensis* 'Cabaret') (3)

Testing Soil

Some soils practically eat mulch in a single season, while on other soils, mulch decomposes slowly over a couple of years. Of course, the type of mulch you use has a huge impact on how quickly it breaks down. Smaller pieces may decompose in a year; larger pieces may take 3 or more years.

Structure and Tilth

To learn more about the nature and tilth of your soil, try this simple squeeze test. Begin by scooping up a handful of soil and squeezing it gently. If the soil compacts into a tight ball and stays that way, then you are dealing with a clay-based soil. Clay soils drain slowly or puddle up when it rains, and they can turn to a cementlike consistency if worked when wet or walked on repeatedly.

If the soil won't hold a shape and pours out of your hand, you have sandy soil. These soils don't retain nutrients well and dry out quickly. If your soil readily forms a loose ball yet crumbles freely, you are lucky enough to have a nice, sandy loam—the kind of soil preferred by many, if not most, plants. Loamy soils have reasonably balanced texture and shouldn't present problems if given good basic care.

Try the squeeze test in several areas of the property where you plan to plant trees and shrubs or where you'd like to add beds and borders, and note

the results in the chart on the opposite page or in your notebook. When you're recording your results, note any differences in color and smell, as well as in texture and clumping ability. In many parts of the country, it is not unusual to have very different kinds of soil in different parts of one yard—so seize the opportunity to grow a wide variety of plants rather than worrying about how to make all of your soil the same.

Soil Drainage

Another brief test will teach you a good deal about the way your property drains. This test should be performed anywhere you are considering placing paths or building beds and borders. In each possible site, dig a hole about 1 foot deep and 6 inches wide, and fill it with water. Let the water drain away. As soon as the water has completely drained, fill the hole again. If the water drains away fast (in less than 15 minutes), your soil is sandy, and you should record that you'll need to add all the humus you can find.

In good sandy loam, the water will drain away within 30 minutes to an hour. This means your soil is healthy and you can grow a wide range of plants. In this situation, raised beds are unnecessary unless they suit your overall garden design.

Should the water remain visible 8 hours later (perhaps even lingering into the next day), you have

heavy clay soil and very poor drainage. You should seriously consider making raised beds throughout your site to avoid a whole host of problems, including root rots.

Soil pH

Before you begin adding lime or fertilizers to your garden, you need to have the soil tested. In most states, gardeners can get their soil tested inexpensively through the Cooperative Extension Service. These tests will provide you with information about the basic nutrients in your soil (nitrogen, phosphorus, and potassium) as well as your soil's pH. (The extension office also offers a host of useful garden advice and information for free.) You can get the local extension office telephone number at your local library, if you can't find it in the phone book. Or you can do a simple soil pH test yourself, with easy-to-use kits that are sold at most nurseries. While home-test kits are not quite as accurate as commercial testing services, they are good enough to help you identify a pH problem.

Home kits can give you quick results on your soil's pH. You'll need to take a soil sample, mix in distilled water to a recommended consistency, and then dip the kit's litmus paper into the soil and water mixture. You'll match the litmus paper to a color-coded chart that comes with the kit to determine your soil's pH.

Soil Samplings

	Squeeze test result	Length of time to drain	pH	Notes
Area 1				
Area 2				
Area 3				
Area 4				
Area 5				
Area 6				

Minding Your Mulch

Mulch is an important way to keep your garden healthy, but it can be difficult to remember how and when you mulched from year to year. Soils in warm climates practically eat organic mulches in a season, while mulch on cooler soils decomposes slowly. Of course, the type of mulch you use has an impact on how quickly it breaks down—nitrogen-rich grass clippings may decompose in a few months, while fibrous wood chips may take 2 years.

This helpful memory jogger will keep track of your mulching activities and will help you plan your routine for next year.

Mulch Minder

Bed or border location	Year	What type of mulch was used?	How much mulch was used?	When was mulch applied?	When did mulch need replenishing?
	1				
	2				
	3				
	1				
	2				
	3				
	1				
	2				
	3				

Keep a Pest Diary

Knowing when a pest is bound to arrive is almost as useful as knowing what to do to control it. Start a pest diary to keep track of problems you've noticed and the solutions you've found to be most effective. Remember, though, that most insects in the garden are beneficial, so dig out your trusty pest identification guide and see what you're dealing with before you devise your battle plan. Controls may not be necessary or may only be necessary when infestations seem poised to destroy the entire plant.

Think carefully, though, before you reach for that spray bottle of organic pesticide; if it kills the invaders, you're bound to lose a few beneficials in the process. Once you find out which pests are regular problems, you can create a plan for dealing with them the next time they appear (or before they appear!). Besides organic controls, the plan may include eliminating troublesome plants or finding pest-resistant species or cultivars.

Use this chart to record what you see in your garden, and be sure to note the weather conditions around the date you noticed the pests and which controls worked best. The more notes you take, the more prepared you'll be for similar problems next year.

Pest Diary

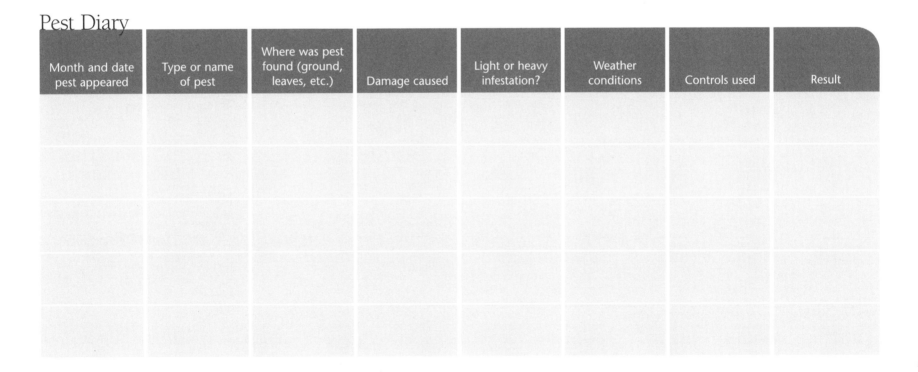

Month and date pest appeared	Type or name of pest	Where was pest found (ground, leaves, etc.)	Damage caused	Light or heavy infestation?	Weather conditions	Controls used	Result

Sources

United States

Abundant Life Seed Foundation
P.O. Box 772
Port Townsend, WA 98368-0772
Phone: (360) 385-5660
Fax: (360) 385-7455
Web site: http://csf.Colorado.edu/
    perma/abundant

American Daylily & Perennials
P.O. Box 210
Grain Valley, MO 64029
Phone: (816) 224-2852 or (800) 770-2777
Fax: (816) 443-2849
Web site: www.americandaylily.com

André Viette Farm & Nursery
P.O. Box 1109
Fishersville, VA 22939
Phone: (800) 575-5538
Fax: (540) 934-0782
Web site: www.viette.com

Antique Rose Emporium
9300 Lueckemeyer Road
Brenham, TX 77833
Phone: (409) 836-9051
Fax: (409) 836-0928

B & D Lilies
P.O. Box 2007
Port Townsend, WA 98368
Phone: (360) 765-4341
Fax: (360) 765-4074
Web site: www.bdlilies.com

Bluestone Perennials
7211 Middle Ridge Road
Madison, OH 44057
Phone/fax: (800) 852-5243
Web site: www.bluestoneperennials.com

Brothers Herbs and Peonies
27015 S.W. Ladd Hill Road
Sherwood, OR 97140
Phone: (503) 625-7548
Fax: (503) 625-5588

Canyon Creek Nursery
3527 Dry Creek Road
Oroville, CA 95965
Phone: (530) 533-2166
Web site: www.canyoncreeknursery.com

Carroll Gardens
444 East Main Street
Westminster, MD 21157
Phone: (800) 638-6334
Fax: (410) 857-4112

Cloud Mountain Nursery
6906 Goodwin Road
Everson, WA 98247
Phone: (360) 966-5859
Fax: (360) 966-0921

Collector's Nursery
16804 N.E. 102nd Avenue
Battleground, WA 98604
Phone: (360) 574-3832
Fax: (360) 571-8540
Web site: www.collectorsnursery.com

Colvos Creek Nursery
P.O. Box 1512
Vashon, WA 98070
Phone: (206) 749-9508
Fax: (206) 463-3917
Web site: www.colvoscreek.qpg.com

Cordon Bleu Daylilies
P.O. Box 2033
San Marcos, CA 92079-2033
Phone: (760) 744-8367
Fax: (760) 744-0510
Web site: www.gardeneureka.com/CORB

Cricklewood Nursery
11907 Nevers Road
Snohomish, WA 98290-6804
Phone: (360) 568-2829

Crystal Palace Perennials, Ltd.
P.O. Box 154
12029 Wicker Avenue
Cedar Lake, IN 46303
Phone: (219) 374-9419
Fax: (219) 374-9052
Web site: www.crystalpalaceperennial.com

Daylily Discounters
6212 West State Road 235
Alachua, FL 32615
Phone: (904) 462-1539
Fax: (904) 462-5111
Web site: www.daylily-discounters.com

Digging Dog Nursery
P.O. Box 471
Albion, CA 95410
Phone: (707) 937-1130 or 937-1235
Fax: (707) 937-2480

Earth's Rising Trees
P.O. Box 334
Monroe, OR 97456-0334
Phone/fax: (541) 847-5950
Web site: www.wolfenet.com/~wind/delbert

Edible Landscaping
P.O. Box 77
361 Spirit Ridge Lane
Afton, VA 22920
Phone: (804) 361-9134 or (800) 524-4156
Fax: (804) 361-1916
Web site: www.eat-it.com

Fancy Fronds
P.O. Box 1090
Gold Bar, WA 98251-1090
Phone: (360) 793-1472
Fax: (360) 793-4243
Web site: www.fancyfronds.com

Forestfarm
990 Tetherow Road
Williams, OR 97544-9599
Phone: (541) 846-7269
Fax: (541) 846-6963
Web site: www.forestfarm.com

Gossler Farms Nursery
1200 Weaver Road
Springfield, OR 97478-9691
Phone: (541) 746-3922
Fax: (541) 744-7924

Great Basin Natives
P.O. Box 114
75 West 300 South
Holden, UT 84636
Phone: (435) 795-2303
Web site: www.grownative.com

Greenmantle Nursery
3010 Ettersburg Road
Garberville, CA 95542
Phone: (707) 986-7504

Heaths & Heathers
East 502 Haskell Hill Road
Shelton, WA 98584-8429
Phone: (360) 427-5318 or (800) 294-3284
Fax: (360) 427-5318
Web site: www.heathsandheathers.com

Heirloom Old Garden Roses
24062 N.E. Riverside Drive
Saint Paul, OR 97137
Phone: (503) 538-1576
Fax: (503) 538-5902
Web site: www.heirloomroses.com

High Country Gardens
2902 Rufina Street
Santa Fe, NM 87505-2929
Phone: (800) 925-9387
Fax: (800) 925-0097
Web site: www.highcountrygardens.com

Joy Creek Nursery
20300 N.W. Watson Road
Scappoose, OR 97056-9612
Phone: (503) 543-7474
Fax: (503) 543-6933

Kurt Bluemel, Inc.
2740 Greene Lane
Baldwin, MD 21013-9523
Fax: (410) 557-9785
Web site: www.bluemel.com

Louisiana Nursery
5853 Highway 182
Opelousas, LA 70570
Phone: (318) 948-3696
Fax: (318) 942-6404
Web site: www.louisiananursery.org

Mellinger's Inc.
2310 W. South Range Road
North Lima, OH 44452-9731
Phone: (330) 549-9861 or (800) 321-7444
Fax: (330) 549-3716
Web site: www.mellingers.com

Milaeger's Gardens
4838 Douglas Avenue
Racine, WI 53402-2498
Phone: (800) 669-9956
Fax: (414) 639-1855
Web site: www.milaegersgardens.com

Musser Forests, Inc.
P.O. Box 340
Indiana, PA 15701-0340
Phone: (412) 465-5685 or (800) 643-8319
Fax: (412) 465-9893
Web site: www.musserforests.com

Naylor Creek Nursery
2610 West Valley Road
Chimacum, WA 98325
Phone: (360) 732-4983
Fax: (360) 732-7171
Web site: www.naylorcreek.com

Niche Gardens
1111 Dawson Road
Chapel Hill, NC 27516
Phone: (919) 967-0078
Fax: (919) 967-4026
Web site: www.nichegdn.com

Nichols Garden Nursery
1190 Old Salem Road
Albany, OR 97321-4580
Phone: (541) 928-9280
Fax: (541) 967-8406

Northern Grown Perennials
Route 1, Box 43
Ferryville, WI 54628
Phone: (608) 734-3178
Web site: mwt.net~ngp/ngp.htm

Old House Gardens
536 West Third Street
Ann Arbor, MI 48103-4957
Phone: (734) 995-1486
Fax: (734) 995-1687
Web site: www.oldhousegardens.com

Park Seed Company
1 Parkton Avenue
Greenwood, SC 29647-0001
Phone: (800) 845-3369
Fax: (800) 275-9941
Web site: www.parkseed.com

Peaceful Valley Farm Supply
P.O. Box 2209
Grass Valley, CA 95945
Phone: (888) 784-1722
Fax: (530) 272-4794
Web site: www.groworganic.com

Plant Delights Nursery
9241 Sauls Road
Raleigh, NC 27603
Phone: (919) 772-4794
Fax: (919) 662-0370
Web site: www.plantdel.com

Plants of the Southwest
Agua Fria Road, Route 6, Box 11A
Santa Fe, NM 87501
Phone: (505) 471-2212 or (800) 788-7333
Fax: (505) 438-8800
Web site: www.plantsofthesouthwest.com

Prairie Nursery
P.O. Box 306
Westfield, WI 53964
Phone: (800) 476-9453
Fax: (608) 296-2741
Web site: www.prairienursery.com

Robyn's Nest Nursery
7802 N.E. 63rd Street
Vancouver, WA 98662
Phone: (360) 256-7399
Web site: www.robynsnestnursery.com

Lon J. Rombough
P.O. Box 365
Aurora, OR 97002-0365
Phone: (503) 678-1410
Web Site: www.hevanet.com/lonrom

Sandy Mush Herb Nursery
316 Surrett Cove Road
Leicester, NC 28748
Phone: (704) 683-2014

Seeds of Change
P.O. Box 15700
Santa Fe, NM 87506-5700
Phone: (888) 762-7333
Fax: (888) 329-4762
Web Site: www.seedsofchange.com

Shooting Star Nursery
444 Bates Road
Frankfort, KY 40601-9446
Phone: (502) 223-1679

Shady Oaks Nursery
P.O. Box 708
112 10th Avenue SE
Waseca, MN 56093
Phone: (800) 504-8006
Fax: (888) 735-4531
Web site: www.shadyoaks.com

Siskiyou Rare Plant Nursery
2825 Cummings Road
Medford, OR 97501-1538
Phone: (541) 772-6846
Fax: (541) 772-4917
Web site: www.wave.net/upg/srpn

Song Sparrow Nursery
13101 East Rye Road
Avalon, WI 53505
Phone: (800) 553-3715
Fax: (608) 883-2257

Stark Bro's Nurseries & Orchards Co.
P.O. Box 10
Louisiana, MO 63353-0010
Phone: (573) 754-5511 or (800) 325-4180
Fax: (573) 754-5290
Web site: www.gardensolutions.com

Thompson & Morgan Inc.
P.O. Box 1308
Jackson, NJ 08527
Phone: (800) 274-7333
Fax: (888) 466-4769
Web site: www.thompson-morgan.com

Wayside Gardens
1 Garden Lane
Hodges, SC 29695-0001
Phone: (800) 845-1124
Fax: (800) 817-1124
Web site: www.waysidegardens.com

White Flower Farm
P.O. Box 50
Litchfield, CT 06759-0050
Phone: (800) 503-9624
Fax: (860) 482-0532
Web site: www.whiteflowerfarm.com

Gilbert H. Wild & Son L.L.C.
P.O. Box 338
3044 State Highway 37
Sarcoxie, MO 64862-0338
Phone: (417) 548-3514 or (888) 449-4537
Fax: (888) 548-6831
Web site: www.gilberthwild.com

William Tricker, Inc.
7125 Tanglewood Drive
Independence, OH 44131
Phone: (800) 524-3492
Fax: (216) 524-6688
Web site: www.tricker.com

Wilkerson Mill Gardens
9595 Wilkerson Mill Road
Palmetto, GA 30268
Phone: (770) 463-9717 or 463-2200
Fax: (770) 463-9717
Web site: www.hydrangea.com

Woodside Gardens
1191 Egg & I Road
Chimacum, WA 98325
Phone/fax: (800) 473-1152
Web site: www.woodsidegardens.com

Wrenwood of Berkeley Springs
Route 4, Box 8055
Berkeley Springs, WV 25411
Phone/fax: (304) 258-3071
Web site: www.wrenwood.com

Canada

Bluestem Nursery
Box 239
Lurier, WA 99146
Phone: (250) 447-6363

Corn Hill Nursery
R.R. #5
Petitcodiac, New Brunswick E0A 2H0
Phone: (506) 756-3635
Fax: (506) 756-1087

Gardens North
5984 Third Line Road North
North Gower, Ontario K0A 2T0
Phone: (613) 489-0065
Fax: (613) 489-1208

Fraser's Thimble Farms
175 Arbutus Road
Salt Spring Island, British Columbia
V8K 1A3
Phone/fax: (250) 537-5788
Web site: www.thimblefarms.com

Hole's Greenhouses and Gardens Ltd.
101 Bellerose Drive
Saint Albert, Alberta T8N 8N8
Phone: (780) 419-6800
Fax: (780) 459-6042
Web site: www.holesonline.com

Hortico, Inc.
723 Robson Road, R.R. #1
Waterdown, Ontario L0R 2H1
Phone: (905) 689-6984 or 689-6002
Fax: (905) 689-6566
Web site: www.hortico.com

Lost Horizons
R.R. #1
Acton, Ontario L7J 2L7
Phone: (519) 853-3085
Fax: (519) 853-2279
Web site: www.eridani.com/losthorizons

Mason Hogue Gardens
3520 Durham Road 1, R.R. #4
Uxbridge, Ontario L9P 1R4
Phone/fax: (905) 649-3532
Web site: www.masonhogue.com

Pickering Nurseries, Inc.
670 Kingston Road
Pickering, Ontario L1V 1A6
Phone: (905) 839-2111
Fax: (905) 839-4807
Web site: www.pickeringnurseries.com

The Perennial Gardens
13139 224th Street
Maple Ridge, British Columbia V4R 2P6
Phone: (604) 467-4218
Fax: (604) 467-3181
Web site: www.perennialgardener.com

Wrightman Alpines
R.R. #3
Kerwood, Ontario N0M 2B0
Phone/fax: (519) 247-3751

FYI

For information about aerobic compost-tea brewers and biotic soil tests, contact any of the following companies:

Soilsoup, Inc.
9792 Edmonds Way #247
Edmonds, WA 98020
Phone: (206) 542-9304 or (877) 711-7687
Fax: (206) 533-0748
Web site: www.soilsoup.com

Growing Solutions
255 Madison Street, Suite A
Eugene, OR 97402
Phone: (888) 600-9558
Fax: (541) 343-8374
Web site: www.growingsolutions.com

Soil Foodweb Inc.
1128 N.E. 2nd Street, Suite 120
Corvallis, OR 97330
Phone: (541) 752-5066
Fax: (541) 752-5142
Web site: www.soilfoodweb.com

For information about gates and garden structures woven with cedar and natural materials, contact:

Sue Skelly
Reflective Gardens
24329 N.E. Snowhill Lane
Poulsbo, WA 98370
Phone: (360) 598-4649

For information about orchard mason bees, contact:

Brian Griffin
Knox Cellars
1607 Knox Avenue
Bellingham, WA 98225
Phone: (425) 898-8802
Fax: (425) 898-8070
Web site: www.knoxcellars.com

For information on wrought iron arches and gardens structures, contact:

Elvis Whittingham
3227 Mahali Court
Port Orchard, WA 98366
Phone: (360) 876-4804

To locate a Master Gardener program in your area, contact your local extension office. You can find this listing in the Blue Pages of your telephone directory under the heading "County Government."

To receive a year's subscription (12 issues) of Ann Lovejoy's Organic Garden School Newsletter, send $15 to:

Ann Lovejoy's Organic Garden School
9010 Miller Road
Bainbridge Island, WA 98110
Phone: (206) 780-6783

Photo Credits

Animals, Animals/Fabio Colombini 192

Animals, Animals/Jack Wilburn 191

Rob Cardillo vi (right), 146, 181 (right), 204 (right), 204 (middle right), 204 (middle), 204 (middle left), 204 (left), 206 (right), 206 (middle right), 206 (middle), 206 (middle left), 206 (left), 215, 222 (middle left), 230

J. C. Carlton/Bruce Coleman Stock 222 (left)

David Cavagnaro 220

Walter Chandoha 223

Richard Day/Daybreak Imagery 180

Dembinsky Photo Associates 222 (right)

Alan and Linda Detrick 222 (middle right)

Ken Druse 140, 143, 171

Garden Picture Library/John Glover 67, 138

Garden Picture Library/Neil Holmes 123

Garden Picture Library/Howard Rice 181 (middle)

Garden Picture Library/J. S. Sira 172-173

Pamela Harper 226

Lynne Harrison vi (middle right), 8 (bottom), 23 (right), 31, 32-33, 34–35, 85, 92, 121 (top), 121 (bottom), 126, 131, 132, 134, 135 (top left), 135 (top right), 135 (bottom), 137, 141, 144–145, 164, 176

Saxon Holt 7, 8 (top), 12, 13, 14, 14–15, 16 (right), 16 (left), 17 (right), 17 (middle), 44, 45, 47, 49, 51, 53, 57, 59, 60 (top left), 60–61, 61, 71, 75, 99, 100–101, 102, 103, 108, 109, 110, 111, 113, 114, 127, 128, 147, 148, 149, 155, 189 (top), 189 (bottom), 196, 197, 207

Janet Loughrey 17 (left), 41, 54, 66, 69, 76, 78, 104, 106, 118, 139, 160, 167

Holly Lynton 193

Mitch Mandel 211, 229

Alison Miksch vi (left), 60 (right), 175, 177, 182, 186, 188, 195, 201, 211, 212, 219, 221, 229

Clive Nichols vii (right), 46, 63, 150, 151 (right), 151 (middle), 151 (left)

John Peden 218

PhotoAlto 42, 43 (all)

Rodale Images 48

Susan A. Roth 48

Susan Seubert ii, v, vi (middle left), vii (left), vii (middle left), vii (middle right), viii, 3, 5, 6, 10-11, 19, 20, 22, 23 (left), 26, 27, 28, 29, 30, 36, 37, 38, 39, 62, 73, 80, 82, 87, 88–89, 90, 91, 92 (left), 94–95, 96, 115, 116, 120, 153, 159, 162, 166, 168–169, 178–179, 181 (left), 184, 208, 209, 217, 225, 231

Rick Wetherbee 227

Kurt Wilson 191, 198 (top), 198 (bottom), 203

Location Credit

Rodale Institute Experimental Farm, Maxatawny, Pennsylvania vi (left), 60 (right), 175, 177, 182, 186, 188, 195, 201, 212, 219, 221

Index

Note: Page references in *italic* indicate charts. **Boldface** references indicate illustrations or photographs.

USDA Plant Hardiness Zone Map

This map is recognized as the best indicator of minimum temperatures available. Look at the map to find your area, then match its pattern to the key below. When you've found your color, the key will tell you what hardiness zone you live in. Remember that the map is a general guide; your particular conditions may vary.

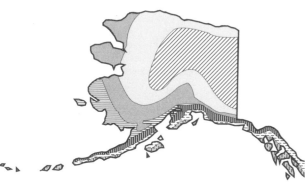

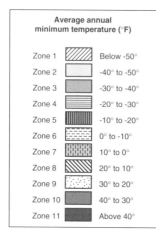

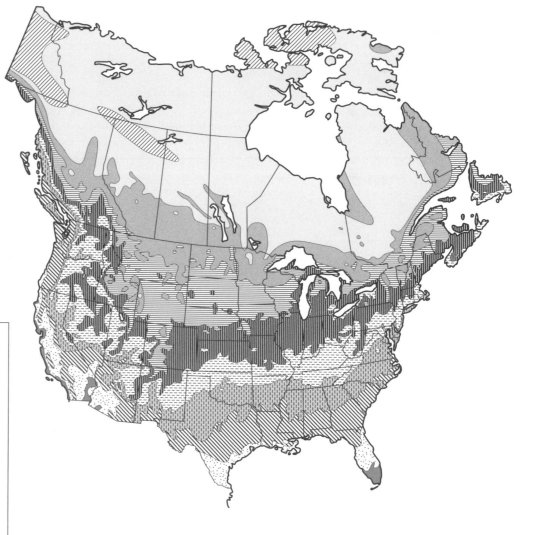

Average annual minimum temperature (°F)

Zone 1		Below -50°
Zone 2		-40° to -50°
Zone 3		-30° to -40°
Zone 4		-20° to -30°
Zone 5		-10° to -20°
Zone 6		0° to -10°
Zone 7		10° to 0°
Zone 8		20° to 10°
Zone 9		30° to 20°
Zone 10		40° to 30°
Zone 11		Above 40°